An Introduction to Economic Dynamics

An examples-driven treatment of introductory economic dynamics for students with a basic familiarity with spreadsheets.

Shone approaches the subject with the belief that true understanding of a subject can be achieved only by students themselves setting out a problem and manipulating it experimentally. Although all economics students now have access to a spreadsheet, they often use it for little more than graphing economic data. This book encourages students to go several stages further and set up and investigate simple dynamic models.

The book presents the essentials of macroeconomic and microeconomic dynamics, including: demand and supply dynamics, Keynesian dynamics, IS-LM dynamics, inflation–unemployment dynamics, dynamics of the firm, rational expectations and saddle-points, fiscal dynamics and the Maastricht Treaty and chaos theory.

The book contains over 50 exercises, with an additional 100 questions contained on the support web site. Material is also provided for a tutor's web site.

RONALD SHONE is Senior Lecturer in Economics at the University of Stirling. He has written nine books on economics covering the areas of microeconomics, macroeconomics, international economics and economic dynamics.

An Introduction to Economic Dynamics

Ronald Shone

PUBLISHED BY THE PRESS SYNDICATE OF THE UNIVERSITY OF CAMBRIDGE
The Pitt Building, Trumpington Street, Cambridge, United Kingdom

CAMBRIDGE UNIVERSITY PRESS
The Edinburgh Building, Cambridge CB2 2RU, UK
40 West 20th Street, New York, NY 10011-4211, USA
10 Stamford Road, Oakleigh, VIC 3166, Australia
Ruiz de Alarcón 13, 28014 Madrid, Spain
Dock House, The Waterfront, Cape Town 8001, South Africa

http://www.cambridge.org

First published 2001

Printed in the United Kingdom at the University Press, Cambridge

Typeface 10/12.5pt Times NR MT   *System* QuarkXPress™   [SE]

A catalogue record for this book is available from the British Library

Library of Congress Cataloguing in Publication data

Shone, Ronald.
    An introduction to economic dynamics / Ronald Shone.
        p.   cm.
    Includes bibliographical references and index.
    ISBN 0 521 80034 X – ISBN 0 521 80478 7 (pb.)
        1. Macroeconomics. 2. Microeconomics. I. Title.
    HB172.5 .S5269 2001
    330–dc21   00-069893

ISBN 0 521 80034 X hardback
ISBN 0 521 80478 7 paperback

Contents

Tables and boxes

Preface

This is a short book. It aims to get across the essential elements of dynamics that are used in modern treatments of the subject. More significantly, it aims to do this through the means of examples. Some of these examples are purely algebraic. But many others consider economic models: both microeconomic and macroeconomic. Macroeconomics is replete with dynamic models – some simple and others quite complex. But this is not true of microeconomics. Microeconomics is still very largely static, with the exception of the cobweb model. In this book we have considered the dynamics of demand and supply and the dynamics of the firm. In terms of the firm we deal only with advertising, diffusion models and the dynamic theory of oligopoly. The macroeconomic models we consider follow the traditional development of the subject matter. The Keynesian fixed-price model is considered first, followed by the IS-LM model. But we also consider the Dornbusch model of the open economy. This model in particular allows us to show how rational expectations enter model construction. It also illustrates the concept of a saddle-point solution to a dynamic model. Other topics of importance are also dealt with such as inflation and unemployment and the fiscal criteria of the Maastricht Treaty. The final chapter (chapter 10) provides an introduction to modern ideas of bifurcation and chaos.

Every student now has access to a spreadsheet. In many colleges and universities, students are trained in the use of the spreadsheet. Often, however, this is for setting out economic data and graphing it. Occasionally a regression equation is undertaken. Rarely is a simple dynamic model set up and investigated. This is what this book is about. I have deliberately set a constraint on the material covered that it must be capable of being investigated on a spreadsheet and that no additional technical software needs to be invoked. This is not as limiting as it may first appear. It may be thought that this restricts our investigation only to discrete models. This is not in fact true. By utilising Euler's approximation, we can investigate quite readily continuous dynamic models. In this book we shall invoke Euler's approximation frequently.

There is a second reason for limiting myself to spreadsheets. Economics, like many subjects, can be more fully appreciated by setting out a problem and manipulating it experimentally. Experimentation is at the heart of this book. But such experimentation is based *only* on the reader setting up the model themselves on their computer. I have found that students like setting models up from scratch. When they get things wrong they must check their model specification relative to the theory. So they read the theory with a more focused mind. They have a reason for getting it right! This is quite a different approach from having a complete model all ready set up. There is a value in such models, but for learning model construction, and for appreciating the properties of a model, there is no better substitute than setting it up from scratch. Of course, there is a cost to this. The models must be relatively simple. I feel this is a cost worth bearing. Complex models may take account of more variables and more interrelationships in the economic system under investigation, but sometimes knowing why a result is the way it is becomes obscured. All one can say is that it is the output of the model. Furthermore, it is not clear what the model assumes unless you were involved in its construction. Listing these assumptions is dry and a turn-off, and such models are best considered by postgraduates and researchers. This book is aimed specifically at undergraduates. It is assumed that the reader will actually set up the model on a spreadsheet and then experiment with it.

Throughout, we have kept things simple. Even some advanced concepts are illustrated by means of simple examples. In doing this special emphasis has been placed on graphically illustrating dynamics. This is where the spreadsheet has been extensively used. Computing large amounts of data points (sometimes 2,000) allows some complex trajectories to be illustrated in the X-Y plane. Seeing how these graphs change when parameter values are altered or when the initial condition is altered is very interactive.

This book is aimed at undergraduates who are pursuing economics either as a single honours subject or as a joint degree. It presupposes familiarity with first-year economics and for some topics a second- or third-year level. It also presupposes a basic familiarity with Excel or an equivalent spreadsheet. It is intended as an accompaniment to all basic economics courses, but it is especially useful to courses in quantitative economics.

Web site
The book, as mentioned, is deliberately short. It provides the essentials. The real learning comes from setting up the models and graphing and/or solving them yourself. There are generally five exercises at the end of each chapter, an additional ten exercises per chapter can be found on the web site for students and a further ten exercises for tutors – around 250 in all! The web site includes solutions to all exercises. The fact that part of the book is in hard copy and part on the web simply takes advantage of modern technology in providing students with a learning environment.

Material for the student
At the end of each chapter there are generally five problems, with brief solutions contained at the end of the book. The Cambridge University Press web site has available:

(1)   Detailed solutions to all end-of-chapter problems.
(2)   An additional ten exercises per chapter and their detailed solutions.

This material can be downloaded from the web site. It is also possible to download the Windows Excel files used to produce the answers.

Material for the tutor

The following material is available to tutors from the Cambridge University web site:

(1)   Microsoft Windows Excel files for *all* problems contained in this book.

(2)   Detailed solutions to all end-of-chapter problems.

(3)   Ten additional exercises per chapter and their detailed solutions – also available to students.

(4)   A further ten exercises and their detailed solutions – available only to tutors.

All this material can be downloaded from the web site.

The author welcomes comments on this book and the material on the web site. He can be contacted by e-mail on <ron.shone@stir.ac.uk>.

Ronald Shone
22 June 2000

Chapter 1

Introduction

In this chapter we shall introduce some basic concepts of dynamics. In order to illustrate these we shall consider just one example. This example is a simple linear model. Why such a linear equation explains what is of interest we shall not consider here. Our main aim is to define and elaborate on dynamic concepts that we shall use throughout this book. Our second aim is to show how such a model can be set up on a spreadsheet and then investigated interactively.

1.1 Definitions and concepts

Dynamics is concerned with how things change over time. The passage of time is a crucial element in any dynamic process. Whether a variable remains the same value at two points in time or whether it is different is not the essential issue, what matters is that time has elapsed between the value of the variable on the first occasion and the value it takes on the second. Time cannot be reversed.

In dynamics we must specify the point in time for any given variable. If we are concerned about national income, price or profits we need to specify the level of income at a point in time, the price at a point in time and profits at some point in time. As time moves on the value these variables take may change. We will specify time in this book by referring to periods: period 0, usually referring to the initial point in time, then period 1, period 2, and so on. Consequently we shall denote this $t = 0$, 1, 2, etc. If our variable of interest is price, say, which we denote as p, then $p(0)$ refers to the price at time period 0, the present, $p(1)$ the price at time period 1, $p(2)$ the price at time period 2, and so on. Unfortunately, referring to price in this way allows us to refer only to *future* prices. Sometimes we wish to talk about what the price was in the previous period, or the price two periods ago. In order to do this we sometimes say that $p(t)$ is the price in period t, the price now, $p(t+1)$ the price in the next period, and $p(t+2)$ the price two periods from now. Doing this then allows us to refer to price in the previous period, $p(t-1)$, and the price two periods in the past, $p(t-2)$, etc. Which we use depends on what we are discussing, but the context should make it quite clear. If our model is continuous, then $p(t)$ is a continuous function of time. There is a price for each instant of time. We consider continuous models in section 1.9.

How a variable changes over time depends on what determines that variable. What determines a variable is formulated by means of models. In other words, a model is an explanation of how the variable comes about: how it takes on the value that it does, how it is related to other variables, and how it changes over time. A model that refers to no passage of time is called a **static model**. Elementary economics has many static models. The model of demand and supply, which determines the equilibrium price, is a typical static model. Equilibrium price is determined by the equality between what is demanded and what is supplied: where the demand curve intersects the supply curve. If demand rises, and the demand curve shifts to the right, then equilibrium price will rise. When we compare one equilibrium with another we are concerned with **comparative statics**. We are simply comparing the two or more equilibrium points. How the variable got to the new equilibrium is not really considered. To do this would require some dynamic process to be specified. Usually in the theory of demand and supply the movement is assumed to be instantaneous. Or, put another way, that adjustment all happens in the *same* time period, so that it is unnecessary to specify time. On the other hand, if we wish to specify the time path of a variable between one equilibrium point and another, then we must set out a **dynamic model** which explicitly explains the movement of the variable over time. In other words, a dynamic model must involve time explicitly.

Notice here that the model comes from the subject. It comes from our understanding of how the world works. The world is a complex place and we simplify by forming a model. The model sets out the relationships between the crucial elements of the system we are interested in. Models involve abstractions and simplifications. An **economic model** will concentrate on the economic aspects of a system while a sociological model would concentrate on the social aspects of the same system. In this book we are concerned only with economic models. The subject matter of economics is usually divided into microeconomics and macroeconomics. Microeconomics is concerned with individual units, such as choices made by individuals, profits made by firms, decisions about supplying labour at different wage rates, and so on. Macroeconomics is concerned with aggregate variables at the economy level such as unemployment, national income and the general price level. A large part of studying economics is coming to an understanding of **microeconomic models** and **macroeconomic models**. In elementary courses in economics these models are usually static models. Time does not enter them explicitly and attention is usually directed towards the determination of equilibrium conditions.

An **equilibrium** of a model is where the system settles down and, once there, there is no reason for the system to move. It is often thought of in mechanical terms as a balance of forces. In demand and supply, for example, demand represents one force and supply another. When demand equals supply then the forces are in balance and the system is in equilibrium. The price that establishes this balance of force is then referred to as the **equilibrium price**. Much attention in economics is paid to what determines the equilibrium of a model and how that equilibrium changes when some feature of the system changes. But most elementary textbooks stop at this point. But consider for a moment. To establish that a system has an equilibrium just establishes whether an equilibrium exists or not. It cannot guarantee that the system will ever achieve that equilibrium. When attention is directed at the attainment or not of the equilibrium we are dealing with its stability or instability. We refer to this simply as the condition of **stability of the equilibrium**. But to consider the stability of an equilibrium we need to know what happens to the variable over time. If a variable over time tends towards the equilibrium value, then we say it is **stable**. If a variable moves away from the equilibrium value then we say it is **unstable**. (We shall explain this more formally later in the book.) Notice that it is the stability of the equilibrium which we are referring to. Furthermore, any discussion of stability must involve the passage of time explicitly, and so stability is a dynamic consideration of the model. To illustrate this in simple terms take a bowl and (gently) drop an egg down the side. The egg will slip down the side, rise up the other, and steadily come to rest at the bottom of the bowl. The movements around the base get smaller and smaller over time. The base of the bowl represents a stable equilibrium. We know it is an equilibrium because the egg stops moving, and will remain there until it is disturbed. Furthermore, if gently moved a little from the base, it will soon return there. Now place the egg carefully on a bowl placed upside down. If placed carefully, then the egg will remain in that position. It is equilibrium. There is a balance of forces. But move the egg just a little and it will topple down the side of the bowl. It does not matter which direction it is moved, once moved the egg will move away from the top of the bowl. In other words, the top of the bowl is an unstable equilibrium. In this book we shall be considering in some detail the stability of equilibrium points. In this example the movement of the egg was either towards the equilibrium or away from it. But in some systems we shall be considering it is possible for a variable to move *around* the equilibrium, neither moving towards it nor away from it! Such systems exhibit **oscillatory behaviour**.

Here we have introduced the reader to only some of the concepts that we will be dealing with. It will be necessary to formalise them more carefully. We shall do this in terms of the economic models we shall consider.

1.2 Dynamic models

Consider the following equation, which we shall assume for the moment comes from some theory of economics explaining the variable x.

$$x(t+1) = 3 + \tfrac{1}{2}x(t) \tag{1.1}$$

Since the variable x at time $t+1$ is related to the same variable in the previous period we call such models **recursive**. This is true even if more than one time period in the past is involved in the relationship. This recursive model is also linear, since the equation itself is a linear equation. In more complex models nonlinear equations can arise, but they are still recursive if they are related to the same variable in early periods. If the relationship is for just one previous period, then we have a **first-order recursive equation**; if it is for two periods, then we have a **second-order recursive equation**, and so on.

Now in itself this is not sufficient to specify the time path of the variable x.

We need to know its *starting value*. For the moment let this be $x(0) = 10$. Obviously, if this is the case then $x(1) = 3 + \frac{1}{2}(10) = 8$ and $x(2) = 3 + \frac{1}{2}(8) = 7$. The sequence of $x(t)$ generated over time is then 10, 8, 7, 6.5, 6.25 ... We can learn quite a bit from this equation. First, the change in the sequence is getting smaller and appears to be getting close to some number. If the series was extended for many more periods it would indicate that the series is getting closer and closer to the number 6. Is this a coincidence? No, it is not. The number 6 is the equilibrium of this system. Can we establish this? Yes, we can. If the system is in equilibrium it is at rest and so the value the variable x takes in each period is the same. Let us call this x^*. Then it follows that $x(t-1) = x(t) = x^*$, and so $x^* = 3 + \frac{1}{2}x^*$ or $x^* = 6$. Mathematicians often call equilibrium points **fixed points** and we shall use the two terms interchangeably. But we can say much more. From the solution we have just derived it is clear that there is only *one* fixed point to this system: one equilibrium.

It is very useful to display first-order recursive systems of this type on a diagram that highlights many features we shall be discussing. On the horizontal axis we measure $x(t)$ and on the vertical axis we measure $x(t+1)$. Next we draw a 45°-line. Along such a line we have the condition that $x(t+1) = x(t)$. This means that any such equilibrium point, any fixed point of the system, must lie somewhere on this line. Next we draw the equation $3 + \frac{1}{2}x(t)$. This is just a straight line with intercept 3 and slope $\frac{1}{2}$. For this exercise we assume a continuous relationship. The situation is shown in figure 1.1. It is quite clear from this figure that the line $3 + \frac{1}{2}x(t)$ cuts the 45°-line at the value 6, which satisfies the condition

$$x(t+1) = x(t) = x^* = 6$$

It is also quite clear from figure 1.1 that this line can cut the 45°-line in only one place. This means that the equilibrium point, the fixed point of the system, is unique.

Given the starting value of $x(0) = 10$, the next value is found from a point on the line, namely $x(1) = 3 + \frac{1}{2}x(0) = 3 + \frac{1}{2}(10) = 8$. At this stage the value of $x(1)$ is read on the vertical axis. But if we move horizontally across to the 45°-line, then we can establish this *same* value on the horizontal axis. Given this value of $x(1)$ on the horizontal axis, then $x(2)$ is simply read off from the equation once again, namely $x(2) = 3 + \frac{1}{2}x(1) = 3 + \frac{1}{2}(8) = 7$. Continuing to perform this operation will take the system to the equilibrium point $x^* = 6$. The line pattern that emerges is referred to as a **cobweb**. We shall consider these in more detail in chapter 2.

It would appear on the face of it that the fixed point $x^* = 6$ is a stable fixed point, in the sense that the sequence starting at $x(0) = 10$ converges on it. But we must establish that this is true for other starting values. This may have been an exception! Suppose we take a starting value below the equilibrium point, say $x(0) = 3$. If we do this, the sequence that arises is 3, 4.5, 5.25, 5.625 ... So once again we note that the sequence appears to be converging on the fixed point of the system. This is also shown in figure 1.1. It is very easy to establish that no matter what the starting value for the variable x, the system will over time converge on the fixed point $x^* = 6$. Not only is this fixed point stable, but

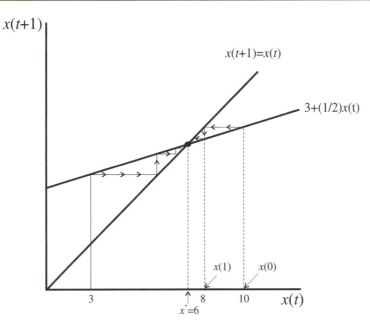

Figure 1.1

also it is said to be **globally stable**. The word 'global' indicates that it does not matter what value of x is taken as a starting value, whether near to the fixed point or far away from the fixed point, the system will always converge on the fixed point.

To reiterate, we have established that the system has an equilibrium point (a fixed point), that there is only one such equilibrium point and that this fixed point is globally stable. This is a lot of information.

1.3 Deterministic dynamical models

We can use the model we have just outlined to clarify more clearly what we mean by a 'dynamic model'. In doing this, however, let us generalise the initial point. Let this be denoted $x(0) = x_0$, then the system can be written

$$x(t+1) = 3 + \tfrac{1}{2}x(t) \quad x(0) = x_0 \tag{1.2}$$

This is a **deterministic dynamical model** (or deterministic dynamical system). It is a dynamic system because it deals with the value of the variable x over time. Given $x(0) = x_0$, then we can trace out the whole series of value of $x(t)$, for all time periods t from period 0 onwards. Notice that the series is crucially dependent on the initial condition. A different initial condition, as in our example above, will lead to quite a different series of numbers, although they will in this instance converge on the same fixed point. Why have we referred to it as 'deterministic'? It is deterministic because given the *same* initial value, the sequence of numbers is always the *same*. The initial condition and the specification of the recursive equation determine the sequence. There is no random element entering the series. Even if we calculate the sequence on a computer the numbers will be identical for the same starting value. It does not matter which software we use or which chip is contained in the computer. The whole system is deterministic.

Let us generalise the model. Suppose

(1.3) $$x(t+1) = a + bx(t) \quad x(0) = x_0$$

This is still a deterministic dynamical system. However, to establish the sequence of $x(t)$ over time we need to know the values of a and b, which are referred to as the **parameters** of the system. Parameters are constants of the system and typically capture the structure of the problem under investigation. They are therefore sometimes called **structural parameters**. We now have the three ingredients that are necessary to specify a deterministic dynamical system. They are:

(1)   the initial condition, namely $x(0) = x_0$
(2)   the values of the parameters, here the values of a and b
(3)   the sequence of values over time of the variable x.

As we shall see later, the fact that the system is deterministic does not mean that it may not appear like a random series. It simply means that given the initial condition and the same values for the parameters, then the sequence of values that are generated will always be the same no matter what they look like.

1.4 Dynamical systems on a spreadsheet

We shall frequently be displaying dynamical systems on a spreadsheet and so we shall use our present model to illustrate how this is done. Spreadsheets are ideal mediums for investigating recursive systems, and a great deal of dynamic investigation can easily be undertaken with their help. Using spreadsheets avoids the necessity of establishing complex formulas for solution paths. Of course the more one understands about such solution methods, the more one can appreciate the nature of the dynamic system under investigation. For individuals wishing to know such solution methods they will find these in my *Economic Dynamics* (Shone, 1997).

From the very outset we want to set up the model in general terms so we can undertake some analysis. This may involve changing the initial value and/or changing the value of one or more of the parameters. The situation is shown in figure 1.2. At the top of the spreadsheet we have the values of the two parameters a and b. The values themselves are in cells C2 and C3, respectively. When using spreadsheets it is essential to understand from the very outset that cells can have absolute addresses or relative addresses. An absolute address is distinguished from a relative address by having the $-sign precede the row and column designation: C3 is a relative address while $C$3 is an absolute address. The importance of this distinction will become clear in a moment.

In the first column we place our time periods, $t = 0, 1, 2$, etc. It is not necessary to type in these values, and it would be tedious to do so if you wanted to investigate the dynamics of a model over 500 time periods or even 2000! Most

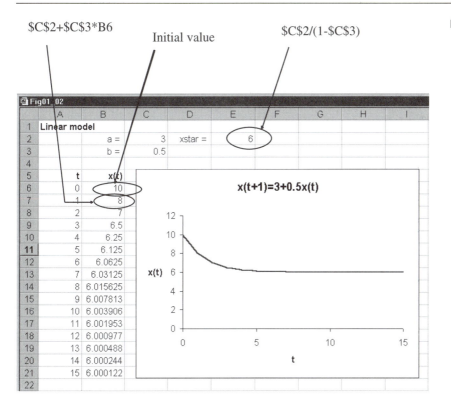

$C$2+$C$3*B6   Initial value $C$2/(1-$C$3)   Figure 1.2

software packages have a 'Fill' command. You simply specify the initial value (here 0) and then block down and request a fill with the incremental value included, here an increment of 1. That is all that is necessary. It is useful to include the time periods because it then becomes easier to graph the series $x(t)$. Since the row headings take place along row 5, the time periods are in cells A6, A7, etc. Next we place in cell B6 the initial value. In this example we insert the value 10.

At this stage it is essential to distinguish the absolute and relative address. Since the parameter values will always be the same, we need to refer to the absolute value in cell C2 and C3, i.e. the parameter a has the value in cell $C$2 while the parameter b has the value in cell $C$3. We now need to write a formula in cell B7. A comparison between the algebraic formula and the spreadsheet formula is useful here. These are for the value $x(1)$

$$= a + bx(0)$$
$$= $C$2 + $C$3*B6$$

Notice that B6 is a relative address, it simply refers to the previous value of x, which in this instance is the initial value 10. Also notice that it is necessary when specifying formulas in a spreadsheet to indicate a multiplication by the 'star' symbol. Once this formula is entered it is replaced by the value it takes, in this example the value 8.

The power of the spreadsheet really comes into play at this point. Consider for a moment what we would do if we wished to calculate the value of $x(2)$.

This value is positioned in cell B8. Again comparing the algebraic specification and the spreadsheet will help clarify what is going on

$$= a + bx(1)$$
$$= \$C\$2 + \$C\$3 * B7$$

Because the parameter values have absolute addresses, their values do not change. However, B7 is a relative address and refers to the cell immediately above. That in turn has already been calculated. But the spreadsheet formula in cell B8 is almost identical to the formula in cell B7, the only difference is the value which x takes, which is always the value in the cell immediately above. If you copy the formula in cell B7 to the clipboard and paste it down for as many periods as you are considering, the computations are immediately carried out, with the value of x changing in the formula each time to be the value of x in the cell immediately above. This can be done because the cell involves a relative address (along with some absolute addresses) and this relative address keeps changing. Absolute addresses do not change. So you can paste down 13, 488 times or even 1,998 times with one click.

We have laboured this point here because it is the feature we shall be using throughout. It also indicates that when dealing with dynamic systems on a spreadsheet it is useful to set out the parameter values and then refer to their absolute addresses and ensure formulas are entered *and changed* to include the appropriate absolute and relative addresses. They need to be changed since all formulas are entered with only relative addresses.

The spreadsheet involves one other computed value, namely the fixed point of the system. Since

$$x^* = a + bx^*$$

then

(1.4) $$x^* = \frac{a}{1-b}$$

In the spreadsheet we label the fixed point as 'xstar=' and its value is placed in cell E2 where this value is

$$= \$C\$2/(1 - \$C\$3)$$

Consequently any change to the parameter values is immediately reflected in a change to the equilibrium value.

Note
It is always useful to check that you have entered formulas in the main body of the computations. This can easily be accomplished. Copy the equilibrium value to the cell containing the value for $x(0)$, cell B6. If your formula is correctly entered then *every* entry in column B should be the same equilibrium value!

One final thing to do is to graph the series of $x(t)$ against time, t. This is simply a X-Y plot with time on the horizontal axis and the variable x on the vertical axis. Here we assume you are familiar with your spreadsheet's graphing facility. Typically spreadsheets allow you either to place a graph on its own sheet, or as a graphic item on the sheet where the calculations are being done. This latter position is very useful when you wish to experiment with your model because then you can see immediately the impact of changing some element of the model. Placing it on its own sheet is useful if you wish to have a printout of the graph. We shall experiment with the model in section 1.5. To insert the graph, block cells A6:B21 and invoke the chart wizard. Choose the X-Y plot and choose the option with the points joined. The wizard automatically knows that the first column (cells A6:A21) is the values on the x-axis. We have also included a title and labels for the two axes. We also have turned the y-axis label through 90°. Figure 1.2 shows the resulting time path of $x(t)$. In order to see the dynamics of the path more clearly, we have suppressed the points and joined the points up with a continuous line. The plot readily reveals the stability of the equilibrium, with the path of $x(t)$ starting at the value 10 and tending to the equilibrium value of 6.

1.5 Experimentation

It is now time to experiment with the model in order to investigate the characteristics of its dynamics. We shall leave this up to the reader, and here just indicate what you should expect to observe.

1.5.1 Changing initial conditions

We stated above that this model was globally stable; that no matter what the initial value was, the system would always converge on the equilibrium value, (1.4). Verify this. Try for example $x(0) = 3$, 0, 7, -2 and 25. No matter what value is chosen, the system will always converge on the value 6. Of course, sometimes it takes a long time to do this. If the initial value were 100, for example, then it takes a much longer time to reach the equilibrium value than if the initial value were 10.

1.5.2 Changing the parameter a

Raising (lowering) the value of the parameter a raises (lowers) the equilibrium value. This readily follows from the formula for the equilibrium value, but it is readily verified on the spreadsheet. It is also apparent from figure 1.1. A rise in the parameter a is a rise in the intercept in the formula $a + bx(t)$, and this will intersect the 45°-line further up. A fall in the parameter a will do the opposite. Such a change alters only the equilibrium value, the value of the fixed point. It has no bearing on the stability properties of that fixed point. The system remains convergent. Verify these statements by changing the value of the parameter a and choose again the same initial values for the variable x.

1.5.3 *Changing the parameter* b

Retain the initial value of $x(0) = 10$ but now let $b = 1.5$. Not only does the equilibrium become negative, with value -6, but also the system diverges away from the equilibrium value. The variable $x(t)$ just grows and grows. Let $b = -\frac{1}{2}$. The equilibrium value falls from 6 to 2. Furthermore, the values that x take oscillate above and below this value, but converge on it. If $b = -1.5$, the system still oscillates, but the oscillations diverge away from the equilibrium value, which is now 1.2. Finally take $b = -1$. Equilibrium becomes 1.5 and the system oscillates either side of this value indefinitely, with values -7 and 10, and the system neither moves towards the equilibrium or away from it.

It is apparent from these experimentations that changing the value of the parameter b can have drastic consequences on the dynamics of this system, far more dramatic an impact than occurs when the parameter a is altered.

Carry out some more experimentation with changes in the value of the parameter b. What you should conclude is the following:

(1)   A value of $0 < b < 1$ leads to the system converging on the equilibrium value.
(2)   A value of $b = 1$ leads to no fixed point. (What does this imply about the graph of $x(t+1)$ against $x(t)$?)
(3)   A value of $-1 < b < 0$ leads to the system oscillating, but converging on the equilibrium value.
(4)   A value of $b = -1$ leads to oscillations between two values, neither moving toward nor away from the equilibrium value.
(5)   A value of $b < -1$ leads to oscillations which diverge further and further from the equilibrium value.

All these statements are true regardless of the initial value taken by the system (other than the equilibrium value).

What began as a very simple linear model has led to a whole diversity of dynamic behaviour. It clearly illustrates that simply demonstrating that a model has an equilibrium point is not sufficient. It is vital to establish whether the system will converge or not converge on this equilibrium. It is essential to investigate the dynamics of the model.

1.6 Difference equations

The recursive system we have been analysing, represented here as (1.5)

(1.5) $$x(t+1) = 3 + \tfrac{1}{2}x(t)$$

can be expressed in a different way which is often very revealing about its dynamics. If we subtract from both sides the same value, then we have not changed the characteristics of the system at all. In particular, the equilibrium value is unchanged and the stability/instability of the system is unchanged. Suppose, then, that we subtract from both sides the value $x(t)$, then we have

$$x(t+1) - x(t) = \Delta x(t+1) = 3 + \tfrac{1}{2}x(t) - x(t) = 3 + \left(\tfrac{1}{2} - 1\right)x(t)$$

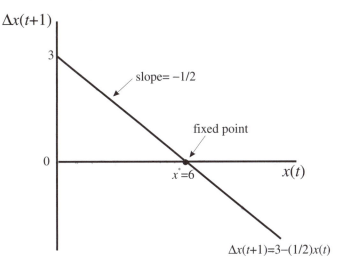

Figure 1.3

or

$$\Delta x(t+1) = 3 - \tfrac{1}{2}x(t)$$ (1.6)

This relationship is referred to as a **difference equation** because it expresses the difference $\Delta x(t+1) = x(t+1) - x(t)$ as a function of $x(t)$. It is also a **first-order difference equation** because we are considering only the first difference. The system is shown in figure 1.3, where we place $x(t)$ on the horizontal axis and $\Delta x(t+1)$ on the vertical axis. Of particular note is that the intercept is the value 3 and the slope of the line is $-\tfrac{1}{2}$.

Let us establish that the properties of the system are the same. Consider first the equilibrium value, the fixed point of the system. In equilibrium we know that $x(t+1) = x(t) = x^*$. Then it follows that $\Delta x(t+1) = x(t+1) - x(t) = 0$. Given this situation, then $0 = 3 - \tfrac{1}{2}x^*$ or $x^* = 6$. We have therefore verified that the equilibrium value is unchanged. In terms of figure 1.3, the equilibrium is where the equation $3 - \tfrac{1}{2}x(t)$ cuts the horizontal axis, because at this point $\Delta x(t+1) = 0$.

Now consider the stability or otherwise of the equilibrium point. Take the typical initial value we have been using of $x(0) = 10$ This value lies above the equilibrium value of 6, and so $\Delta x(t+1)$ is negative. If $\Delta x(t+1) < 0$ then $x(t+1) < x(t)$ and so $x(t)$ is falling over time. In fact this will continue to be so until the fixed point is reached. If, on the other hand, we take $x(0) = 3$, then $\Delta x(t+1) > 0$ and so $x(t+1) > x(t)$, and hence $x(t)$ is rising over time. Again, this will continue to be so until the fixed point is reached. Once again, therefore, we have demonstrated that the fixed point is 6 and that it is stable. Even more, no matter what value of $x(0)$ we take, the system will converge on the equilibrium. The equilibrium is unique and globally stable. The characteristic to take note of here is that the line that passes through the equilibrium in figure 1.3 is *negatively sloped* and cuts the x-axis at only one point.

Consider next the situation where $b = 1.5$. In this case

$$x(t+1) - x(t) = \Delta x(t+1) = 3 + 1.5x(t) - x(t) = 3 + \left(1.5 - 1\right)x(t)$$

or

(1.7) $\Delta x(t+1) = 3 + 0.5x(t)$

Is the equilibrium unchanged? No, it changes since

$$0 = 3 + 0.5x^*$$
$$x^* = -6$$

Also the line $3 + 0.5x(t)$ is *positively sloped*. At $x(0) = 10$ $\Delta x(t+1) > 0$ and so $x(t)$ is rising. The system is moving further away (in the positive direction) from the equilibrium value. A value of $x(t)$ less than -6 will readily reveal that $\Delta x(t+1) < 0$ and so $x(t)$ is falling, and the system moves further away (in the negative direction) from the equilibrium point. A linear system with a positively sloped difference equation, therefore, exhibits an unstable fixed point.

To summarise, for *linear* difference equations of the first order, if the difference equation has a nonzero slope, then a unique fixed point exists where the difference equation cuts the horizontal axis. If the difference equation is *negatively* sloped, then the fixed point of the system is unique and globally stable. If the linear difference equation is *positively* sloped, then the fixed point of the system is unique and globally unstable. We have demonstrated all this in previous sections. If $b = 1$ the slope is zero and no fixed point is defined. All we have done here is to show the same characteristics in a different way. It may not at this point seem obvious why we would do this. It is worth doing only if it gives some additional insight. It gives some, but admittedly not very much. Why we have laboured this approach, however, is that when we turn to two variables, it is much more revealing. We shall see this in later chapters.

1.7 Attractors and repellors

We noted that in our example if $-1 < b < 1$ then the system is stable and the sequence of points converges on the fixed point. It converges either directly if b is positive or in smaller and smaller oscillations if b is negative. If a trajectory (a sequence of points) approaches the fixed point as time increases, then the fixed point is said to be an **attractor**. On the other hand, if the sequence of points moves away from the fixed point, then the fixed point is said to be a **repellor**.

We can illustrate these concepts by means of the **phase line**. In constructing the phase line we make use of the difference equation representation of our recursive model. Our model is

(1.8) $x(t+1) = 3 + \frac{1}{2}x(t)$ $x(0) = 10$

and the difference equation version of it is

(1.9) $\Delta x(t+1) = 3 - \frac{1}{2}x(t)$ $x(0) = 10$

This is shown in the upper part of figure 1.4. The fixed point, denoted x^*, is where the line $3 - \frac{1}{2}x(t)$ cuts the horizontal axis, which is at the value 6. The phase line simply denotes the variable $x(t)$, and on this line is marked any fixed

Figure 1.4

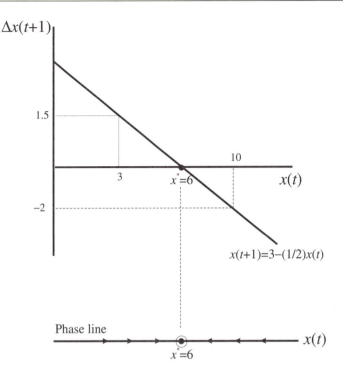

points (here we have only one), and arrows indicating the path of $x(t)$ over time. To the left of x^*, $\Delta x(t)$ is positive, and so $x(t)$ is rising over time. The arrows are therefore shown pointing to the right. Similarly, when the initial point is to the right of x^*, $\Delta x(t)$ is negative and so $x(t)$ is falling over time. The arrows are therefore shown pointing to the left. The phase line thus illustrates that the fixed point is attracting the system from any position on either side. We have already established that this is the only fixed point and that it is globally stable. Hence, for any initial value not equal to the equilibrium, the system will be attracted to the fixed point.

Consider next the recursive model

$$x(t+1) = 3 + 1.5x(t) \quad x(0) = 10 \tag{1.10}$$

with the difference equation version

$$\Delta x(t+1) = 3 + \tfrac{1}{2}x(t) \quad x(0) = 10 \tag{1.11}$$

The equilibrium point is $x^* = -6$, and the relationship $3 + \tfrac{1}{2}x(t)$ is positively sloped. The situation is shown in figure 1.5. Once again we place the phase line in the diagram below. For any initial point to the right of -6, then $\Delta x(t+1)$ is positive, and so $x(t)$ is rising over time. The arrows are therefore shown pointing to the right and the system is moving away from the fixed point. Similarly, when the initial point is to the left of x^*, $\Delta x(t)$ is negative and so $x(t)$ is falling over time. The arrows are therefore shown pointing to the left and once again the system is moving away from the fixed point. The phase line thus illustrates that the fixed point is repelling the system for any initial value not equal to the equilibrium value.

Figure 1.5

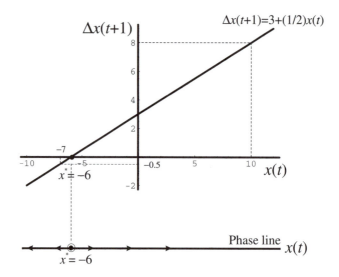

Fixed points that are attracting indicate stability while fixed points that repel indicate instability. But a fixed point can be neither of these, even in simple linear models. We noted this above when b was equal to minus unity. The system oscillated between two values: one above the equilibrium and one below the equilibrium. The system neither moved towards the fixed point nor away from it. In this case we observe a **periodic cycle**, and in this example the period is 2.[1]

1.8 Nonlinear dynamical systems

Although a considerable amount of analysis has taken place concerning linear models, it must always be kept in mind that in general the world is nonlinear, and it is necessary to model the topic of interest with nonlinear equations. Nonlinear models lead to far more diverse behaviour. They can lead to more than one equilibrium point, they can lead to a system exhibiting both stability or instability in different neighbourhoods and they can lead to cyclical behaviour of orders greater than two.

Our intention in this section is to present some introductory remarks about nonlinear systems and to introduce some new concepts. A fuller treatment will occur in later sections of this book. Although nonlinear systems are more complex and lead to more diverse behaviour, they can still be investigated in a fairly easy fashion with the aid of a spreadsheet.

Consider the following nonlinear recursive model

(1.12) $$x(t+1) = c + ax^2(t) \quad x(0) = x_0$$

As earlier, the equilibrium of the system is found by setting $x(t+1) = x(t) = x^*$, then

---

[1] Period cycles are explained more fully in chapter 10.

$$x^* = c + ax^{*2}$$
$$ax^{*2} - x^* + c = 0$$

with solutions

$$x_1^* = \frac{1 + \sqrt{1 - 4ac}}{2a} \text{ and } x_2^* = \frac{1 - \sqrt{1 - 4ac}}{2a} \tag{1.13}$$

We immediately see from (1.13) that there are *two* fixed points to this system. Second, the fixed points are real valued only if $1 - 4ac \geq 0$. But if there are two fixed points to the system, then any consideration of stability or instability cannot be global; it must be in relation to a particular fixed point. When there is more than one fixed point we refer to **local stability** and **local instability**. The word 'local' indicates that we are considering stability only in a (small) neighbourhood of the fixed point.

Consider the following nonlinear recursive system

$$x(t+1) = 2 - \tfrac{1}{2}x^2(t) \quad x(0) = x_0 \tag{1.14}$$

which leads to equilibrium points $x_1^* = -1 + \sqrt{5} = 1.23607$ and $x_2^* = -1 - \sqrt{5} = -3.23607$ (see box 1).

Box 1 Solving quadratic equations with a spreadsheet

We shall be solving quadratic equations frequently in this book and so it will be useful to set the solutions up on a spreadsheet. Let any quadratic equation be written in the form

$$ax^2 + bx + c = 0$$

then we know that the solutions are given by

$$x_1 = \frac{-b + \sqrt{b^2 - 4ac}}{2a}, x_2 = \frac{-b - \sqrt{b^2 - 4ac}}{2a}$$

Now set up a spreadsheet with the parameters a, b and c, as shown below. Let their values be placed in cells F3, F4 and F5. (To the left we insert the formulas as a reminder.) Then in cells F7 and F8 place the results, i.e.

F7	$= \left(-b + \sqrt{b^2 - 4ac}\right)/2a$
	$= (-\$F\$4 + SQRT(\$F\$4\^2 - 4*\$F\$3*\$F\$5))/(2*\$F\$3)$
F8	$= \left(-b - \sqrt{b^2 - 4ac}\right)/2a$
	$= (-\$F\$4 - SQRT(\$F\$4\^2 - 4*\$F\$3*\$F\$5))/(2*\$F\$3)$

Save this spreadsheet. It can now be used to solve any quadratic of the form $ax^2 + bx + c = 0$

	A	B	C	D	E	F	G
	Quadratic						
1	Quadratic						
2							
3		$ax^2 + bx + c = 0$				a =	1
4						b =	-2
5		$x = \dfrac{-b \pm \sqrt{b^2 - 4ac}}{2a}$				c =	-3
6							
7						x1 =	3
8		$x_1 = \dfrac{-b + \sqrt{b^2 - 4ac}}{2a}$				x2 =	-1
9							
10		$x_2 = \dfrac{-b - \sqrt{b^2 - 4ac}}{2a}$					
11							
12							
13							

The cobweb representation of this nonlinear system is shown in figure 1.6, where we have the curve $2 - \frac{1}{2}x^2(t)$ and the 45°-line denoting $x(t+1) = x(t)$.

In order to investigate what is happening in the neighbourhood of the fixed points let us set this problem up on a spreadsheet in just the same manner as our linear example, as shown in figure 1.7. Once again we set this up in general terms, placing the parameters a and c above the data we are deriving. Also included are the formulas for the two fixed points of the system. These are entered in cells E2 and E3 with the instructions

$$(1 + SQRT(1 - 4*\$C\$2*\$C\$3))/(2*\$C\$3)$$
$$(1 - SQRT(1 - 4*\$C\$2*\$C\$3))/(2*\$C\$3)$$

We next place the initial value in cell B6, which is here equal to 1.25.

In considering what to place in cell B7, consider the algebraic representation and the spreadsheet representation of the problem

$$= 2 - \tfrac{1}{2}x^2(0)$$
$$= \$C\$2 + \$C\$3*B6\hat{}2$$

Notice that cell C3 includes the minus sign and that we specify powers in spreadsheets by using the 'caret' symbol. Although the system we are investigating is more complex, there is fundamentally no difference in the way we set it up on the spreadsheet. We can now copy cell B7 to the clipboard and then copy down for as many periods as we wish. To verify we have done all this correctly, copy one of the equilibrium values and place it in cell B6 for the initial value. If all is OK, then *all* values should be 1.23607 (or approximately so depending on the decimal places you have specified for your results). Having performed this test satisfactorily, replace $x(0)$ by 1.25 once again and then experimentation can begin.

1.8.1 A change in the initial value

Let us consider first the lower equilibrium point, $x_1^* = -3.23607$ and an initial value of $x(0) = -3.5$. Given this initial value, the system declines very rapidly,

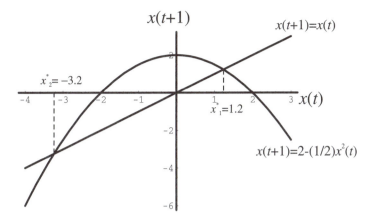

Figure 1.6

Figure 1.7

	A	B	C	D	E	F	G	H	I
1	Nonlinear dynamics								
2		c =	2	xstar1 =	-3.23607				
3		a =	-0.5	xstar2 =	1.236068				
4									
5	t	x(t)							
6	0	1.25							
7	1	1.21875							
8	2	1.257324							
9	3	1.209568							
10	4	1.268473							
11	5	1.195488							
12	6	1.285404							
13	7	1.173869							
14	8	1.311016							
15	9	1.140618							
16	10	1.349495							
17	11	1.089432							
18	12	1.406569							
19	13	1.010781							
20	14	1.48916							
21	15	0.891201							

moving further in the negative direction. What about a value slightly larger than -3.2? Consider the value $x(0) = -3.1$. The system certainly moves away from the fixed point, but then begins to oscillate between the values 0 and 2. For the moment we shall not concern ourselves with the oscillatory behaviour, and we shall take up this point later. All we are establishing here is that for initial values a little larger than -3.23607 the system moves away from it, which it certainly does. Hence, the fixed point $x_1^* = -3.23607$ is *locally* unstable.

What about the fixed point $x_2^* = 1.23607$? Consider first a value 0.9. Very soon the system settles into an oscillatory behaviour, oscillating once again between 0 and 2. Consider an initial point above $x_2^* = 1.23607$, say 1.5. The system once again converges on the oscillation between 0 and 2. What if we

Figure 1.8

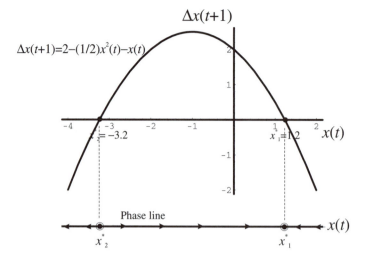

choose values even closer to the fixed point? Consider values 1.2 and 1.25, respectively. With initial value 1.2 the system once again settles down to the cycle 0 and 2 by about period 25. With initial point 1.25 the system settles down to the same cycle by about period 30. The fixed point $x_2^* = 1.23607$ is neither an attractor nor a repellor.

In order to see what is taking place let us consider the difference equation version of the model. This is

(1.15)
$$\Delta x(t+1) = 2 - \tfrac{1}{2}x^2(t) - x(t) \quad x(0) = x_0$$

In equilibrium $\Delta x(t+1) = 0$ and so

$$2 - \tfrac{1}{2}x^{*2} - x^* = 0$$
$$\text{or } x^{*2} + 2x^* - 4 = 0$$

with solutions

$$x_1^* = -1 + \sqrt{5} \quad x_2^* = -1 - \sqrt{5}$$

The same equilibrium points have once again been established. The phase diagram representation of the problem is drawn in figure 1.8. The curve represents the equation $2 - \tfrac{1}{2}x^2(t) - x(t)$. Here we are treating the curve as continuous. ***This is important.*** To the left of $x_2^* = -3.23607$ $\Delta x(t+1) < 0$, which indicates that $x(t)$ is falling, so the system is moving even further in the negative direction. Slightly to the right of $x_2^* = -3.23607$ then $\Delta x(t+1) > 0$ and so $x(t)$ is rising, i.e. moving away from the fixed point. From this perspective the fixed point $x_2^* = -3.23607$ is locally unstable and is a repellor.

Now turn to the larger of the fixed points, $x_1^* = 1.23607$. Slightly to the left of this fixed point, in its neighbourhood, $\Delta x(t+1) > 0$ and so $x(t)$ is rising. Slightly to the right of the fixed point, $\Delta x(t+1) < 0$ and so $x(t)$ is falling. In terms of this *continuous* representation it appears that the fixed point $x_1^* = 1.23607$ is locally stable and is an attractor. But this seems in contradiction to our spreadsheet investigation – at least for the higher fixed point! Why is this?

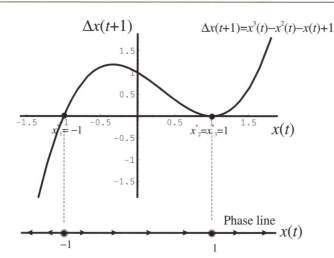

Figure 1.9

What has been illustrated here is that the properties of continuous models are **not** necessarily the same for their discrete counterpart. In fact, for many discrete nonlinear models oscillatory behaviour arises. We shall see why in later chapters. For the present all we wish to do is point out that if you are interested in continuous models, then the difference representation of the model with its accompanying phase line is sufficient to establish fixed points and their local stability or instability. If, however, the model is in discrete time, then it should be investigated on a spreadsheet to establish whether some of the fixed points exhibit oscillations.

Let us take one further example to illustrate these points. Consider the non-linear recursive model

$$x(t+1) = x^3(t) - x^2(t) + 1 \quad x(0) = x_0 \tag{1.16}$$

The difference form of the model is

$$\Delta x(t+1) = x^3(t) - x^2(t) - x(t) + 1 \quad x(0) = x_0 \tag{1.17}$$

In equilibrium $\Delta x(t+1) = 0$ and so we have

$$x^{*3} - x^{*2} - x^* + 1 = 0$$
$$\text{or } (x^* - 1)^2(1 + x^*) = 0$$

Since the difference equation is to the power three, then there are three solutions to this equation. These are

$$x_1^* = -1, \quad x_2^* = 1, \quad x_3^* = 1$$

The reason why two fixed points are the same is clearly shown in figure 1.9, which plots the equation $x^3(t) - x^2(t) - x(t) + 1$ and shows the phase line below.

Consider first the continuous form of the model as shown in figure 1.9. To the left of $x^* = -1$ $\Delta x(t+1) < 0$ and so $x(t)$ is falling. To the right of $x^* = -1$ $\Delta x(t+1) > 0$ and so $x(t)$ is rising. The fixed point $x^* = -1$ is locally unstable and is a repellor. Now consider the fixed point $x^* = 1$. To the left of this point $\Delta x(t+1) > 0$ and so $x(t)$ is rising. To the right of $x^* = 1$ $\Delta x(t+1) > 0$ and so $x(t)$

is still rising. The unusual nature of the fixed point $x^* = 1$ is shown by the phase line with its arrows. The arrows are moving towards the fixed point $x^* = 1$ and then away from it to the right. It is as if the system is being 'shunted along'. For this reason, the fixed point $x^* = 1$ is referred to as a **shunt**.

Does the discrete form of the model reveal these properties? In setting up the model on a spreadsheet simply enter the initial value for the variable x, and then in the cell immediately below the initial value, type in the formula – moving the cursor to the cell above when placing in the variable x. Then copy this cell to the clipboard and paste down for as many periods as you wish. Doing this reveals the following. A value to the left of -1, say -1.2, leads the system ever more in the negative direction. A value just above -1, say -0.9, leads the system towards the upper fixed point $x^* = 1$. Taking a value just to the left of the upper fixed point, say 0.5, leads the system to the fixed point $x^* = 1$. Taking a value just above this fixed point, say 1.1, soon leads the system into ever-higher values. Once again we have verified the same properties for this specific model. In particular, we have illustrated that the lower fixed point is a repellor, and is locally unstable, while the upper fixed point (strictly two) is a shunt. In this particular example, therefore, there is no disparity in the conclusions drawn between the continuous form of the model and the discrete form.

1.9 Continuous models

In section 1.8 we talked about continuous models but used a discrete representation of them. We need to be more precise about continuous models and how to represent them. This is the purpose of this section. In section 1.10 we shall consider a spreadsheet representation of continuous models using Euler's approximation. This will be found especially useful when we consider systems of equations in chapter 4 and later.

If a variable x varies continuously with time, t, then $x(t)$ is a continuous variable. If we know, say from theory, that the change in $x(t)$ over time, denoted $dx(t)/dt$, is

(1.18)
$$\frac{dx(t)}{dt} = f[x(t)]$$

then we have a **first-order differential equation**. If t does not enter explicitly as a separate variable, then the differential equation is said to be an **autonomous differential equation**.[2]

By way of example, suppose

(1.19)
$$\frac{dx(t)}{dt} = 4 - 2x(t)$$

[2] This is the mathematicians' use of the word 'autonomous'. They mean independent of time. When an economist refers to a variable being autonomous they mean being independent of income.

Figure 1.10

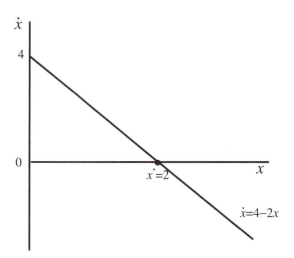

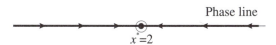

Phase line

then this is a first-order differential equation. $dx(t)/dt$ simply denotes the change in $x(t)$ over time, and $4 - 2x(t)$ gives the formula for this change. Since time does not enter explicitly in this equation then it is autonomous. A non-autonomous equation would be something like

$$\frac{dx(t)}{dt} = 4 - 2x(t) + 2t \tag{1.20}$$

where t enters explicitly. In this book we shall consider only autonomous differential equations as defined here. Since x is always assumed to be a function of t, then we can drop the time designation and write (1.19) more succinctly as

$$\frac{dx}{dt} = 4 - 2x \tag{1.21}$$

A convention used in mathematics, and one we shall use too, is to denote dx/dt by the dot-symbol, i.e. $\dot{x}$. This now means that (1.21) can be written as

$$\dot{x} = 4 - 2x \tag{1.22}$$

The fixed point, the equilibrium point, of this model is where x is unchanging, which means where $\dot{x} = 0$. This gives the fixed point

$$0 = 4 - 2x^*$$
$$x^* = 2$$

Furthermore, this fixed point is globally stable. We establish this in exactly the same way as we did with our discrete models. The situation is shown in figure 1.10.

The model has only one fixed point, namely $x^*=2$. The relationship between the change in x, denoted $\dot{x}$, and the variable x is shown in the upper diagram in figure 1.10. Given $x(0)$ for period 0, the initial period, where we assume $x(0)<2$, then $\dot{x}>0$ and so x is rising. For any initial point above $x^*=2$, then $\dot{x}<0$ and so x is falling. This is true no matter what value of x we take on the real line (other than the equilibrium point itself). Hence, $x^*=2$ is an attractor and is globally stable.

If the model includes the initial condition, then

(1.23) $\dot{x}=f(x)$ $x(0)=x_0$

and (1.23) is referred to as the **initial value problem**. If $f(x)$ is linear and negatively sloped, then there is a unique fixed point which is globally stable. If $f(x)$ is linear and positively sloped, then there is a unique fixed point which is globally unstable. If $f(x)$ is nonlinear and more than one equilibrium exists, then we can refer only to local stability or instability in just the same way as we did with the discrete models earlier in this chapter.

Return to the example of the shunt. In its continuous form, we have the model

(1.24) $\dfrac{dx}{dt}=\dot{x}=x^3-x^2-x+1$ $x(0)=x_0$

where x is a continuous function of time. The model is the same as that shown in figure 1.9 with the one exception that we place $\dot{x}$ on the vertical axis and not $\Delta x(t+1)$. All the remaining dynamics is the same.

1.10 Continuous differential equations on a spreadsheet

Return to the simple example of section 1.9, with the initial condition $x(0)=1$

(1.25) $\dot{x}=4-2x$ $x(0)=1$

Now this is a simple differential equation and there are known techniques for solving it.[3] We are not concerned about that here, and we shall simply state that the solution is

(1.26) $x(t)=2-e^{-2t}$ or $x(t)=2-\exp(-2t)$

Of course if we did know this we could plot the path of $x(t)$ for some length of time. This is illustrated in figure 1.11. The solution curve $x(t)$ goes through the point $x(0)=1$, which is our initial condition, and shown by point P. Now let an interval of time pass, which we shall denote by Δt. If we did know the solution curve, then at a value of $t=0.01$, i.e. $\Delta t=0.01$, the value of x would be

$$2-e^{-2(0.01)}=1.0198$$

This is shown by point Q. But suppose we do not know the solution curve. Can we find an approximate value for point Q? Yes, we can. The change in x over

---

[3] See Shone (1997, ch.2).

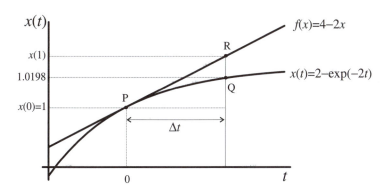

Figure 1.11

time is the slope of the solution curve at any particular point. Consequently, the slope of the solution curve when $t=0$ is $4-2(1)=2$, since $x(0)=1$. Then the value Q is approximated by $x(1)$, and shown by the point R. But then

$$\text{slope at } P = \frac{x(1)-x(0)}{\Delta t}$$

$$f[x(0)] = \frac{x(1)-x(0)}{\Delta t}$$

$$\therefore \quad x(1) = x(0) + f[x(0)]\Delta t$$

In our example,

$$x(1) = 1 + (4-2(1))(0.01) = 1.02$$

which is not a bad approximation. In fact, we can always improve on the approximation by taking smaller intervals of time. More generally, our approximation is

$$x(t+1) = x(t) + f[x(t)]\Delta t \tag{1.27}$$

which is **Euler's approximation** to a differential equation. This approximation can be used for any linear or nonlinear single-variable differential equation.[4]

1.10.1 Solution path on a spreadsheet

The advantage of the Euler approximation is that it applies to any linear or nonlinear differential equation even if we cannot explicitly solve the model. Furthermore, it is in such a form that it can readily be set out on a spreadsheet. Before we begin, notice the importance of the initial condition. This sets the solution path to pass through this point and only one such solution path can go through the initial condition for autonomous differential equations – and these are the only types of differential equations we shall be dealing with. This gives us the value of x at time period 0. We label the time *periods* 0, 1, 2, ... and the value for the variable, x by $x(0)$, $x(1)$, $x(2)$, etc. The elapse of time, however,

---

[4] We shall see in chapter 4 how it can be adapted for two-variable models.

Figure 1.12

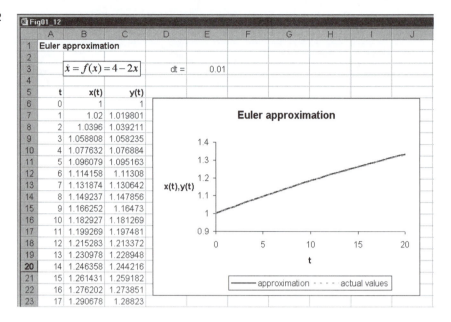

is only 0.01 between any two periods. The spreadsheet representation of our example is shown in figure 1.12.

In cell D3 we have the label 'dt =' to represent the symbol Δt, and set this value equal to 0.01 in cell E3. In cell B6 we place our initial value, $x(0) = 1$. Given this value, and the interval of time, we can calculate $x(1)$ in cell B7 as follows

$$= x(0) + f[x(0)]\Delta t$$
$$= B6 + (4 - 2*B6)*\$E\$3$$

This is then copied to the clipboard and pasted down. Here we have $t = 0, 1,$ ... 20. To see how good the approximation is we have also included the computations for the true solution curve in column C, i.e. (1.26). Again we place the initial condition in cell C6. Cell C7 then has the formula

$$= 2 - \exp(-2t)$$
$$= 2 - EXP(-2*A7*\$E\$3)$$

Notice that time t is given by A7*$E$3. This cell is then copied to the clipboard and pasted down. Given the small interval of time we have chosen, 0.01, there is virtually no noticeable difference between the true values and our approximation, which is very reassuring.[5] We shall utilise this approximation for two-variable models in chapter 4 and later.

---

[5] There are other superior approximations available that are given in books on differential equations.

1.11 Conclusion

In this chapter we have defined dynamic models, particularly deterministic dynamic models. It is not sufficient to demonstrate that a model has an equilibrium, a fixed point, it is also important to establish whether the fixed point is stable or not. By means of some simple examples we highlighted the concepts of global stability and global instability, attractors and repellors and periodic cycles.

Discrete dynamic models are recursive and can be represented in a number of ways. In this chapter we represented such systems as cobwebs, as a difference equation model and in a spreadsheet. The spreadsheet representation of a dynamical model allows a considerable amount of experimentation to be undertaken. The difference equation representation allows us to introduce the concept of the phase line. We next considered two nonlinear dynamical models, highlighting the more complex and more diverse behaviour to which they can give rise. Finally, we outlined continuous dynamic models of one variable, showing how the solution paths of such differential equations can be set up on a spreadsheet.

Exercises

(1)   Establish the fixed points of the following discrete systems and show the path of the system from the given initial condition

    (i) $x(t+1) = 5 - 0.2x(t)$ $x(0) = 2$

    (ii) $x(t+1) = -2 + 3x(t)$ $x(0) = 0.5$

    (iii) $x(t+1) = 3 + \dfrac{x(t)}{2}$ $x(0) = 1$

(2)   Establish whether the systems in qu.1 are globally stable or globally unstable.

(3)   Represent a phase line for the periodic solution to the linear equation

    $x(t+1) = 3 - x(t)$ $x(0) = 1$

(4)   Establish the fixed points of the following nonlinear discrete systems and establish their stability/instability properties

    (i) $x(t+1) = 3 + x^2(t) - 5x(t)$

    (ii) $x(t+1) = x^3(t) + 2x^2(t) - 2$

    (*Note*: $x^3 + 2x^2 - x - 2 = (x-1)(x^2 + 3x + 2)$, or plot the function $x^3 + 2x^2 - x - 2$ for $-3 < x < 3$)

(5)   Establish the fixed points of the following continuous models and their stability/instability properties

(i) $\dot{x} = 5 - 2x$

(ii) $\dot{x} = x^2 + x - 5$

(iii) $\dot{x} = x^3 + 2x^2 - x - 2$

Chapter 2
Demand and supply dynamics

2.1 Beyond the textbook

The first market studied in economics is that of demand and supply. With demand indicated by a downward sloping demand curve and supply represented by an upward sloping supply curve, then equilibrium in this market is where demand equals supply. But elementary textbooks tend to be rather unclear on what happens when the market is not in equilibrium. One typical story is that at a price below the equilibrium, where there is excess demand, price rises. This continues until the market is cleared. Where price is above the equilibrium, where there is a situation of excess supply, price falls. This continues until the market is cleared. This story is even less clear on what is happening to the *quantity traded* during this adjustment process. Consider for a moment a price that is below the equilibrium price. Here there is a situation of excess demand. It is this excess demand that puts pressure on price to rise. One assumption we can make is to assume that price rises by a proportion of the excess demand. Let us make all this clear with a simple linear demand and supply model.

Let

$$qd(t) = 20 - 4p(t)$$
$$qs(t) = 5 + 2p(t) \tag{2.1}$$

Equilibrium in this model is where demand is equal to supply. So we can establish immediately that

$$20 - 4p^* = 5 + 2p^*$$
$$p^* = 2.5$$
$$q^* = 10$$

where p^* and q^* denote equilibrium price and quantity, respectively. Turning to the dynamics, we have argued that price adjusts proportionally to the excess demand. More formally we can write this

$$\Delta p(t+1) = p(t+1) - p(t) = a(qd(t) - qs(t)) \quad a > 0 \tag{2.2}$$

What this equation clearly reveals is that when there is excess demand price rises by a proportion a of this excess demand. Price will continue to rise so long as there is excess demand. Similarly, if there is excess supply, or a negative excess demand, then price will fall, and will continue to fall until equilibrium is attained. The parameter a denotes the **speed of adjustment**, and the higher this value the faster the market approaches equilibrium and vice versa.

But what is *traded* at these nonequilibrium prices? Take a price below the equilibrium price, say a price of 2. At this price the quantity demanded is 12 and the quantity supplied is 9. But only *one* quantity can be traded on the market at any particular price. What quantity do we choose? This depends on what we assume about quantities traded. If no stocks exist in this market, then no matter what the level of demand is, sales cannot exceed what is supplied, and so only a quantity of 9 will be traded. On the other hand, if price is above the equilibrium, say a price of 4, then the quantity demanded is 4 and the quantity supplied is 13. Firms cannot force people to buy what they do not want. They can of course entice them to do so by altering the price, but for any given price, such as $p=4$, the quantity traded must be what is demanded, namely 4. If we are assuming no stocks, as we presently are, then the excess supply simply perishes. Of course, in some markets where goods can be stored, such excess supply can become part of inventories. Then, when there is excess demand, some (or all) of that excess demand can be met out of stocks. In this case, however, the quantity traded can be anywhere between the quantity supplied and the quantity demanded depending on the level of stocks available and how much of these stocks will be released to satisfy the excess demand. But such a model would need to set out clearly assumptions about stock behaviour. Here we shall just pursue the model under the assumption of no stocks.

With no stocks, we note from our discussion above that where there is excess demand then it is the quantity supplied which is traded and when there is excess supply it is the quantity demanded which is traded. In each instance it is the 'short side of the market' which is traded. Let $q(t)$ denote the quantity traded at any particular price, then

(2.3) $$q(t) = \min(qd(t), qs(t))$$

It has been necessary to labour this point about the quantity traded, because in the dynamics of demand and supply we are considering adjustment towards the equilibrium and while this is taking place the market is *out of equilibrium*, and we must establish at any particular price what quantity is traded.

To continue with our example, let $a=0.05$ then our model is

$$qd(t) = 20 - 4p(t)$$
$$qs(t) = 5 + 2p(t)$$
$$\Delta p(t+1) = 0.05(qd(t) - qs(t))$$
(2.4) $$q(t) = \min(qd(t), qs(t))$$

Given this model then we can express the price in period $t+1$ in terms of the price in period t as follows

$$p(t+1) - p(t) = 0.05(20 - 4p(t) - 5 - 2p(t))$$

or

(2.5) $$p(t+1) = p(t) + 0.05(15 - 6p(t))$$

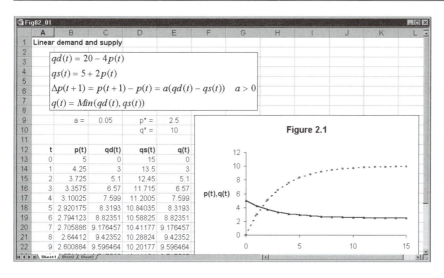

Figure 2.1

Starting from any initial price we can establish (a) the quantity demanded and supplied, (b) the rise in price and hence the price in the next period and (c) the quantity traded. For instance, if the initial price is 5, then the quantity demanded and supplied are $qd(0) = 20 - 4(5) = 0$ and $qs(0) = 5 + 2(5) = 15$, respectively, while the quantity traded is $q(0) = \min(0,15) = 0$. All this is shown in figure 2.1 where $p(0) = 5$. In cell C9 we place the value of a, and in cells E9 and E10 the equilibrium price and quantity as a reminder. In cells A13 to A28 we place our time periods – utilising the fill command in doing so. In cell B13 we place the initial price of $p(0) = 5$. In cell B14 we write the formula

$$= p(0) + a(15 - 6p(0))$$
$$= B13 + \$C\$9*(15 - 6*B13)$$

This is then copied to the clipboard and pasted down in cells B15:B28. The quantity demanded in cell C13 is simply

$$= 20 - 4p(0)$$
$$= 20 - 4*B13$$

while the quantity supplied in cell D13 is simply

$$= 5 + 2p(0)$$
$$= 5 + 2*B13$$

Finally, in cell E13 we place the quantity traded, which is

$$= \min(qd(t), qs(t))$$
$$= MIN(C13, D13)$$

Cells C13 to E13 are then copied to the clipboard and pasted down into cells C14:E28.

The inserted graph is not only a multiple X-Y graph but also is produced using noncontiguous cells in the spreadsheet. We will often be using this procedure in this book and so we shall explain it in detail here. First, what is the meaning of 'noncontiguous cells'? If I simply wanted to plot the price, then all I would do is block cells A13:B28. Columns A and B are next to each other: they are contiguous. What I wish to do, however, is plot the price series (column B) against time (column A) *and* the quantity traded (column E) against time (column A). Clearly, column A is common and represents the values on the *x*-axis. The procedure in Microsoft Excel is to block cells A13 to B28, then holding the control key down move the cursor to cell E13 and, while retaining hold of the control key, block down cells E13 to E28. What you will observe is a dotted rectangle shown around *each* of the blocks. The programme automatically chooses column A as the *x*-axis data. With the data now identified, invoke the chart wizard, choose the X-Y option and choose the points joined up. During the wizard, I included a title and labels for the axes and moved the legend to the bottom (since the default is on the right-hand side). Once the graph was inserted on the page, I realigned the vertical axis label, turning it through 90°. The inserted graph displays the path of prices and quantities traded over time. What is revealed here is that the price adjusts downwards towards its equilibrium value of 2.5 and the quantity traded rises upwards towards the equilibrium value of 10.

Given the spreadsheet representation of the model it is possible to experiment with different initial prices and changes in the speed of adjustment. For example, a starting price of unity leads to a rise in price towards its equilibrium value, and a *rise* in the quantity traded towards its equilibrium quantity. In fact, no matter what the initial price is, the market will always tend to its equilibrium price and quantity. This market is globally stable.

We can establish this also by considering the difference version of the model, as in chapter 1. We have

(2.6) $$\Delta p(t+1) = 0.05(15 - 6p(t)) = 0.75 - 0.3\, p(t)$$

This is shown in the upper part of figure 2.2. The phase line is shown in the lower part of this figure. The difference equation is negatively sloped. The equation $0.75 - 0.3p(t)$ cuts the horizontal axis at the value 2.5, which denotes the equilibrium price. Any price to the left of this value results in $\Delta p(t+1) > 0$ and so $p(t)$ is rising over time. If the price is above the equilibrium value then $\Delta p(t+1) < 0$ and the price is falling. The fixed point $p^* = 2.5$ is globally stable and is an attractor. Since the price tends to equilibrium over time then it must be the case that the quantity traded tends to the equilibrium quantity over time.

2.1.1 *Different adjustment speeds*

The value taken by the parameter *a* has no bearing on the equilibrium price and quantity. This follows immediately from the fact that in equilibrium $\Delta p(t+1) = 0$. Where it is of major importance is the *speed* with which the market approaches the equilibrium. Return to an initial price of $p(0) = 5$, but

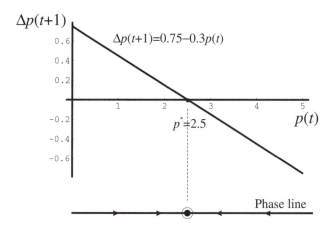

Figure 2.2

now increase the size of the parameter a to 0.1. The inserted graph immediately alters to reflect this, and it is clearly seen that the equilibrium is approached much faster. This is a general result in this model. A rise in the parameter a increases the speed of adjustment and equilibrium is approached much sooner.

Two alternative diagrammatic representations of increasing the speed of adjustment are illustrated in figure 2.3. Figure 2.3(a) shows the cobweb version of the model, (2.5), while figure 2.3(b) shows the difference equation representation of the model, (2.6). Figure 2.3(a) illustrates more dramatically what is shown in figure 2.2. However, figure 2.3(b) can be a simpler way to demonstrate this phenomenon. It is clear from figure 2.3(b) that a higher value for the parameter a increases the absolute value of the slope. Therefore, if price is to the left of the equilibrium, not only do we know that the price will rise, but we can see quite clearly that with a higher value for the parameter a the price in the next period is higher than for a smaller value of this parameter. Or, just as simply, there is a greater change in the price. If on the other hand, price is above the equilibrium price, then it is the case that price will fall, and will fall faster the higher the value of a. Of course, the faster price adjusts to its equilibrium the faster the quantity traded will approach the equilibrium quantity.

2.2 The linear cobweb model[1]

The cobweb model of demand and supply arose from the consideration of agricultural markets, although the analysis applies to other markets as well. The basic idea is that farmers determine how much to supply in the present period, period t, based on what they expect the price to be in period t. This is because they have to sow seeds earlier and how much they sow depends on

---

[1] Cobweb models are discussed only in discrete time. We avoid, therefore, any use of the difference equation formulation of the model, which we have been using for *continuous* models. Their application gives quite different answers to the dynamics! (See Shone, 1997, chs. 2, 3 and 7).

Figure 2.3

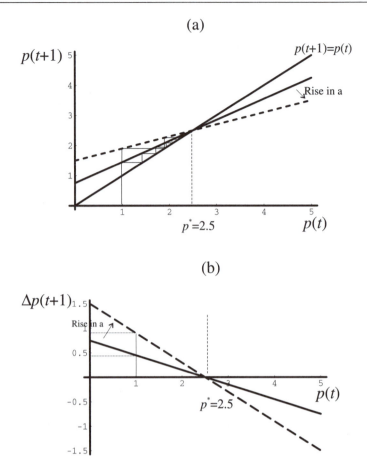

(a)

(b)

what price they think they can get on the market. The simplest assumption of all about expected price is that it is the same as it was in the previous period. Consider then the following simple linear model of demand and supply

$$qd(t) = 20 - 4p(t)$$
$$qs(t) = 2 + 2.5p^e(t)$$
$$p^e(t) = p(t-1)$$
(2.7)
$$q(t) = qd(t) = qs(t)$$

The first and second equations specify demand and supply, respectively, the third equation indicates the assumption made about how expectations are formed and the final equation gives the equilibrium condition.

We wish to set system (2.7) up on a spreadsheet. We intend to do this in general terms so that we can consider a variety of models of the same structure but with different parameter values. We therefore consider the more general model as

$$qd(t) = a - bp(t) \quad a,b > 0$$
$$qs(t) = c + dp^e(t) \quad c,d > 0$$
$$p^e(t) = p(t-1)$$
(2.8)
$$q(t) = qd(t) = qs(t)$$

Let us pursue this general model for a moment. First we can replace the expected price in the second equation by the price in the previous period. Next, since in equilibrium demand is equal to supply, we can equate these two. The result is

$$a - bp(t) = c + dp(t-1)$$

or

$$p(t) = \frac{a-c}{b} - \left(\frac{d}{b}\right)p(t-1) \tag{2.9}$$

If the system is in equilibrium then $p(t) = p(t-1) = \ldots = p^*$, leading to an equilibrium price and quantity of

$$p^* = \frac{a-c}{b+d}, \quad q^* = \frac{ad+bc}{b+d} \tag{2.10}$$

The spreadsheet results are illustrated in figure 2.4. Alongside the parameter values we supply the equilibrium price and quantity, with spreadsheet formulas, respectively

$$= (\$E\$3 - \$E\$5)/(\$E\$4 + \$E\$6)$$
$$= (\$E\$3*\$E\$6 + \$E\$4*\$E\$5)/(\$E\$4 + \$E\$6)$$

The initial price is given in cell B11 and then in cell B12 we specify the following formula for $p(1)$ (we give here both its algebraic form and the form in the spreadsheet)

$$= \frac{a-c}{b} - \left(\frac{d}{b}\right)p(0)$$

$$= (\$E\$3 - \$E\$5)/\$E\$4 - (\$E\$6/\$E\$4)*B11$$

This price is then copied to the clipboard and then pasted down for as many periods as you wish to consider, here we have the series going down as far as period 20. The quantities traded are given in column C. These are taken from the supply curve. Hence, cell C12 has the formula

$$= c + dp(t-1)$$
$$= \$E\$5 + \$E\$6*B11$$

Again we copy this to the clipboard and then paste down. Finally, we block all the data, here cells A11 to C31 denoting 21 periods of data, and then click on the graphics button to create the inserted chart shown in figure 2.4 – after some manipulation of the graph! Figure 2.4 shows that price and quantity oscillate, but converge on the equilibrium price and quantity.

As in chapter 1, we can represent this model (2.7) in its cobweb form, as shown in figure 2.5. This places $p(t)$ on the vertical axis and $p(t-1)$ on the horizontal axis. Two lines are drawn: one for the equation $4.5 - 0.625p(t-1)$ and the other representing a 45°-line. It is clear from the web (which is why such diagrams are called cobwebs) that the path of price and quantity converges on the equilibrium.[2]

---

[2] Notice that this cobweb representation of the model is a little different from the economic textbook representation, which has the web forming around the demand and supply curves. See for example Beardshaw *et al.* (1998).

Figure 2.4

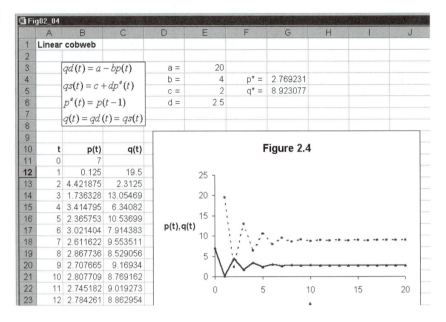

Figure 2.5

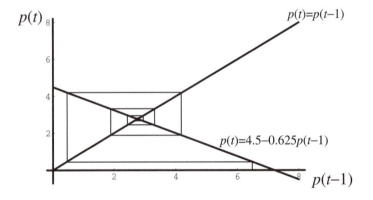

2.3 Experimentation

It is now time to experiment with this model. Since we have set the linear model up in the most general terms in our spreadsheet, we can change the parameters and see the results. In each case you should draw both the cobweb version of the model, and the path of price and quantity. It will be assumed here that the reader will do these exercises, and we shall simply highlight some features of importance.

Consider a rise in the parameter d from 2.5 to 6, all else remaining constant – including the initial price. The spreadsheet readily reveals that the system still oscillates but it is now unstable and both price and quantity diverge from the equilibrium. In noting why this happens in comparison to the early version of the model of (2.7), notice that before we had $d/b = -0.625$ (*less* than the slope of the 45°-line in absolute terms) while in the present case we have $d/b = -1.5$ (*greater* than the slope of the 45°-line in absolute terms). The crucial consideration, therefore, in considering the stability/instability of the fixed point is to consider the ratio d/b. If this is less than unity in absolute terms, then the system is oscillatory but convergent. If the ratio is greater than unity in absolute terms, then the system is oscillatory but divergent. The values of the parameters a and c have no bearing on the stability/instability of the fixed point. They simple change the equilibrium values. Experiment with different values of the parameters a and c and show that if the system is convergent (divergent) with the given values of the parameters b and d, then the systems will remain so even after the change in either a or c.

Return to the cobweb representation of the model. It appears that the pattern of the web depends very much on the (absolute) slope d/b relative to unity. What happens if the slope of the demand curve is identical to the slope of the supply curve, so that $d/b = 1$? Try this first on the spreadsheet, let $b = 2$ and $d = 2$, with a and c remaining the same. Start again with an initial price of $p(0) = 7$. Equilibrium price and quantity become $p^* = 4.5$ and $q^* = 11$. But now both price and quantity oscillate between two values. The price oscillates between 7 and 2 while quantity oscillates between 6 and 16. This repeated oscillation would always arise in the present model when the slope of the demand curve is equal to the slope of the supply curve. But is it a coincidence that one of the two prices is the same as our initial price? Experiment with different initial prices, some above the equilibrium price and some below. It is readily revealed that it is *always* the case that one of the two prices is the initial price of the system.

2.4 Different expectations

The supply curve had the quantity supplied dependent on the expected price. In our earlier discussion we made the simplifying assumption that the expected price in period t was equal to the price in the previous period. This is only one possible specification of the *formation* of expectations. Another possibility is to take account of the *trend* in prices and adjust the previous expectation accordingly. In other words, if the previous expectation was too low, then raise the present expectation by some margin of the error. This is an **adaptive expectation** formulation. More specifically we can assume that

$$p^e(t) = p^e(t-1) - \lambda(p^e(t-1) - p(t-1)) \quad 0 \le \lambda \le 1 \tag{2.11}$$

Writing it in this way clearly illustrates that we are adjusting the previous expectation by a fraction of the forecast error. If the previous price turned out to be lower than expected, so that $p^e(t-1) - p(t-1) < 0$, then the previous expected price is raised by a fraction λ of this difference. If the previous price turned out to be higher than the expected price, so that $p^e(t-1) - p(t-1) > 0$, then the previous expected price is lowered by a fraction λ of this difference.

Of particular note is the situation where $\lambda=1$. In this case $p^e(t)=p(t-1)$, which is the assumption we made above in terms of model (2.8). This can be thought of then as a special case of the present model.

Return to our example but now with this new specification for the formation of expectations. The model is

$$qd(t)=20-4p(t)$$
$$qs(t)=2+2.5p^e(t)$$
$$p^e(t)=p^e(t-1)-\lambda(p^e(t-1)-p(t-1)) \quad 0\le\lambda\le1$$
(2.12)
$$q(t)=qd(t)=qs(t)$$

Although a little more involved, it is still a straightforward linear model. First let us establish whether this new formulation of expectations formation changes the equilibrium of the model. Before we can do this, however, we must eliminate any unknown variables. We cannot have a model involving expected prices, since these are nonobservable. Our previous version, in which the expected price in period t is equal to the price in the previous period, simply and easily replaced an unknown expected price with a price that was known. We must therefore eliminate all expected prices, both present and past expected prices.

To do this we note that we can re-arrange the expectations equation (2.11) into

(2.13)
$$p^e(t)=(1-\lambda)p^e(t-1)+\lambda p(t-1)$$

This way of expressing the expected price indicates that it is a weighted average of the previous expected price and the previous actual price. Next we can re-arrange the supply curve to express the expected price, and then substitute demand into supply since this is the equilibrium condition. Thus

$$p^e(t)=\frac{qs(t)-2}{2.5}=\frac{20-4p(t)-2}{2.5}=7.2-1.6p(t)$$

If this is true for period t then in period $t-1$ we must have the condition

$$p^e(t-1)=7.2-1.6p(t-1)$$

Substituting this into (2.13) gives

$$p^e(t)=(1-\lambda)(7.2-1.6p(t-1))+\lambda p(t-1)$$

and we now have an expression for the unknown expected price in period t in terms of price in the previous period and the parameter λ.

Equating demand and supply we have

$$20-4p(t)=2+2.5[(1-\lambda)(7.2-1.6p(t-1))+\lambda p(t-1)]$$

or

$$p(t)=4.5\lambda+(1-1.625\lambda)p(t-1)$$

Setting $p(t)=p(t-1)=p^*$ readily establishes that $p^*=2.76923$ and is independent of the parameter λ. We can verify this by setting up the model on a spreadsheet. Here we shall concentrate solely on the price variable and consider different values for λ. The model is illustrated in figure 2.6.

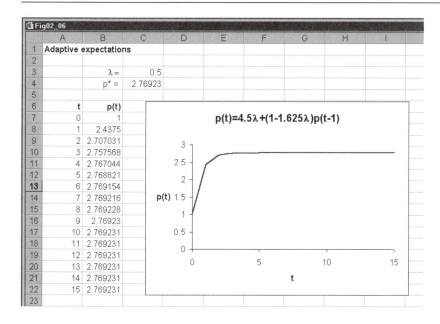

Figure 2.6

If $\lambda = 0.5$ the model rapidly converges on the equilibrium. The oscillatory behaviour we observed earlier seems to have disappeared! Confirm this by taking initial values below and above the equilibrium. If we take a smaller value of λ then the convergence is still gradual but takes longer to reach the equilibrium. Now consider a value of $\lambda = 0.8$: the oscillations return. Furthermore, the oscillations are greater the higher the value of λ. Of course, when $\lambda = 1$, we are back to the previous model. Can we establish the value of λ at which oscillations begin? Yes, we can. Once the coefficient of $p(t-1)$ becomes negative then oscillations will occur. This is approximately 0.62. Confirm this by taking values for λ just above 0.62 and values just below.

2.5 The Goodwin model of expectations

Of course there are many different types of assumptions we can make about the formulation of expectations. We shall consider just one more because it leads to our first example of a second-order recursive equation. In this formulation, we are attempting to take the trend in price changes into account. We therefore postulate the following (Goodwin, 1947)

$$p^e(t) = p(t-1) + r(p(t-1) - p(t-2)) \tag{2.14}$$

Notice first that the expected price is expressed purely in terms of known prices in the past, along with the parameter r. If $r = 0$, then we have our original specification of expectations formation. If $r > 0$ then price is expected to move in the same direction as in the past. On the other hand, if $r < 0$, then price is expected to reverse itself. The extent of the price movements is accordingly very dependent and very sensitive to the value of the parameter r.

Figure 2.7

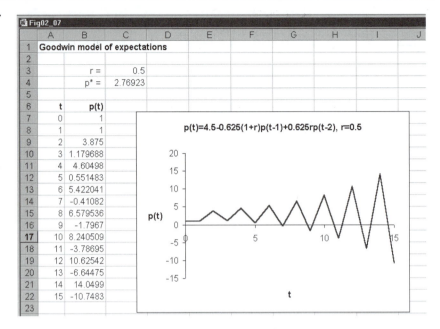

Let us use our existing model given in (2.12) to consider the difference in price behaviour under the present assumption about expected prices. Our model is

$$qd(t) = 20 - 4p(t)$$
$$qs(t) = 2 + 2.5p^e(t)$$
(2.15)
$$p^e(t) = p(t-1) + r(p(t-1) - p(t-2))$$
$$q(t) = qd(t) = qs(t)$$

Substitute the expectations equation into the supply curve and then equate demand and supply. Doing this gives

$$20 - 4p(t) = 2 + 2.5(p(t-1) + r(p(t-1) - p(t-2)))$$
(2.16)   or
$$p(t) = 4.5 - 0.625(1 + r)p(t-1) + 0.625rp(t-2)$$

This is a second-order recursive equation.

The first consideration is whether the respecification of expectations formation leads to a different equilibrium condition. Setting $p(t) = p(t-1) = p(t-2) = p^*$ and solving for p^* readily reveals that the equilibrium is unaltered.

Now set this model up on a spreadsheet in just the same way as the previous one, as shown in figure 2.7. Again we concentrate only on the price behaviour. The only essential difference is that two initial conditions have to be given, $p(0)$ and $p(1)$. Cell B9 has the formula (here expressed both algebraically and as entered on a spreadsheet)

$$= 4.5 - 0.625(1 + r)p(1) + 0.625rp(0)$$
$$= 4.5 - 0.625*(1 + \$C\$3)*B8 + 0.625*\$C\$3*B7$$

In figure 2.7 we have set the value of r to be 0.5 and the initial prices in period 0 and period 1 to be unity. The result is a divergent oscillatory price path. Now leave the values of $p(0)=1$ and $p(1)=1$, and change the value of the parameter r. Experiment with the following values: $r=-3, -0.1, 0.1, 1$. What you will find is a whole variety of paths. A far richer set of solution paths is now possible.

2.6 Nonlinear cobwebs

One of the advantages of using a spreadsheet is that even more complex nonlinear models can often be investigated in more or less the same manner as the linear model. In doing this we shall return to our simple specification of expectations and assume that the expected price suppliers have is equal to the price in the previous period. Consider the model

$$qd(t)=4-3p(t)$$
$$qs(t)=(p^e)^2(t)$$
$$p^e(t)=p(t-1)$$
$$q(t)=qd(t)=qs(t) \tag{2.17}$$

The model contains two fixed points, one at -4 and another at unity. Since price cannot be negative we shall consider only the model in the location of the upper fixed point, $p^*=1$. One way to establish the fixed points is to consider the recursive nature of the model. Substituting the expectations formation into the supply curve and then equating demand and supply readily gives the recursive equation

$$p(t)=(4/3)-(1/3)p^2(t-1) \tag{2.18}$$

which is a first-order nonlinear recursive equation. Setting $p(t)=p(t-1)=p^*$ leads to a quadratic with solutions -4 and 1.

Now set this recursive equation up on a spreadsheet. Set the initial price at $p(0)=1.5$, as shown in figure 2.8. There are no unknown parameters in this model, and so cell B6 has the following entry

$$=(4/3)-(1/3)*B5^2$$

which is then copied to the clipboard and pasted down for as many periods as you wish – here we have just $t=0$ to 15. The fact that we have a nonlinear model in no way changes the structure of the way we set up the spreadsheet. All it does is result in a more complex equation in cell B6. It is quite clear from the inserted graph that the system oscillates but settles down at the equilibrium value.

Now look at the problem in terms of the cobweb formulation, as shown in figure 2.9. We place $p(t-1)$ on the horizontal axis and $p(t)$ on the vertical axis. We draw in two relationships, one the equation we have just derived, namely $(4/3)-(1/3)p^2(t-1)$ and the other just the 45°-line. Since prices must be positive, we do this only for the positive quadrant, and so only the one fixed point is shown, $p^*=1$. Starting at the price $p(0)=1.5$, the web spins in towards the fixed point. This fixed point is locally stable and an attractor. This statement, however, holds only for a small neighbourhood of the fixed point.

Figure 2.8

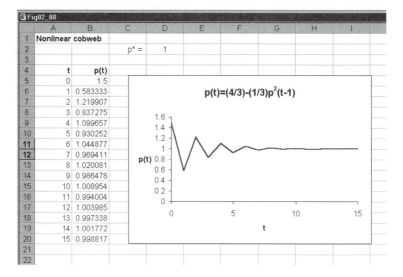

Figure 2.9

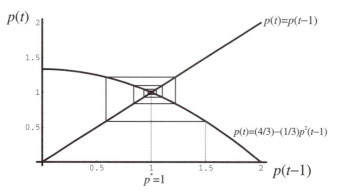

One must be very careful with nonlinear systems because they can exhibit far more complex behaviour. For instance, set the initial price to $p(0)=4$ on the spreadsheet, then the system immediately shoots down to the negative fixed point and stays there! For initial values 'close to' unity, however, the system oscillates but converges on the equilibrium price of unity.[3] However, with nonlinear systems, double-period oscillations can be more in evidence.

2.7 Ceilings and floors

An important nonlinearity that can arise in markets is that of price ceilings and price floors (Waugh, 1964). Consider the following simple linear model

$$qd(t) = 42 - 4p(t)$$
$$qs(t) = 2 + 6p^e(t)$$
$$p^e(t) = p(t-1)$$
(2.19) $$q(t) = qd(t) = qs(t)$$

---

[3] It should be noted that if $f(p)=(4/3)-(1/3)p^2$, then $f'(p^*=1)=2(-1/3)(1)=-2/3$. Consequently the slope of the curve at the fixed point is $-2/3$, which in absolute terms is less then unity. We showed earlier for the linear model that when the absolute value of the slope for the equation was less than unity we had a stable fixed point.

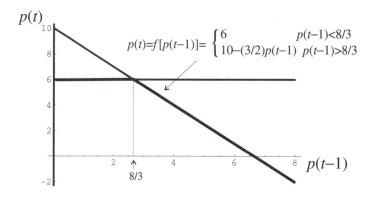

Figure 2.10

This leads to the following recursive equation

$$p(t) = 10 - (3/2)p(t-1) \tag{2.20}$$

Letting $p(t) = p(t-1) = p^*$ leads to $p^* = 4$ and $q^* = 26$. Since the coefficient of $p(t-1)$ is greater than unity in absolute value, then this model has an unstable equilibrium. Use the spreadsheet for figure 2.4 to verify this.

Now suppose a price ceiling of $p^U = 6$ is imposed and so the price in any period cannot exceed this value. The situation is clarified in the cobweb diagram shown in figure 2.10. The *lowest* value that $p(t-1)$ can take is 8/3. At this value the price in period t is $10 - (3/2)(8/3) = 6$. Any lower price in period $t-1$ will lead to a price in period t exceeding the ceiling price of $p^U = 6$. Our recursive equation now takes the form

$$p(t) = f[p(t-1)] = \begin{cases} 6 & p(t-1) < 8/3 \\ 10 - (3/2)p(t-1) & p(t-1) \geq 8/3 \end{cases} \tag{2.21}$$

The heavy line in figure 2.10 shows the relationship $f[p(t-1)]$. This kinked relationship is nonlinear and is also not continuous at the point $p(t-1) = 8/3$.

How can we set up this model on a spreadsheet? This is quite straightforward and is shown in figure 2.11. Place the value of the ceiling in cell E11, here we have a price of 6. We do this so we can change this value and see the result. Next the formula is going to be placed in cell B14, the initial value already having been put in cell B13, which we have assumed is 3.8. If we entered the formula $10 - (3/2)*B13$ in cell B14, then we would obtain the price in period 1. If we copied this down, the price would rise and fall. But we know that whatever the price in period $t-1$, the price in period t cannot exceed the ceiling price, here 6 contained in cell E11. Hence the formula we actually enter in cell B14 is

$$= MIN(10 - (3/2)*B13, \$E\$11)$$

and it is this which is copied down.

Figure 2.11 shows that the price initially explodes but once the ceiling price is reached, a two-period cycle emerges. Is the feature of an emerging two-cycle typical? It is. Change the value of the ceiling and you will note that once again a two-cycle emerges. Furthermore, the upper price of the two-cycle is *always* the ceiling price.

Figure 2.11

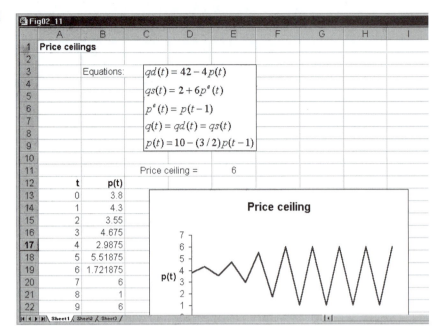

Price floors can also arise. A typical example is in the labour market where the government imposes a minimum wage. Assume the same model holds for the labour market so that the model is

$$Ld(t) = 42 - 4w(t)$$
$$Ls(t) = 2 + 6w^e(t)$$
$$w^e(t) = w(t - 1)$$
(2.22)
$$L(t) = Ld(t) = Ls(t)$$

Carrying out the same manipulation as above, we derive the recursive equation

(2.23)
$$w(t) = 10 - (3/2)w(t - 1)$$

Since the model is the same, we have $w^* = 4$ and $L^* = 26$, and this model has an unstable equilibrium and so without government intervention there will arise an explosive cobweb.

With a wage floor of $w^F = 2$, the *highest* value $w(t - 1)$ can take is $(16/3)$. At this value, the wage in period t is $10 - (3/2)(16/3) = 2$. At any higher wage in period $t - 1$ the wage in period t will fall below the minimum wage imposed by the government. Our recursive equation now takes the form

(2.24)
$$w(t) = f[w(t-1)] = \begin{cases} 10 - (3/2)w(t - 1) & w(t - 1) < (16/3) \\ 2 & w(t - 1) \geq (16/3) \end{cases}$$

The model is illustrated in figure 2.12 and takes the same pattern as figure 2.11. The only differences are that in cell E11 we have the value of the wage floor, which is set by the government at 2; and in cell B14 we have the formula

$$= MAX(10 - (3/2)*B13, \$E\$11)$$

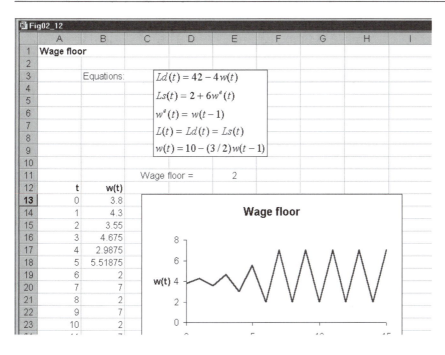

Figure 2.12

which is copied down. Notice once again that a two-period cycle results after an explosive period, and that the lower wage for the cycle is the minimum wage set by the government.

2.8 Cobwebs in interrelated markets

It is sometimes the case, especially in agricultural markets, that two or more markets are interrelated. An early example was the corn–hog market. Corn is grown in part for the feed of hogs. So although the hog market does not directly affect the corn market, it is the case that the corn market will influence the hog market. This is a typical model which applies to animal-feed interaction. Furthermore, these agricultural markets have the same problem we discussed above about expected prices. Farmers supply in both markets according to the expected price. In the corn market farmers supply in time period t according to the expected price in the corn market in time period t. In the hog market, farmers supply hogs in time period t according to what they expect the price of hogs to be in time period t *and* what they expect the price of corn to be in time period t. To simplify our expectations, we assume in all cases that the expected price is the price in the previous period. We can illustrate the model in terms of the following example

Corn market
$$d^c(t) = 24 - 5p^c(t)$$
$$s^c(t) = -4 + 2p^c(t-1)$$
$$q^c(t) = d^c(t) = s^c(t)$$

Hog market
$$d^h(t) = 20 - 5p^h(t)$$
$$s^h(t) = 2.5 + 2.5p^h(t-1) - 2p^c(t-1)$$
$$q^h(t) = d^h(t) = s^h(t)$$

where

$$d^c = \text{demand for corn} \qquad d^h = \text{demand for hogs}$$
$$s^c = \text{supply of corn} \qquad s^h = \text{supply of hogs}$$
$$p^c = \text{price of corn} \qquad p^h = \text{price of hogs}$$

Equating demand and supply in both markets, we can derive two recursive equations. Consider first the corn market

$$24 - 5p^c(t) = -4 + 2p^c(t-1)$$
$$p^c(t) = 5.6 - 0.4p^c(t-1)$$

Next consider the hog market

$$20 - 5p^h(t) = 2.5 + 2.5p^h(t-1) - 2p^c(t-1)$$
$$p^h(t) = 3.5 - 0.5p^h(t-1) + 0.4p^c(t-1)$$

Our two recursive equations are therefore

(2.25)
$$p^c(t) = 5.6 - 0.4p^c(t-1)$$
$$p^h(t) = 3.5 - 0.5p^h(t-1) + 0.4p^c(t-1)$$

For both markets to be in equilibrium at the same time we must have

$$p^c(t) = p^c(t-1) = p_c^* \quad \text{and} \quad p^h(t) = p^h(t-1) = p_h^*$$

which leads to two equations in two unknowns

$$p_c^* = 5.6 - 0.4p_c^*$$
$$p_h^* = 3.5 - 0.5p_h^* + 0.4p_c^*$$

with solutions

$$p_c^* = 4 \quad \text{and} \quad p_h^* = 3.4$$

But are the two interrelated markets stable or not?

The way we go about answering this question by means of a spreadsheet is illustrated in figure 2.13. Since we have two interrelated markets we must specify two initial conditions: one for each market. In figure 2.13 the initial conditions are $p^c(0) = 2$ and $p^h(0) = 1$, which are placed in cells B10 and C10, respectively. In cell B11 we write the formula for the first recursive equation. As we have done throughout this chapter we indicate here both its algebraic form and the form as written in the spreadsheet. Cell B11, therefore, has the formula

$$= 5.6 - 0.4p^c(t-1)$$
$$= 5.6 - 0.4*B10$$

Next we enter the formula for the recursive equation for the hog market. In cell C11 we have

$$= 3.5 - 0.5p^h(t-1) + 0.4p^c(t-1)$$
$$= 3.5 - 0.5*C10 + 0.4*B10$$

Notice in particular that both initial prices are required for the hog market. Now we simply copy *both* cells B11 and C11 to the clipboard and paste down.

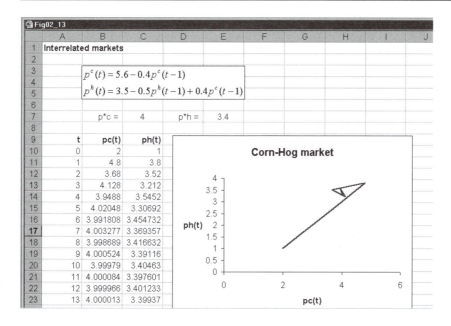

Figure 2.13

The paste down will paste prices for *both* the corn market and the hog market simultaneously. Since we wish to know whether both markets simultaneously come into equilibrium, we need to graph the corn price and hog price on the one diagram. Blocking the data in cells B10 to C25 (which then includes 15 periods in addition to the initial period) and clicking the graphics button allows a construction of the inserted chart, as shown in figure 2.13.

With initial prices $p^c(0) = 2$ and $p^h(0) = 1$ it is clear the market soon stabilises at the equilibrium values. Experiment with a whole variety of prices in both markets, some below the equilibrium and some above. It will be verified that no matter what prices are chosen, the system will be attracted to the fixed point.

We shall return to this market again in chapter 4 when we consider trajectories in more detail. What we wish to illustrate here is how to set up a model involving two variables that are interrelated. What figure 2.13 illustrates is that it is fundamentally the same as a single variable; the only difference is that we require two initial conditions and deal with both markets on the spreadsheet at the same time. It is even possible to have nonlinear relationships in both markets. The procedure to follow would still be the same. What we have here is a very powerful technique for analysing two markets simultaneously. We shall consider many more as the book progresses.

Exercises

(1)   Given the model

$$qd(t) = 100 - 2p(t)$$
$$qs(t) = -20 + 3p(t)$$
$$\Delta p(t+1) = 0.1(qd(t) - qs(t))$$
$$q(t) = \min(qd(t), qs(t))$$

(i)   Establish the equilibrium price and quantity.

(ii)   Use a spreadsheet to plot $p(t)$ and $q(t)$, given $p(0) = 10$. Do these values tend to their equilibrium values?

(iii) Raise the speed of adjustment to 0.2. What do you observe?

(2)   Set up the following cobweb model on a spreadsheet for $t = 0$ to 10

$$qd(t) = 18 - 3p(t)$$
$$qs(t) = -10 + 4p^e(t)$$
$$p^e(t) = p(t-1)$$
$$q(t) = qd(t) = qs(t)$$

(i)   What is the equilibrium price and quantity?

(ii)   Given $p(0) = 3$, does the market tend to equilibrium?

(3)   Set up the following adaptive expectations model on a spreadsheet

$$qd(t) = 100 - 2p(t)$$
$$qs(t) = -20 + 3p^e(t)$$
$$p^e(t) = p^e(t-1) - \lambda(p^e(t-1) - p(t-1))$$
$$q(t) = qd(t) = qs(t)$$

(i)   If $\lambda = 0.5$, what is the equilibrium price and quantity? Are these values the same as those in qu. 1(i)?

(ii)   If $p(0) = 10$, does this system converge on the equilibrium values?

(iii) Does the system show the same pattern if $\lambda = 0.8$?

(4)   For the Goodwin model in section 2.5, set $p(0) = 2$ and $p(1) = 2$. If $r = 0.5$, does the system still exhibit a divergent oscillatory price path? Is this true for $r = -3, -0.1, 0.1$ and 1?

(5)   Given the following nonlinear cobweb model

$$qd(t) = 24 - 5p(t)$$
$$qs(t) = -4 + 2(p^e)^2(t)$$
$$p^e(t) = p(t-1)$$
$$q(t) = qd(t) = qs(t)$$

(i)   Establish the recursive equation for $p(t)$.

(ii)   What are the fixed points for this recursive equation and are they all economically meaningful?

(iii) If $p(0) = 2.6$, establish whether the fixed point in the neighbourhood of this initial value is locally stable or not.

(6)   Given the cobweb model

$qd(t) = 18 - 3p(t)$
$qs(t) = -10 + 4p^e(t)$
$p^e(t) = p(t-1)$
$q(t) = qd(t) = qs(t)$

(i)   Establish the recursive equation for $p(t)$.

(ii)   If a ceiling price of $p^U = 5$ is set, establish the new recursive equation for $p(t)$.

(iii)   Set up this model on a spreadsheet and establish that the ceiling leads to a two-cycle solution with the upper value on price equal to the ceiling price.

Chapter 3
Simple Keynesian dynamics

3.1 The Keynesian-cross diagram

The first model a student of macroeconomics is introduced to is the Keynesian model of income determination – sometimes called the Keynesian-cross diagram. In simple terms the model is

$$C = a + bY$$
$$E = C + I + G$$
$$Y = E$$

(3.1)

where C = consumption expenditure, Y = national income, E = total expenditure, I = investment expenditure and G = government expenditure. Investment and government spending are treated as exogenous variables. The constant a denotes autonomous consumption and the parameter b denotes the marginal propensity to consume. Consumption is substituted into the second equation and then total expenditure is equated with total income to solve for national income

$$E = a + bY + I + G$$
$$Y = a + bY + I + G$$
$$Y^* = \frac{a + I + G}{1 - b}$$

The model is represented in figure 3.1.

Analysis proceeds by allowing some element to change. A rise in investment, for example from I_1 to I_2, raises the expenditure line up parallel to itself, leading to a higher level of equilibrium income, Y_2 as against Y_1. The rise in equilibrium income is established to be

$$Y_1^* = \frac{a + I_1 + G}{1 - b} \quad Y_2^* = \frac{a + I_2 + G}{1 - b}$$

$$\Delta Y = Y_2^* - Y_1^* = \frac{a + I_2 + G}{1 - b} - \frac{a + I_1 + G}{1 - b} = \frac{I_2 - I_1}{1 - b} = \frac{\Delta I}{1 - b}$$

and so the multiplier, denoted k, is

$$k = \frac{\Delta Y}{\Delta I} = \frac{1}{1 - b}$$

(3.2)

Usually the diagram is accompanied by a brief description of how the economy gets from equilibrium point E_1 to equilibrium point E_2. This goes

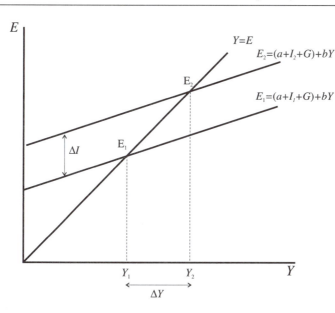

Figure 3.1

along the following lines. The initial rise in investment, ΔI, raises the expenditure line up by exactly this amount. This is the vertical distance between the two lines at the income level Y_1. At the existing level of income and higher level of expenditure, there is excess demand in the economy and so stocks begin to fall. Note that in this model the price level is being held constant. In order to replenish stocks, supply (in the next period) is raised. Output is raised by existing labour or more labour is taken on to produce it (which makes sense only if we assume the economy is not fully employed). National income accordingly rises. In the next round (notice here the implied dynamics), expenditure is still above income, but less than it was before. Accordingly, stocks are still running down. As stock levels are replenished, income rises. This process will continue until the new equilibrium level of income is reached, namely Y_2. Had investment fallen, the adjustment story is put in reverse. At the existing initial level of income, expenditure falls short of income and so stocks are rising. With the rise in inventories, retailers put in for fewer orders (in the next period). Output, and hence income, falls. This process will continue until the newer lower level of income is reached. The same story is often used to explain adjustment to the equilibrium when the economy is out of equilibrium.

As with demand and supply, some textbooks assume adjustment is instantaneous, in which case adjustment immediately (or in the *same* time period) adjusts from one equilibrium to the next. In other words, the model is a static model. If all adjustment takes place in the same time period, then explicitly denoting variables in time is irrelevant. But if, as we have done above, given a story about stock adjustments in the next period, then there is a definite dynamic process being referred to, which needs spelling out. Part of the purpose of this chapter, therefore, is to reconsider some basic Keynesian income-determination models and clearly lay out the dynamics of such models in simple terms, using a spreadsheet to clarify the time path of the variables.

3.2 Some simple dynamics

We begin by reconsidering the model in a simple dynamic context. We shall assume that consumption expenditure in period t is related to income in the same period, $Y(t)$, and we retain the assumption that investment expenditure and government expenditure are exogenous. Total expenditure at time t, $E(t)$, is defined as the sum of all expenditures in time period t. Finally, we assume that income adjusts by a proportion λ of the excess demand, where excess demand is $E(t) - Y(t)$. Our dynamic model is then

$$C(t) = a + bY(t)$$
$$E(t) = C(t) + I + G$$
(3.3)
$$\Delta Y(t+1) = \lambda(E(t) - Y(t)) \quad \lambda > 0$$

First notice that in equilibrium we have $\Delta Y(t+1) = 0$ and so $E(t) = Y(t)$ for all t, which is the same as our equilibrium condition in section 3.1. Substituting the first equation into the second, and the second into the third leads to the following difference equation

(3.4)
$$\Delta Y(t+1) = \lambda[a + bY(t) + I + G - Y(t)] = \lambda(a + I + G) - \lambda(1-b)Y(t)$$

But does this dynamic model have the same equilibrium as our static model of section 3.1? It would be unfortunate to set up a dynamic model with different properties to its static counterpart. In equilibrium we know that $\Delta Y(t+1) = 0$, and so

$$0 = \lambda(a + I + G) - \lambda(1-b)Y^*$$

or

(3.5)
$$Y^* = \frac{a + I + G}{1 - b}$$

which is the same as our result for the static model. Notice that the value of λ has no bearing on the equilibrium condition!

In order to see the adustment process in operation, and in order to set this up on a spreadsheet, we need to express the difference equation as a recursive equation. To do this all we need to do is add to $Y(t)$ both sides of (3.4). Doing this results in the recursive equation

(3.6)
$$Y(t+1) = \lambda(a + I + G) + [1 - \lambda(1-b)]Y(t)$$

We have not changed the equilibrium condition, which is easily verified by setting $Y(t+1) = Y(t) = Y^*$ and solving for Y^*.

We are now in a position to see the dynamics of this model in *three* different variants, which are illustrated in figure 3.2. The top diagram is the recursive equation and is the cobweb representation of the dynamic model (see chapter 1). Basically this is the version of section 3.1, where $\lambda = 1$. The second diagram represents the difference equation version of the model. Notice in particular that the line has a *negative* slope if $b < 1$ and that it passes through the horizontal axis at the equilibrium level of income. The third diagram represents the phase line of the dynamic model, which is derived from the diagram above it.

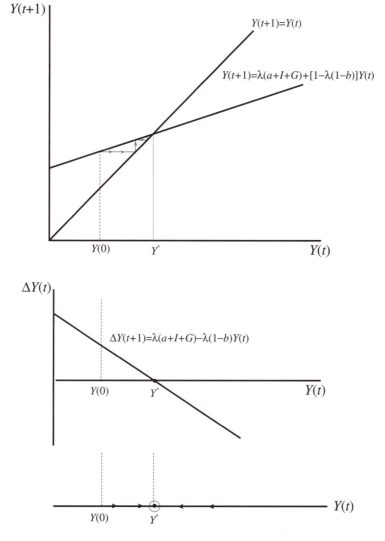

Figure 3.2

Take any initial value for income, denoted $Y(0)$, which would be measured on the horizontal axis. Let this be below the equilibrium level. In this case $E(0) - Y(0) > 0$, and so income in period 1 is a proportion λ of this difference. Since $\lambda > 0$, then income in period 1 is higher than it was in period 0. This same information is shown in the middle diagram. At income level $Y(0)$, $\Delta Y(t+1) > 0$ and so income must be rising. Finally, this information is shown by the arrows on the phase line pointing to the right in the third diagram in figure 3.2. In all instances, the economy is experiencing a rise in income and is moving towards the equilibrium level of income. Choosing an initial level of income above the equilibrium would indicate $E(0) - Y(0) < 0$, and so income falling; $\Delta Y(t+1) < 0$, and so income falling; and the arrows on the phase line pointing to the left.

Let us verify all this using a simple numerical example, which will also be set up on a spreadsheet to allow experimentation. This is shown in figure 3.3.

On the spreadsheet we shall set up the model in general terms and place the values of a, b, λ, I and G in cells, so that they can be changed. This will become clear as we proceed with the example. The model we intend to consider is

$$C(t) = 110 + 0.75\,Y(t)$$
$$E(t) = C(t) + I + G$$
$$I = 200 \quad G = 100$$
(3.7)
$$\Delta Y(t+1) = E(t) - Y(t)$$

where we have assumed the adjustment coefficient $\lambda = 1$. The equilibrium level of income is readily found to be 1640. This too is given on the spreadsheet in cell H4. Cell H4 has the formula

$$= (a + I + G)/(1 - b)$$
$$= (\$F\$3 + \$F\$5 + \$F\$6)/(1 - \$F\$4)$$

We have set the initial level of income $Y(0) = 1000$ which is below the equilibrium level. Since income satisfies the recursive equation (3.6), we derive the whole series for income by first writing the following formula in cell B15

$$= \lambda(a + I + G) + (1 - \lambda(1 - b))\,Y(0)$$
$$= \$F\$7*\,(\$F\$3 + \$F\$5 + \$F\$6) + (1 - \$F\$7*\,(1 - \$F\$4))*\,B14$$

This is then copied to the clipboard and pasted down for as many periods as you wish. In our spreadsheet we have $t = 0 \ldots 30$. The spreadsheet contains many more computations, however. We have in columns C, D and E the computations for consumption, total expenditure and excess demand. The following summarises the entries for cells C14, D14 and E14

Cell C14	Cell D14	Cell E14
$C(t)$	$E(t)$	$E(t) - Y(t)$
$= \$F\$3 + \$F\$4*B14$	$= C14 + \$F\$5 + \$F\$6$	$= D14 - B14$

Having derived these values, making sure that you have clearly identified absolute and relative addresses, copy cells C14, D14 and E14 to the clipboard and then paste down. You will now have all the same computations as shown in figure 3.3.

It is now time to experiment with the model.

3.3 Experimentation: 1

Take values close to and further away from the equilibrium, such as $Y(0) =$ 1600, 500, 1700, and 2000. It is readily verified that the equilibrium value of 1640 is approached in all cases – even if it is not attained for some time! Now set the initial value to be the equilibrium value. All values in any given column become constant. Certainly all the values in column B should be equal to the equilibrium level of income. If this is not the case, then you have made a

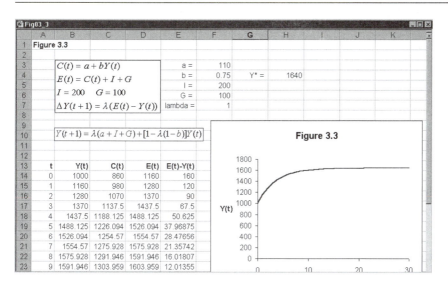

Figure 3.3

mistake on entering the formula. This is also true for any other column. This is always a good check to make after you have entered all the formulas. Now raise the level of investment by 20 to 220. Equilibrium income changes to 1720, and the time path of income moves from 1640 to the new equilibrium level. Return investment to the same level and raise government spending by 20 to the value of 120. The new equilibrium level of income is once again equal to 1720 and the time path of income is the same as it was for the rise in investment by the same amount. In fact, this is also true of a rise in autonomous consumption by 20. Verify this statement. What we have verified here is that for *any* rise in autonomous expenditure (a) equilibrium income rises by the same amount, and (b) the time path of *all* variables is the same.

Next consider changing the value of λ. This coefficient indicates the *speed* with which income adjusts to the difference between total expenditure and income. The higher the value of λ, the sooner the economy will reach its new equilibrium. You can verify this for yourself by increasing the value of λ. Try values such as 1.5, 2 and even 5. Reduce the value of λ below unity and verify that income takes much longer to reach its new equilibrium value. What we conclude with this experiment is that although the value of λ has no bearing on the actual equilibrium value, it is most important in determining how *long* it takes the economy to reach this equilibrium.

A most important parameter to consider is that of the marginal propensity to consume, parameter b. Raise the value of b to 0.8. The first thing that should be noted is that the equilibrium value of income rises. This should not be surprising. A rise in the marginal propensity to consume increases the slope of the expenditure function, and this then cuts the 45°-line at a higher level of income. The implication can be seen in terms of figure 3.2. In the top diagram, the cobweb version of the model, the expenditure line, as just indicated, pivots upwards. At the initial level of income we now have excess demand, which puts pressure on income to rise. This will continue until the new level of $Y^* = 2050$ is reached. In the middle diagram this change pivots the difference equation on the vertical axis upward. So once again, at the initial level of income, $\Delta Y(t)$ is now positive, and so income is rising. This will continue until the new higher level of income is reached. The new equilibrium is shown on the phase line further to the right, and so the rightward arrows will continue to move along the phase line.

What happens when $b = 1$? The first notable difference is that the equilibrium level of income has '#DIV/0!' This is because equilibrium income involves division by $(1-b)$, and so when $b = 1$ this term is zero, and so the equilibrium value of income is undefined. In terms of the cobweb version of the model, the top diagram in figure 3.2, the total expenditure line is parallel to the 45°-line, and so they never intersect! In fact, aggregate expenditure is always above income by exactly the same amount, as shown in column E of your spreadsheet. Economic theory argues that b is generally less than unity. The word 'generally' is important. There are some occasions, usually short-run occasions, when the marginal propensity to consume exceeds unity. What happens to the dynamics if this were the case? Let $b = 1.1$. In this instance the equilibrium level of income becomes negative! But, more importantly, from the starting value of $Y(0) = 1000$ income grows rapidly and continuously. Aggregate expenditure forever outstrips national income, so putting pressure on income to rise. Of course, in real life this would soon come to an end as there would arise a situation of full employment and pressure would soon be put on prices to rise. But this takes us well beyond the present model.

The conclusion we come to is that if $b < 1$, which is most often the case, then this model exhibits global stability and the fixed point, the equilibrium point, is attracting.

3.4 The dynamic multiplier

In section 3.1 we defined the income multiplier with respect to a change in investment by

$$k = \frac{\Delta Y}{\Delta I}$$

i.e. (3.2). In the model presented in figure 3.3 the multiplier is 4. This simply tells us that if investment rises by 20, as we established in section 3.3, then the rise in equilibrium income is $4 \times 20 = 80$ and so equilibrium income rises from 1640 to 1720. This we also established in section 3.3.

Of course, this result is after *all* adjustment has taken place. But such adjustment can take quite some time. Suppose we define a **period multiplier** (or **dynamic multiplier**) in the following way

(3.8) $$k(t) = \frac{\Delta Y(t)}{\Delta I} = \frac{Y(t) - Y_1^*}{\Delta I}$$

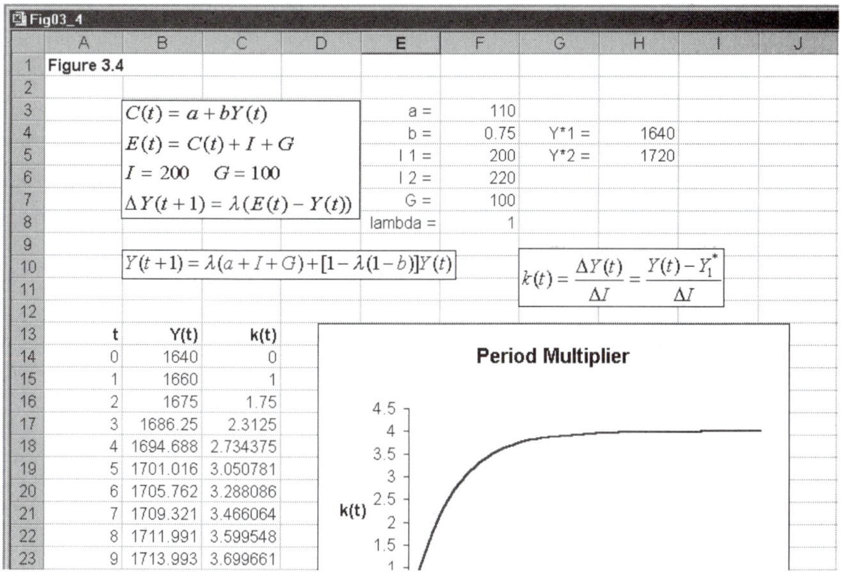

Figure 3.4

The spreadsheet shows:

	A	B	C	D	E	F	G	H	I	J
1	Figure 3.4									
2										
3		$C(t) = a + bY(t)$				a =	110			
4		$E(t) = C(t) + I + G$				b =	0.75	Y*1 =	1640	
5						I 1 =	200	Y*2 =	1720	
6		$I = 200 \quad G = 100$				I 2 =	220			
7		$\Delta Y(t+1) = \lambda(E(t) - Y(t))$				G =	100			
8						lambda =	1			
9										
10		$Y(t+1) = \lambda(a+I+G) + [1-\lambda(1-b)]Y(t)$					$k(t) = \dfrac{\Delta Y(t)}{\Delta I} = \dfrac{Y(t)-Y_1^*}{\Delta I}$			
11										
12										
13		t	Y(t)	k(t)						
14		0	1640	0						
15		1	1660	1						
16		2	1675	1.75						
17		3	1686.25	2.3125						
18		4	1694.688	2.734375						
19		5	1701.016	3.050781						
20		6	1705.762	3.288086						
21		7	1709.321	3.466064						
22		8	1711.991	3.599548						
23		9	1713.993	3.699661						

where Y_1^* denotes the *initial equilibrium* level of income. This multiplier is shown in figure 3.4.

We have distinguished two different levels of investment, labelled I_1 and I_2, respectively, and two equilibrium levels of income, Y_1^* and Y_2^*. Y_1^* is the initial level of income. This initial level is placed in cell B14. In cell B15 we enter the formula

$$= \lambda(a + I_2 + G) + [1 - \lambda(1-b)]\, Y(0)$$
$$= \$F\$8 * (\$F\$3 + \$F\$6 + \$F\$7) + (1 - \$F\$8 * (1 - \$F\$4)) * B14$$

Notice that the only relative address is for income. This is then copied to the clipboard and pasted down. In cell C14 we enter the formula

$$= \frac{Y(t) - Y_1^*}{I_2 - I_1}$$
$$= (B14 - \$H\$4)/(\$F\$6 - \$F\$5)$$

This too is copied to the clipboard and then pasted down. Finally, we identify and block cells A14:A44,C14:C44 click the chart button and insert the chart, which is then suitably changed. As can be seen from figure 3.4, the period multiplier tends to 4 in the limit.

One important conclusion we draw, however, from figure 3.4 is that the multiplier of 4 is really too large if we are considering a short period – say 2 to 5 years. (Recall the length of a Parliament is only 5 years!) For this period the multiplier is more realistically thought of in the region of 1.75 to 2.5. It is also possible to experiment with this spreadsheet to see what happens to the period multiplier when various autonomous variables and/or parameters change, as well as the speed of adjustment, λ. We leave this as an exercise for the reader.

3.5 A dynamic model with taxes

There is really little point in considering a model with government spending without including taxes as well. In this section we add direct taxes to the model. In doing this we now need to distinguish between national income and disposable income, where the latter is income *less* direct tax. Let Y denote income and Yd denote disposable income. Since we are reserving the symbol t for time, we need to define taxes suitably. We shall use the combined symbol Tx for total taxes, i.e. total tax *receipts*, and tx for the *marginal rate of tax*. In particular we define

$$Yd(t) = Y(t) - Tx(t)$$
$$Tx(t) = Tx_0 + tx.Y(t)$$

where Tx_0 is the level of autonomous taxes, tx the marginal rate of tax and $tx.Y(t)$ induced taxes. In general terms our model is now

$$C(t) = a + b\,Yd(t)$$
$$Yd(t) = Y(t) - Tx(t)$$
$$Tx(t) = Tx_0 + tx.Y(t)$$
$$E(t) = C(t) + I + G$$

(3.9)
$$\Delta Y(t+1) = \lambda(E(t) - Y(t)) \quad \lambda > 0$$

Once again we are treating investment and government spending as exogenous – which is why we have not given them a time dimension. Once we have determined the level of income $Y(t)$ for any time period t, then we have determined the level of taxes from the equation for $Tx(t)$. Given $Y(t)$ and $Tx(t)$, then we have determined $Yd(t)$, which in turn is used to derive $C(t)$. Once this is determined, we can derive $E(t)$, which along with $Y(t)$, allows us to determine $Y(t+1)$. The starting point in all of this is clearly to determine the level of income for each time period t. But this is done in just the same way as we did in section 3.2. Before we see this on a spreadsheet, however, let us first consider the change in equilibrium income.

Substitute the tax equation into the equation for disposable income; substitute this result into the consumption function, which in turn is substituted into the total expenditure function. Thus

$$Yd(t) = Y(t) - [Tx_0 + tx.Y(t)] = -Tx_0 + (1 - tx)Y(t)$$
$$C(t) = a + b[-Tx_0 + (1 - tx)Y(t)] = (a - b.Tx_0) + b(1 - tx)Y(t)$$
$$E(t) = (a - b.Tx_0) + b(1 - tx)Y(t) + I + G$$
$$= (a - b.Tx_0 + I + G) + b(1 - tx)Y(t)$$

We now substitute this result into the income adjustment equation

$$\Delta Y(t+1) = \lambda[(a - b.Tx_0 + I + G) + b(1 - tx)Y(t) - Y(t)]$$
$$= \lambda(a - b.Tx_0 + I + G) - \lambda[1 - b(1 - tx)]Y(t)$$

Notice that this difference equation is identical to our earlier one, (3.4) if $Tx_0 = 0$ and $tx = 0$. Adding to both sides $Y(t)$ turns this into a recursive equation

(3.10)
$$Y(t+1) = \lambda(a - b.Tx_0 + I + G) + [1 - \lambda(1 - b(1 - tx))]Y(t)$$

Given an initial level of income $Y(0)$ and values for all the exogenous variables and parameters, allows us to solve for income level $Y(1)$, etc. Before we do this, however, we have still yet to determine the equilibrium level of income. This is achieved by setting $\Delta Y(t+1)=0$ and solving for income

$$0=\lambda(a-b.Tx_0+I+G)-\lambda[1-b(1-tx)]Y^*$$

$$Y^*=\frac{a-b.Tx_0+I+G}{1-b(1-tx)}$$

This is compatible with our earlier result, (3.5), as can be verified by setting $Tx_0=0$ and $tx=0$. Also notice that once again the parameter λ has no bearing on the value that the equilibrium level of income takes.

We set up this much richer model on a spreadsheet, as shown in figure 3.5. The numerical model we are using is

$$C(t)=110+0.75\,Yd(t)$$
$$Yd(t)=Y(t)-Tx(t)$$
$$Tx(t)=-80+0.2\,Y(t)$$
$$I=200 \quad G=300$$
$$E(t)=C(t)+I+G$$
$$\Delta Y(t+1)=0.8(E(t)-Y(t)) \tag{3.11}$$

The spreadsheet uses the general model and utilises the values as set out at the top of the spreadsheet. As before, we include the equilibrium level of income, whose value is placed in cell I4. This is given by the formula

$$=\frac{a-bTx_0+I+G}{1-b(1-tx)}$$

$$=(\$G\$2-\$G\$3*\$G\$4+\$G\$6+\$G\$7)/(1-\$G\$3*(1-\$G\$5))$$

which includes only absolute addresses, and has a value 1675. (The value of Y^* in the spreadsheet is different because this has I set at the level 250.)

The model is basically the same as before. So here we shall simply summarise some of the important cell entries (do take note, however, of absolute and relative addresses)

B15	initial equilibrium
B16	$G$8*($G$2−$G$3*$G$4+$G$6+$G$7)+ (1−$G$8*(1−$G$3*(1−$G$5)))*B15
C15	$G$4+$G$5*B15
D15	B15−C15
E15	$G$2+$G$3*D15
F15	E15+$G$6+$G$7
G15	$G$8*(F15−B15)
H15	$G$7−C15

Figure 3.5

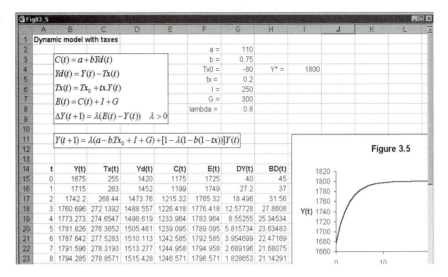

Once these have been entered then B16 can be copied to the clipboard and pasted down. Cells C15 to H15 can be copied to the clipboard and pasted down in one operation! Finally, the inserted chart can be created from cells A15:B45. Column G, which has the heading '$DY(t)$' stands for $\Delta Y(t)$ and column H has $BD(t)$ denoting the budget deficit, which is defined as

$$BD(t) = G - Tx(t)$$

3.6 Experimentation: 2

We can obviously do similar experiments as we did above, and the reader should try these. The same conclusions generally hold. More specifically, for stability in this model we require that

$$b(1 - tx) < 1$$

This ensures that the aggregate expenditure line is less steep than the 45°-line, or that the difference equation is negatively sloped. If this is true, then the equilibrium is unique and globally stable.

What we wish to do here is investigate some features about tax behaviour. First set the initial income at the equilibrium level, namely $Y(0) = 1675$. Now raise the marginal rate of tax, tx, from 0.2 to 0.3. First equilibrium income falls to 1410.5. This should not be surprising; a rise in the marginal rate of tax reduces the slope of the expenditure line, which pivots downwards (the intercept is unaltered by this policy change). As a result it intersects the 45°-line at a lower level of income. In this model tax receipts rise. Why is this? Over time income is falling, but tx has risen, which is more than enough to compensate for the fall in income. Hence the government's budget deficit has gone from a deficit of 45 to almost a surplus of the same order. (Note that a surplus occurs if $BD(t)$ is negative, indicating tax receipts exceed government spending.)

Return the marginal rate of tax to 0.2 and consider a fall in autonomous taxes, say from –80 to –100. It is clearly seen that this leads to a rise in equilibrium income to 1712.5. A fall in autonomous tax is a shift up in the aggregate expenditure function, since $- b.Tx_0$ rises, which shifts up parallel to itself. Tax receipts fall and the rise in income is not sufficient to compensate for the fall in autonomous taxes, so the budget deficit worsens.

For the next experiment, set $tx = 0$ (we intend to consider a model with only autonomous taxes here) and return autonomous taxes to –80. Equilibrium income is then 2680. Set this value for initial income. For this experiment we wish to increase government spending by 50 and increase autonomous taxes by 50 to finance it. On the face of it, it might be thought that this has no impact on the economy – after all, the government are taking an extra 50 and spending it. But let us see whether or not this is so. Change the value for G to 350 and autonomous taxes to -30. Equilibrium income rises rather than remains constant. It eventually rises to the level 2730. But notice that this is exactly 50 above its original equilibrium level. This is not a coincidence! Note, however, from the dynamic path of income that it takes over ten periods before this is true. What we have illustrated here is the famous **balanced budget multiplier**. Taking each impact separately for this 'restricted model' we have

$$\frac{dY}{dG} = \frac{1}{1-b} \quad \text{or} \quad dY_G = k.dG$$

$$\frac{dY}{dTx_0} = \frac{-b}{1-b} \quad \text{or} \quad dY_T = -b.k.dTx_0$$

But the total change in income is $dY = dY_G + dY_T$ and furthermore, $dG = dTx_0$. So

$$dY = dY_G + dY_T = (1-b)kdG = dG$$

$$\frac{dY}{dG}\bigg|_{dG=dTx} = 1$$

The first line tells us that the change in income is equal to the change in government spending (which is equal to the change in total tax receipts). In our example, this is 50. The second equation tells us that the multiplier for a balanced budget change, i.e. a change in government spending matched by an equal change in *total tax receipts*, is unity.[1] We have emphasised here that it must be total tax receipts that match the change in government spending. If the marginal rate of tax was not zero, then raising government spending by 50 and reducing autonomous taxes by 50 would not lead to the change in total tax receipts being matched by the change in government spending. This is because we know from our previous analysis that income will rise, but this in turn will lead to a rise in *induced* taxes (the component $tx.Y(t)$), and so taxes

---

[1] This is not quite true. It is true only for a closed economy. In an open economy the multiplier is less than unity, but still positive.

Figure 3.6

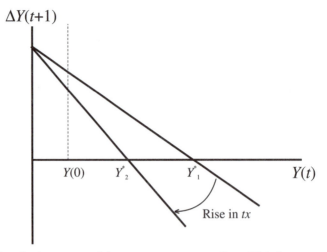

will in fact be in excess of the government spending. This is a more involved exercise, which is why we set the marginal rate of tax to be zero.

3.6.1 Stabilising influence of taxes

Taxes can have a stabilising influence on the economy. We have just seen that a rise in the marginal rate of tax reduces the equilibrium level of income. Furthermore a rise in the marginal rate of tax will reduce the autonomous expenditure multiplier. This multiplier in the present model is given by

(3.12)
$$k = \frac{1}{1 - b(1 - tx)}$$

then

$$tx \uparrow \rightarrow (1 - tx) \downarrow \rightarrow (1 - b(1 - tx)) \uparrow \rightarrow k \downarrow$$

But these comments concentrate only on the equilibrium conditions. Equally importantly, the influence on income on each round is reduced. This is shown more clearly in the difference equation form of the model, shown in figure 3.6. The rise in the marginal rate of tax pivots the difference line in towards the origin. Not only does this reduce the equilibrium level of income, but for any $Y(0)$ below the equilibrium, the change income is now smaller.

3.7 The multiplier–accelerator model

One of the few dynamic models considered in elementary textbooks of economics is that of the multiplier–accelerator model. There are two main differences from our earlier discussion. First, consumption is assumed to depend on the level of lagged income. Second, investment, far from being exogenous, is treated as endogenous and depends on the difference between income in the previous period and what it was two periods ago.[2] More explicitly, we assume

---

[2] Samuelson (1939), who first outlined this model, related investment to the difference in consumption in the previous period and consumption two periods ago.

$$C(t) = a + bY(t-1)$$
$$I(t) = v(Y(t-1) - Y(t-2)) \quad v > 0$$

Here we are reverting to our simpler model with no taxes. The second equation is clearly the new element in this model. The idea is that if firms notice that income is rising, they have positive expectations and this leads them to invest more. If income is falling over time, then they invest less. The parameter v is referred to as the accelerator coefficient. Our full model is then

$$C(t) = a + bY(t-1)$$
$$I(t) = v(Y(t-1) - Y(t-2))$$
$$E(t) = C(t) + I(t) + G$$
$$Y(t) = E(t) \tag{3.13}$$

Notice that we have also simplified the equilibrium condition. We assume that in equilibrium income in period t is equal to expenditure in that same period.

Substituting $C(t)$ and $I(t)$ into the expenditure equation, and then substituting this into the equilibrium condition, we derive the second-order recursive equation

$$Y(t) = (a + G) + (b + v)Y(t-1) - vY(t-2) \tag{3.14}$$

Does this change our static equilibrium level of income? Set

$$Y(t) = Y(t-1) = Y(t-2) = Y^*$$

then

$$Y^* = (a + G) + (b + v)Y^* - vY^*$$

$$Y^* = \frac{a + G}{1 - b}$$

and so there is no change to the equilibrium level of income. What is the difference of making investment depend on the path of income? The variety of paths that income can take depends on the combinations of the parameters b and v (Shone, 1997, pp. 94–7). The following table gives just some examples

Parameter values		Pattern
$b = 0.8$,	$v = 0.1$	Damped and nonoscillatory
$b = 0.8$,	$v = 0.75$	Damped and oscillatory
$b = 0.8$,	$v = 0.3$	Explosive and nonoscillatory
$b = 0.75$,	$v = 1.5$	Explosive and oscillatory

Let us set up the model on a spreadsheet to verify these values and the pattern expected. The model we shall use is the following

$$C(t) = 50 + bY(t-1)$$
$$I(t) = v(Y(t-1) - Y(t-2))$$
$$G = 100$$
$$E(t) = C(t) + I(t) + G$$
$$Y(t) = E(t) \tag{3.15}$$

Substituting we readily derive the following recursive equation

$$Y(t) = 150 + (b + v) Y(t-1) - v Y(t-2)$$

First derive the equilibrium value of nation income by setting $Y(t) = Y^*$ for all t. Then

$$Y^* = 150 + (b + v) Y^* - v Y^*$$

$$Y^* = \frac{150}{1-b}$$

and so the equilibrium level of income is independent of the parameter v. However, the path that income takes to this equilibrium *is* dependent on this parameter.

The model is shown in figure 3.7. The parameter values of interest are placed in cells F3 and F4 for b and v respectively. Equilibrium income is in cell F6 and has the formula

$$= \frac{150}{1-b}$$

$$= 150/(1 - \$F\$3)$$

In order to derive the series for income in this model we require two initial values: one for income in period 0 and the other for income in period 1. We set these both at the value 700, which we know is below the equilibrium value of 750. In cells C13 and D14 we enter the following formulas, respectively

C13	D14
$= 50 + \$F\$3*B12$	$= \$F\$4*(B13 - B12)$

Copy each separately to the clipboard and then paste down.

Changing the values of b and v as set out in this table readily verifies the expected pattern indicated. In particular, figure 3.7 shows the pattern for the values $b = 0.8$ and $v = 0.75$, with income damped but oscillatory. Of course, if income is oscillatory, then so is consumption and investment that depend on the level of income. These oscillations also are damped.

We could incorporate this multiplier–accelerator model in the model with tax, with consumption depending on lagged *disposable* income. Using our earlier model, this would imply that tax in the *previous* period was

$$Tx(t-1) = Tx_0 + tx\, Y(t-1)$$

with disposable income and consumption

$$Yd(t-1) = Y(t-1) - Tx(t-1) = -Tx_0 + (1-tx) Y(t-1)$$
$$C(t) = a + b\, Yd(t-1) = a - b\, Tx_0 + b(1-tx) Y(t-1)$$

Investment would be endogenous, and taking the accelerator form

$$I(t) = v(Y(t-1) - Y(t-2))$$

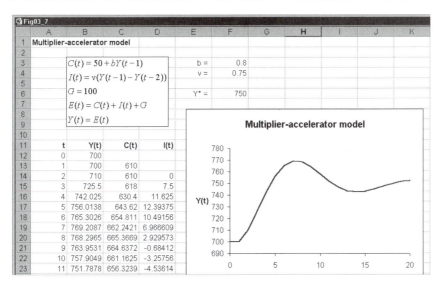

Figure 3.7

The remainder of the model is basically the same. We leave this as an exercise for the reader. What we would expect with the parameters $b=0.8$ and $v=0.75$ is taxes oscillating and the budget deficit oscillating. It is even possible, of course, that if v were in the region of 1.5 the system would become explosive.

3.8 Introduction of net exports

So far we have considered only a closed economy, i.e. an economy that does not engage in international trade. But most economies engage in international trade and they have a large impact on the domestic economy. Since income in macroeconomic models usually denotes gross *domestic* product, for an open economy exports must be added to the total expenditure on goods and services since these are produced *domestically* even though they are consumed overseas. On the other hand, $C+I+G$ includes expenditure on imported goods that were not produced domestically, and therefore do not belong to gross *domestic* product. We must therefore subtract imports. Our definition of total expenditure, equal to gross domestic product, is therefore

$$E(t)=C(t)+I(t)+G(t)+X(t)-M(t)$$
$$=C(t)+I(t)+G(t)+NX(t)$$

where $X(t)$ denotes exports of goods and services, $M(t)$ the import of goods and services and $NX(t)=X(t)-M(t)$ denoting net exports. Let us return to the assumption that investment is exogenous and set at the level I; and government spending is exogenous and set at the level G. Now we make further assumptions about imports and exports. We assume exports are exogenous and set at the level X and imports are related to income according to

Figure 3.8

	A	B	C	D	E	F	G	H	I
	Fig03_8								
1	**Open Economy**								
2						a =	110		
3		$C(t) = a + bYd(t)$				b =	0.75		
4		$Yd(t) = Y(t) - Tx(t)$				Tx0 =	-80		
5						tx =	0.2	Y* =	1766.667
6		$Tx(t) = Tx_0 + tx.Y(t)$				m =	0.2		
7		$NX(t) = X + mY(t)$				I =	300	k =	1.666667
8		$E(t) = C(t) + I + G + NX(t)$				G =	200		
9						X =	400		
10		$\Delta Y(t+1) = \lambda(E(t) - Y(t))\quad \lambda > 0$				M0 =	10		
11						lambda =	0.8		
12									
13		$Y(t+1) = \lambda(a - bTx_0 + I + G + X - M_0) + [1 - \lambda(1 - b(1-tx) + m)]Y(t)$							
14									
15									
16	t	Y(t)	Tx(t)	Yd(t)	C(t)	M(t)	NX(t)	E(t)	E(t)-Y(t)
17	0	1000	120	880	770	210	190	1460	460
18	1	1368	193.6	1174.4	990.8	283.6	116.4	1607.2	239.2
19	2	1559.36	231.872	1327.488	1105.616	321.872	78.128	1683.744	124.384
20	3	1658.867	251.7734	1407.094	1165.32	341.7734	58.22656	1723.547	64.67968
21	4	1710.611	262.1222	1448.489	1196.367	352.1222	47.87781	1744.244	33.63343
22	5	1737.518	267.5035	1470.014	1212.511	357.5035	42.49646	1755.007	17.48939
23	6	1751.509	270.3018	1481.207	1220.906	360.3018	39.69816	1760.604	9.09448

(3.16) $$M = M_0 + mY(t)$$

where M_0 denotes autonomous imports and m is the marginal propensity to import. Our model is now

$$C(t) = a + b\,Yd(t)$$
$$Yd(t) = Y(t) - Tx(t)$$
$$Tx(t) = Tx_0 + tx.\,Y(t)$$
$$M(t) = M_0 + m\,Y(t)$$
$$NX(t) = X - M(t)$$
$$E(t) = C(t) + I + G + NX(t)$$

(3.17) $$\Delta Y(t+1) = \lambda(E(t) - Y(t))\quad \lambda > 0$$

Doing the same substitutions as we have done throughout, we can derive the following difference equation

$$\Delta Y(t+1) = \lambda(a - bTx_0 + b(1-tx)Y(t) + I + G + X - M_0 - mY(t) - Y(t))$$
$$= \lambda(a - bTx_0 + I + G + X - M_0) - \lambda[1 - b(1-tx) + m]Y(t)$$

Adding $Y(t)$ to both sides turns this difference equation into a recursive equation

(3.18) $$Y(t+1) = \lambda(a - bTx_0 + I + G + X - M_0) + [1 - \lambda(1 - b(1-tx) + m)]Y(t)$$

Although this looks rather daunting, it is a simple linear first-order recursive equation that can readily be set up on a spreadsheet in just the same way as we have done with earlier models. The model and the data computations are shown in figure 3.8.

The first task is to establish the equilibrium condition. This is done by setting $\Delta Y(t+1) = 0$ and solving for Y^*. This is readily found to be

$$0 = \lambda(a - bTx_0 + I + G + X - M_0) - \lambda[1 - b(1 - tx) + m]Y^*$$

$$Y^* = \frac{a - bTx_0 + I + G + X - M_0}{1 - b(1 - tx) + m}$$

Once again we observe that the adjustment coefficient λ has no bearing on the equilibrium level of income. What now affects equilibrium income are exogenous exports, autonomous imports and the marginal propensity to import.

The numerical version of the model set out in figure 3.8 is

$$C(t) = 110 + 0.75\,Yd(t)$$
$$Yd(t) = Y(t) - Tx(t)$$
$$Tx(t) = -80 + 0.2\,Y(t)$$
$$I = 300 \quad G = 200 \quad X = 400$$
$$M(t) = 10 + 0.2\,Y(t)$$
$$E(t) = C(t) + I + G + X - M(t)$$
$$\Delta Y(t+1) = 0.8(E(t) - Y(t)) \tag{3.19}$$

Equilibrium income is defined in cell I5, with the formula

$$= \frac{a - bTx_0 + I + G + X - M_0}{1 - b(1 - tx) + m}$$

$$= (\$G\$2 - \$G\$3*\$G\$4 + \$G\$7 + \$G\$8 + \$G\$9 - \$G\$10)/$$
$$(1 - \$G\$3*(1 - \$G\$5) + \$G\$6)$$

which has the value 1766.667; and the autonomous expenditure muliplier, k, is defined in cell I7 with the formula

$$= \frac{1}{1 - b(1 - tx) + m}$$

$$= 1/(1 - \$G\$3*(1 - \$G\$5) + \$G\$6)$$

which has a value 1.667. Cell B17 sets initial income at the level 1000, which we know is below the equilibrium level of income. The remaining cells in which formulas are entered are as follows

B18	$\$G\$11*(\$G\$2 - \$G\$3*\$G\$4 + \$G\$7 + \$G\$8 + \$G\$9 - \$G\$10)$ $+ (1 - \$G\$11*(1 - \$G\$3*(1 - \$G\$5) + \$G\$6))*B17$
C17	$\$G\$4 + \$G\$5*B17$
D17	B17–C17
E17	$\$G\$2 + \$G\$3*D17$
F17	$\$G\$10 + \$G\$6*B17$
G17	$\$G\$9$–F17
H17	$E17 + \$G\$7 + \$G\$8 + \$G\$9$–F17
I17	H17–B17

Now copy B18 to the clipboard and then paste down. Having done this, copy cells C17 to I17 to the clipboard and paste down in one operation. This will conclude all the computations for this model.

Notice that this model is stable if the slope of the difference equation is negative, i.e. if

$$1 - b(1 - tx) + m < 1$$

or

$$b(1 - tx) - m > 0$$

This is not automatically guaranteed. The higher the marginal rate of tax and/or the higher the marginal propensity to import, the more likely this condition is violated and the slope becomes positive. If this should happen then the system becomes unstable. One could argue, therefore, that openness has a *destabilising* influence on economies. Also note that along with early models, the fixed point is either globally stable or globally unstable. With a one-period lag, no oscillations can occur.

Experimentation can now begin.

3.9　Experimentation: 3

First check that the formulas have been entered correctly. This can be done as usual by placing in cell B17 the equilibrium level of income (the value in cell I5). All values for each column should then display constant values for each time period, namely the equilibrium values for each variable. Now raise government spending by 50 to 250 and plot the resulting paths for income, consumption and net exports – showing that income steadily rises to its new equilibrium level (here 1850), as does consumption, and that net exports declines to its new lower equilibrium level. Of course, this last result arises because the rise in income raises the level of imports over time. With exports exogenous and constant, then net exports will decline.

Return all variables to those shown in figure 3.8 and set initial income at the equilibrium level of 1766.667. Now suppose domestic residents have a sudden liking for imported goods, resulting in a rise in the marginal propensity to import. What is the result of this? Suppose *m* rises from 0.2 to 0.25. From the spreadsheet we immediately see that equilibrium income falls to 1630.8 and the multiplier falls to 1.54. Income gradually falls to its new lower equilibrium level, as does consumption, while net exports gradually rise to their new equilibrium level.

Return all variables and parameters to their original levels. Raise exports by 50 to the new level of 450. It is readily seen that this has the same impact on equilibrium income and consumption as did the 50 rise in government spending. The impact on net exports is not the same, however. The rise in imports arising from the rise in income is partly offset by the rise in exports. One might wonder whether the rise in exports that stimulated the growth in income could be more than swamped by the rise in imports, so worsening the net export position. Let the increase in exports be denoted ΔX, and the autonomous expenditure multiplier denoted as usual by k, then

$$\frac{\Delta Y}{\Delta X} = k \quad \text{or} \quad \Delta Y = k \Delta X$$

Turning to the change in net exports, we have

$$\Delta NX = \Delta X - \Delta M = \Delta X - m \Delta Y$$
$$= \Delta X - mk \Delta X = (1 - mk) \Delta X$$

and so long as $mk < 1$, then net exports will improve. In our numerical model we have $mk = (0.2)(1.667) = 0.3334$. Not only does net exports improve, but by less than the increase in exports. But what the spreadsheet reveals, however, is that this improvement is spread out over a reasonably long time period.

Many more experiments can be carried out with this model. We did not include budgetary computations in the table in figure 3.8, but this could easily be done. It is then possible to consider policy changes that will improve the government budget and see what implications this will have on net exports. One important aspect revealed by our model so far is that whenever some domestic policy is undertaken, such as a change in investment, there will always be an impact on net exports, and this impact will be spread out over relatively long intervals of time. The converse is also true: policies that are implemented to deal with balance of payments deficits will have implications for the domestic economy and for government budgets.

Exercises

(1) Use the spreadsheet used to express model (3.7) to analyse the following model

$$C(t) = 200 + 0.8\,Y(t)$$
$$E(t) = C(t) + I + G$$
$$I = 150 \quad G = 250$$
$$\Delta Y(t+1) = 0.5(E(t) - Y(t))$$

(i) Establish the equilibrium level of Y and C.

(ii) Plot the path of $Y(t)$ and $C(t)$ given $Y(0) = 2000$; and establish that these approach your results in part (i).

(iii) Is the equilibrium income attained if $Y(0) = 4000$?

(2) Use the model in qu. 1 to verify the following propositions. Take $Y(0) = 3000$

(i) A rise in autonomous consumption spending or a rise in investment or a rise in government spending by 50 leads to the *same* impact on equilibrium income and to *identical* adjustment paths for $Y(t)$.

(ii)   For a rise in investment of 50, and a lower value for λ of 0.4, there is no difference in the equilibrium value of income, but income takes longer to reach this new equilibrium.

(3)   Use the model in qu. 1 with $I_1 = 150$. Set initial income at the equilibrium level. Derive the dynamic multiplier $k(t)$ as defined by (3.8) for a rise in investment of 50. Comment on your result.

(4)   Use the spreadsheet used to express model (3.9) to analyse the following model

$$C(t) = 200 + 0.8\,Yd(t)$$
$$Yd(t) = Y(t) - Tx(t)$$
$$Tx(t) = 10 + 0.25\,Y(t)$$
$$I = 250 \quad G = 500$$
$$E(t) = C(t) + I + G$$
$$\Delta Y(t+1) = 0.5(E(t) - Y(t))$$

(i)   Establish the equilibrium level of C, Y, Yd and Tx.

(ii)   Let $Y(0) = 1500$ and plot the path of $Yd(t)$ and $Y(t)$ on the same graph.

(iii)   Plot the path of the budget deficit, $BD(t)$.

(5)   Use the model of section 3.7 on the multiplier–accelerator. Let $b = 0.7$ and $v = 1.5$ and let $Y(0) = 300$. Derive the level of income, $Y(t)$, consumption, $C(t)$, and investment, $I(t)$. Form the series $C(t) - C^*$ and $I(t) - I^*$, where C^* and I^* denote equilibrium consumption and investment, respectively. Plot these deviations on the same graph and hence show that in this instance, consumption is the most volatile component of national income.

(6)   Use the model of section 3.8 embodied in model (3.17) and (3.19). Set initial income at its equilibrium level of 1766.667. Let government spending rise from $G = 200$ to $G = 300$. Plot the resulting dynamic path of net exports, $NX(t)$. Comment on your results.

Chapter 4

Constructing trajectories in the phase plane

4.1 Trajectories and fixed points

In chapter 2 we considered two interrelated markets, the corn market that was animal feed for the hog market, and so it was necessary to consider these markets *simultaneously*. There are many such markets in economics, both in microeconomics and macroeconomics. Because they are so pervasive we need to set up a relatively simple framework in which to consider their dynamics. As in chapter 1, we shall here be general and simply refer to a market for x and a market for y, where these markets are interrelated. In other words, in order to solve for an equilibrium in market x we need to know not only the value of x but also the value for y; and to determined the equilibrium for market y we need to know not only the value of y but also the value for x.

We also mentioned in chapter 1 that we can specify models either in discrete time or in continuous time, but that sometimes these give different dynamics – even if the comparative statics appears the same. This is especially true when dealing with two or more relationships. We shall consider in this book models with only two fundamental dynamic relationships. It is much easier to establish the time path of models of two markets if we set the model up in terms of continuous time. Of course, if the model is naturally a discrete time model, as in the case of the corn–hog markets with one-period supply lags, then we must also consider the dynamics of two markets which involve discrete time. In this chapter we shall cover both types – with some warnings about considering the *same* model from the two perspectives.

By way of example, and we shall pursue this example in some detail, suppose

$$\dot{x}(t) = \frac{dx(t)}{dt} = 9 - 2x(t) - y(t)$$

$$\dot{y}(t) = \frac{dy(t)}{dt} = 3 - y(t) + x(t) \tag{4.1}$$

or, more simply

$$\dot{x} = 9 - 2x - y$$
$$\dot{y} = 3 - y + x \tag{4.2}$$

where it is assumed that all variables are related to time. This system of equations indicates how both x and y change over time. It indicates that the change in x not only depends on the level of x but also on the level of y. Similarly, how y changes over time depends not only on the value of y but also on the value of x.

69

Figure 4.1

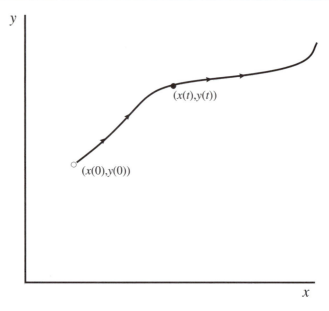

The first thing we note about this model is that time does not occur as a separate variable. If we had, for example

$$\dot{x}(t) = 9 - 2x(t) - y(t) + 2t$$

then it would. When time does not occur as a separate variable in an equation we say that such an equation is autonomous.[1] If this is true for all equations in the system (in the model), then we say that the system (or model) is autonomous. All economic models we shall be dealing with in this book are autonomous in the sense just described. Second, we cannot know the value of x at time t without knowing the value of y at time t, and vice versa. This means that we must consider $x(t)$ and $y(t)$ at time t *simultaneously*. To do this geometrically we place the variable x on the horizontal axis and the variable y on the vertical axis. This (x,y)-space now refers to the phase plane. It is the two-dimensional counterpart to the phase line we outlined in chapter 1. The system moves in the phase plane starting at time 0. The point $(x(0), y(0))$ is referred to as the **initial point**. The path of the system over time plots the curve $\{x(t), y(t)\}$ as t varies continuously and is referred to as the **trajectory** of the system, sometimes called the **orbit**. One such trajectory is shown in figure 4.1. With autonomous systems, given an initial point, there is only *one* trajectory that passes through this initial point.

It is important to realise that the trajectory does not refer to either of the two equations necessarily, and most usually does not. It denotes the time path of x and y. This will become clear in a moment.

Return to the example. Does this simultaneous system have an equilibrium point, a fixed point? In our single-variable models, we defined a fixed point as the condition where $x(t) = x^*$ for all t. In the present system, we require that

---

[1] This is the mathematicians' use of the word autonomous. They mean independent of time. When economists talk about a variable being autonomous they mean being independent of income.

$$x(t) = x^* \quad \text{and} \quad y(t) = y^* \quad \text{for all } t$$

When this is true $\dot{x} = 0$ and $\dot{y} = 0$. Substituting these conditions, we have

$$0 = 9 - 2x^* - y^*$$
$$0 = 3 - y^* + x^*$$

with solutions (see box 2)

$$x^* = 2 \quad \text{and} \quad y^* = 5$$

Of course, all that this establishes is that a fixed point, an equilibrium point, exists. It in no way guarantees that the system starting at some initial point $(x(0), y(0))$, will tend towards it or even reach it. To establish this feature, we must look at the system's dynamics.

Box 2 Solving two linear simultaneous equations with a spreadsheet

In this and later chapters we will be solving many linear simultaneous equations involving two variables. Rather than do each one separately, it is useful to set up the solution on a spreadsheet. To do this, however, we need to specify the equations in the same common format. Let the two equations be written as follows

$$a_1 x + a_2 y = a_3$$
$$b_1 x + b_2 y = b_3$$

Then set up a spreadsheet as follows. Place the equations and their solutions just under the title on the left. These are the equations above and the solution equations

$$x^* = \frac{a_3 b_2 - a_2 b_3}{a_1 b_2 - a_2 b_1} \quad y^* = \frac{a_1 b_3 - a_3 b_1}{a_1 b_2 - a_2 b_1}$$

Then in cells D3:D5 and D7:D9 place the name of the parameters and in cells E3:E5 and E7:E9 their values. Then in cells D11 and D12 place the descriptors '$x^* =$' and '$y^* =$' and in cells E11 and E12 place the formulas for the solution values, i.e.

E11 $= (a_3 b_2 - a_2 b_3)/(a_1 b_2 - a_2 b_1)$
     $= (\$E\$5*\$E\$8 - \$E\$4*\$E\$9)/(\$E\$3*\$E\$8 - \$E\$4*\$E\$7)$

E12 $= (a_1 b_3 - a_3 b_1)/(a_1 b_2 - a_2 b_1)$
     $= (\$E\$3*\$E\$9 - \$E\$5*\$E\$7)/(\$E\$3*\$E\$8 - \$E\$4*\$E\$7)$

Save the spreadsheet. It can now be used to solve any set of two linear simultaneous equations.

We now show such a spreadsheet for solving the equilibrium for model (4.2).

	A	B	C	D	E	F
			Box_2			
1	**Solving simultaneous equations**					
2						
3		$a_1x + a_2y = a_3$		a1 =	2	
4		$b_1x + b_2y = b_3$		a2 =	1	
5				a3 =	9	
6						
7		$x^* = \dfrac{a_3b_2 - a_2b_3}{a_1b_2 - a_2b_1}$		b1 =	1	
8				b2 =	-1	
9				b3 =	-3	
10						
11		$y^* = \dfrac{a_1b_3 - a_3b_1}{a_1b_2 - a_2b_1}$		x* =	2	
12				y* =	5	
13						

4.2 Isoclines and vector forces: continuous models

If we concentrate just on the market for x we know that this market is in equilibrium when $\dot{x} = 0$. If we impose this condition, then there will exist a relationship between x and y that guarantees that the market for x is in equilibrium. Notice that we are not in any way saying that the market for y is in equilibrium, only that the market for x is in equilibrium. Furthermore, in specifying this relationship we are not concerned with time, we are merely concerned with the condition for equilibrium to be satisfied in the market for x, and the relationship between x and y for this to be so. The relationship is found by solving

$$0 = 9 - 2x - y$$
$$y = 9 - 2x$$

This relationship is referred to as an isocline, or simply as an equilibrium condition. To make it clear that it is the isocline for market x we write

(4.3) $\qquad y = 9 - 2x \quad \dot{x} = 0$

We can derive the isocline for market y in just the same way. This, too, denotes the relationship between x and y for which market y is in equilibrium and so satisfying the condition, $\dot{y} = 0$. Hence

$$0 = 3 - y + x$$
$$y = 3 + x$$

and the isocline for market y is denoted

(4.4) $\qquad y = 3 + x \quad \dot{y} = 0$

We can now summarise what we have done so far. We have derived a relationship between x and y, an isocline for market x, which denotes all combi-

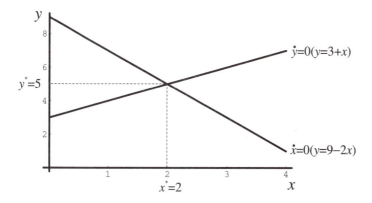

Figure 4.2

nations of x and y which preserves equilibrium in market x. We have derived a similar isocline for market y, which also denotes combinations of x and y for which market y is in equilibrium. We can now draw these isoclines in the (x, y)-plane as shown in figure 4.2, which is referred to as the phase plane. If the two isoclines intersect then both markets can be in equilibrium at the same time, in which case an equilibrium for the system (model) exists. This will generally be the case – it will not be the case only if the two isoclines are parallel. It is quite clear from our derivation of the isoclines that they will intersect at the values $x^* = 2$ and $y^* = 5$.

But we now have much, much more information contained in figure 4.2. Along any isocline we know that that particular market is in equilibrium. If we are not on the line, either above it or below it (or to the left or right of the line) then we know that that market cannot be in equilibrium and there will be forces in play moving the system in some direction. The same is true for the other isocline. This, too, divides the diagram into areas above and below (to the left and to the right). We therefore have four quadrants, which are marked in figure 4.3 as I–IV, and we have four representative points a, b, c and d in each of the four quadrants, respectively.

Consider just the market for x and consider the situation when $\dot{x} > 0$. When this is true we have

$$9 - 2x - y > 0$$
$$y < 9 - 2x$$

This means that when the system is *below* the x-isocline, x is *rising*. This is shown by the horizontal arrows emanating from points c and d and pointing to the right. Clearly when $\dot{x} < 0$ we are at a point *above* the x-isocline, and here x is *falling*. This is shown by horizontal arrows emanating from points a and b and pointing to the left. Turning next to market y, if $\dot{y} > 0$ then

$$3 - y + x > 0$$
$$y < 3 + x$$

This means that when the system is *below* the y-isocline, y is rising. This is shown by the vertical arrows emanating from points b and c and pointing upward. Similarly, when $\dot{y} < 0$ we are at a point *above* the y-isocline, and here

Figure 4.3

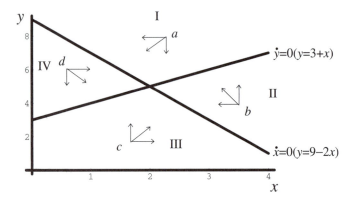

y is *falling*. This is shown by the vertical arrows emanating from points *a* and *d* and pointing downward. These vector forces show the force acting on the system in the *x*-direction and *y*-direction, respectively. The system in any quadrant will be somewhere between these extreme forces, as indicated by the central arrow emanating from the four points *a, b, c* and *d*. At this stage the vector forces indicate a counterclockwise movement of the system in the phase plane. In other words, the trajectory of the system starting at some initial point will traverse the phase space in a counterclockwise movement. At this stage, however, we do not know whether the trajectory will tend towards the equilibrium point or away from it. In fact, qualitatively, this is all we can say. We can say a fixed point exists and that trajectories in the phase plane will be counterclockwise. But this is a lot of information. To go further, we need to establish some actual trajectories.

4.3 Constructing continuous trajectories with a spreadsheet

In chapter 1 we discussed Euler's approximation to a differential equation and showed how we could use this to construct a solution curve to the differential equation. But the model we are discussing

$$\dot{x}(t) = \frac{dx(t)}{dt} = 9 - 2x(t) - y(t)$$

(4.5)
$$\dot{y}(t) = \frac{dy(t)}{dt} = 3 - y(t) + x(t)$$

is just a set of two differential equations, each equation relating the change in a variable to both *x* and *y*. Let us write the system as

(4.6)
$$\dot{x} = f(x,y) = 9 - 2x - y$$
$$\dot{y} = g(x,y) = 3 - y + x$$

Given *x*(0) and *y*(0), then

$$f(x(0),y(0)) = 9 - 2x(0) - y(0)$$
$$g(x(0),y(0)) = 3 - y(0) + x(0)$$

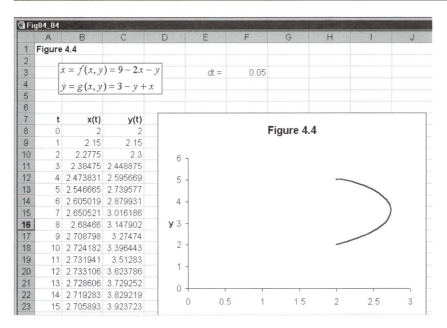

Figure 4.4

and we can approximate $x(1)$ and $y(1)$ in just the same way as we did in chapter 1. In other words

$$x(1) = x(0) + f(x(0),y(0))\Delta t$$
$$y(1) = y(0) + g(x(0,y(0))\Delta t$$

where Δt is the time interval used for the approximation. Suppose we wish to consider the trajectory starting from the point $(x(0), y(0)) = (2,2)$. Then

$$x(1) = 2 + (9 - 4 - '2)(0.05) = 2.15$$
$$y(1) = 2 + (3 - 2 + 2)(0.05) = 2.15$$

while

$$x(2) = 2.15 + (9 - 2(2.15) - 2.15)(0.05) = 2.2775$$
$$y(2) = 2.15 + (3 - 2.15 + 2.15)(0.05) = 2.3$$

and we can continue with such calculations. Of course, this is easier to do on a spreadsheet, and we illustrate just such computations in terms of figure 4.4. The use of the spreadsheet is here particularly convenient since we have computed periods 0 to 200 to plot the trajectory with time interval $\Delta t = 0.05$.

In cells B8 and C8 we have the initial values for x and y. In cells B9 and C9 we have the following formulas

Cell B9	Cell C9
$= x(0) + f(x(0),y(0))\Delta t$	$= y(0) + g(x(0),y(0))\Delta t$
$= B8 + (9 - 2*B8 - C8)*\$F\$3$	$= C8 + (3 - C8 + B8)*\$F\$3$

These are then copied to the clipboard and pasted down for as many periods as you wish to consider. Finally, we block cells B8:C208 and click the chart button to insert the chart denoting the phase plane and the trajectory we have just computed. The counterclockwise movement is quite evident. What is also quite evident is that the trajectory tends towards the equilibrium point, the fixed point of the system.

4.4 Isoclines and vector forces: discrete models

In chapter 2 we considered two interrelated markets: the corn market and the hog market, in which there was a one-period lag on the supply side in both markets. We established the following two recursive equations

(4.7)
$$p^c(t) = 5.6 - 0.4p^c(t-1)$$
$$p^h(t) = 3.5 - 0.5p^h(t-1) + 0.4p^c(t-1)$$

Let us generalise this model slightly and let $x = p^c$ and $y = p^h$, and consider the model in terms of a difference equation. Then

(4.8)
$$\Delta x(t) = x(t) - x(t-1) = 5.6 - 1.4x(t-1)$$
$$\Delta y(t) = y(t) - y(t-1) = 3.5 - 1.5y(t-1) + 0.4x(t-1)$$

First we verify that the model has a fixed point, an equilibrium point. This is where $\Delta x(t) = 0$ *and* $\Delta y(t) = 0$, giving the fixed point

$$0 = 5.6 - 1.4x^*$$
$$0 = 3.5 - 1.5y^* + 0.4x^*$$
$$x^* = 4 \quad and \quad y^* = 3.4$$

which is the result we established in chapter 2.

But now consider this problem in terms of isoclines and vector forces. If we consider just equilibrium in market x, then we have the isocline $\Delta x(t) = 0$, which is vertical at the value $x = 4$. Of course, the reason why this isocline is vertical is because market x in this example is independent of market y. Turning to market y, this market is in equilibrium when $\Delta y(t) = 0$ and this occurs when

$$0 = 3.5 - 1.5y + 0.4x$$
$$y = 2.333 + 0.267x$$

Our two isoclines are therefore

(4.9)
$$x = 4 \quad \Delta x(t) = 0$$
$$y = 2.333 + 0.267x \quad \Delta y(t) = 0$$

It is easy to verify that these intersect at the fixed point $(x^*, y^*) = (4, 3.4)$. The situation is shown in figure 4.5.

The isoclines divide the phase space into four quadrants, which we have labelled I–IV. Now consider just market x and consider the situation when $\Delta x(t) > 0$. When this is true we have

$$5.6 - 1.4x > 0$$
$$x < 4$$

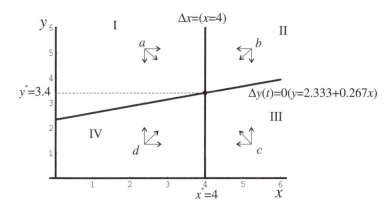

Figure 4.5

Accordingly, to the left of the x-isocline variable x is rising while to the right of the x-isocline the variable x is falling. This information is shown by right-pointing arrows emanating from points a and d and left-pointing arrows emanating from points b and c. Turning next to the market for y, if $\Delta y(t) > 0$ then

$$3.5 - 1.5y + 0.4x > 0$$
$$y < 2.333 + 0.267x$$

and so below the y-isocline the variable y is rising while above it the variable y is falling. This information is shown by the upward arrows emanating from points c and d and the downward arrows emanating from points a and b. In general the system in any quadrant will move somewhere between these two extremes, as shown by the central arrows in each quadrant.

It is immediately noticed from these vector forces that the system in all quadrants is directing it towards the fixed point, towards the equilibrium. We established that in chapter 2. We shall do so once again for this general system to illustrate solving such discrete models on a spreadsheet.

4.5 Constructing discrete trajectories with a spreadsheet

The procedure for constructing discrete trajectories on a spreadsheet is a little easier. First we convert the difference equations to recursive equations by adding $x(t-1)$ to both sides of the first equation in (4.8) and to $y(t-1)$ the second equation. This gives us the simultaneous recursive model

$$x(t) = 5.6 - 0.4x(t-1)$$
$$y(t) = 3.5 - 0.5y(t-1) + 0.4x(t-1)$$

(4.10)

The construction of the trajectory is shown in figure 4.6. Cells C7 and E7 contain the equilibrium values and cells B10 and C10 contain the initial values for x and y, here 2 and 1, respectively – a point in quadrant IV. Cells B11 and C11 have formulas

Cell B11	Cell C11
$= 5.6 - 0.4x(t-1)$	$= 3.5 - 0.5y(t-1) + 0.4x(t-1)$
$= 5.6 - 0.4 * B10$	$= 3.5 - 0.5 * C10 + 0.4 * B10$

Figure 4.6

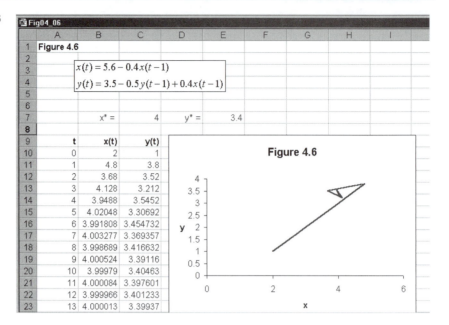

In this particular model we only have relative addresses. Cells B11 and C11 are then copied to the clipboard and pasted down. We have pasted down up to $t = 15$. Finally, we insert the chart by blocking cells B10:C25 and clicking the chart button. The sequence of points

$$\{(x(0),y(0)), (x(1),y(1))), (x(2),y(2)), \cdots\}$$

makes up the discrete trajectory of the system. We plot this in the phase plane as shown in figure 4.6, where we have joined up the points to form a 'continuous-looking' trajectory.

Taking a point in any of the four quadrants will readily reveal that the system always converges on the equilibrium. The fixed point is globally stable and is an attractor. The reader should verify this by taking a variety of initial points in all the four quadrants.

4.6 A cautionary note

On the face of it there appears only a little difference between the continuous terms

$$\frac{dx(t)}{dt} \quad and \quad \frac{dy(t)}{dt}$$

and the discrete difference terms

$$\Delta x(t+1) = x(t+1) - x(t) \quad and \quad \Delta y(t+1) = y(t+1) - y(t)$$

Both sets indicate the change in x and y over time. But it should never be assumed that simply converting a continuous model to a discrete model gives the same dynamic results. It is true that the isoclines are identical and the

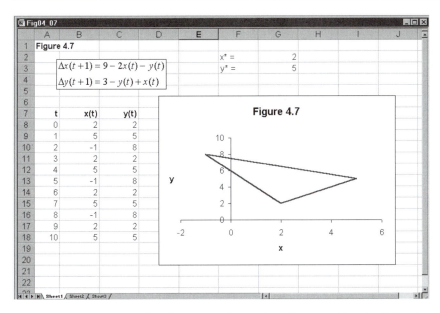

Figure 4.7

vector forces appear to give the same information. But consider the following discrete counterpart to our continuous example we discussed above in terms of (4.6)

$$\Delta x(t+1) = 9 - 2x(t) - y(t)$$
$$\Delta y(t+1) = 3 - y(t) + x(t)$$

(4.11)

The discrete trajectory from this model is set out in figure 4.7 along identical lines as we set up the model in figure 4.6. It is clear, however, that this system is cyclical, forming a three-cycle around the fixed point. The trajectory in figure 4.4, which illustrated a trajectory from the continuous model, has the trajectory tending towards the fixed point.

What we conclude from this brief note is that vector forces should be confined to continuous models *in general*.

4.7 A variety of trajectories

There is quite a diversity of trajectories that can occur in a two-dimensional phase space, some of which are sufficiently common to have names attached to them. In this section we shall consider some of these. Not only will they show a diversity of paths, but they also will help reinforce the isocline and vector forces' diagrammatic treatment that can be so useful when considering dynamic systems. In this section we consider only continuous models.

Let us begin with the simplest case of all. Suppose

$$\dot{x} = x$$
$$\dot{y} = y$$

(4.12)

It immediately follows that the isoclines are the two axes, and the equilibrium point is the origin. In effect, these two markets are independent of one another.

Figure 4.8

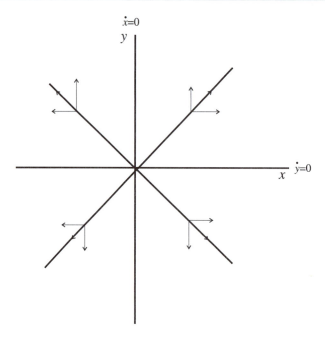

Even so, let us continue to identify the vector forces in the four quadrants shown in figure 4.8. If $\dot{x}>0$ then $x>0$ and x is rising, and vice versa. So to the right of the vertical axis, x is rising and to the left of this axis x is falling. This is shown by the right- and left-pointing arrows, respectively. Similarly, if $\dot{y}>0$ then $y>0$ and y is rising, and vice versa. So above the horizontal axis, y is rising and below the horizontal axis y is falling. This is shown by the up- and down-pointing arrows, respectively. In this example the origin is a repellor and the system is unstable.

This pattern is verified by the spreadsheet shown in figure 4.9. What this shows is that the trajectory starting at point (0.5,0.5) moves outward along a straight line. This is true for any point in the positive quadrant, as we have already indicated in figure 4.8. Experiment by taking a number of points in the positive quadrant. Now take points in the south-west quadrant, say point $(-0.5,-0.5)$. It will immediately be seen that the trajectory remains a straight line, but now moving further away from the fixed point. Similar results follow when taking points in the other quadrants. What we have here is an **unstable star**. It is unstable because all trajectories move away from the fixed point. Taking a whole range of trajectories forms outgoing lines from the fixed point, making a diagram looking like a star, hence the name.

Consider next the following continuous model

$$\dot{x}=-2x+y$$
(4.13)
$$\dot{y}=x-2y$$

Again we set this continuous model up on a spreadsheet as illustrated in figure 4.10 in just the same way as we have done earlier. The initial point for the trajectory shown is $(x(0), y(0))=(2,6)$. The only fixed point is the origin. The two isoclines are

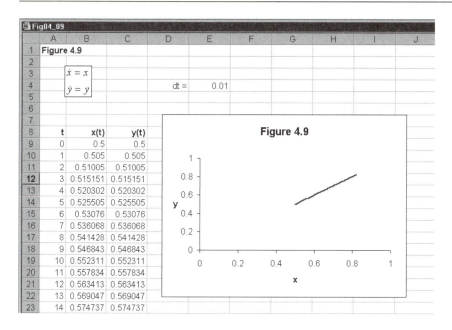

Figure 4.9

$$y = 2x \quad \dot{x} = 0$$
$$y = (1/2)x \quad \dot{y} = 0$$

All trajectories, no matter where the initial point is (other than the origin) will be drawn to the fixed point. This figure illustrates a **stable proper node**. It should be noted that any such trajectory for this problem remains in the quadrant in which the initial point is located.

As another illustration, consider the model

$$\dot{x} = -4x - y$$
$$\dot{y} = x - 2y \tag{4.14}$$

which is illustrated in figure 4.11. Once again, the only fixed point is the origin. Taking an initial point $(x(0), y(0)) = (2,2)$. This is an example of a **stable improper node**. The approach to the fixed point seems to lie along a line that is negatively sloped. To see this, take an initial point $(-2,-2)$. The negatively sloped line can be identified by taking an initial point $(-2,2)$ and another $(2,-2)$. It will be noted that the trajectories are straight lines directed towards the origin.

The next example illustrates a spiral, with fixed point at the origin. The model is

$$\dot{x} = -x + 4y$$
$$\dot{y} = -4x - y \tag{4.15}$$

and is illustrated in figure 4.12. Although this model is fairly similar to the previous one, the trajectories are quite different – taking a spiralling motion to the fixed point. In figure 4.12 our initial point is once again $(x(0), y(0)) = (2,2)$. But taking any initial point different from the origin will have a trajectory drawn to the origin in a clockwise motion. The reader is encouraged to try

Figure 4.10

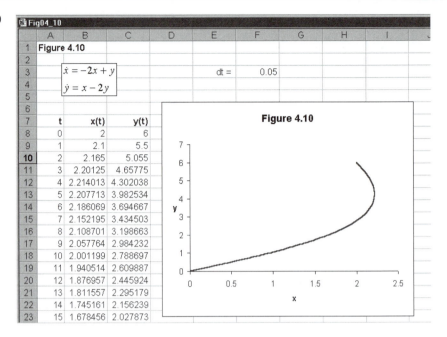

Figure 4.11

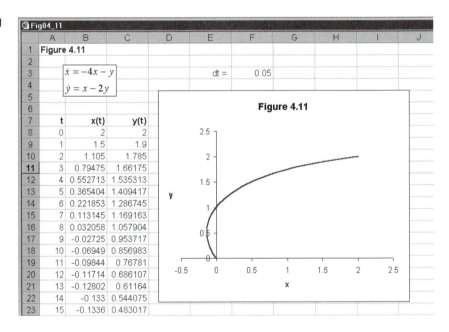

initial points $(-2,2)$, $(-2,-3)$, $(-2,4)$. All trajectories are clockwise spirals to the origin. What we have here is a **spiral**, with a clockwise motion.

An explosive spiral will arise with the following model

$$\dot{x} = x + 4y$$

(4.16) $$\dot{y} = -4x + y$$

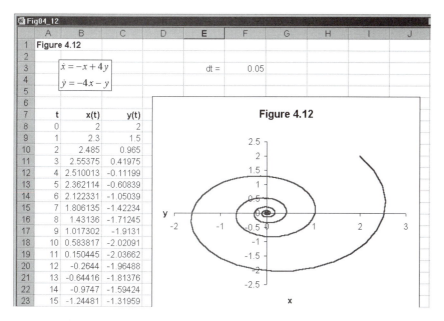

Figure 4.12

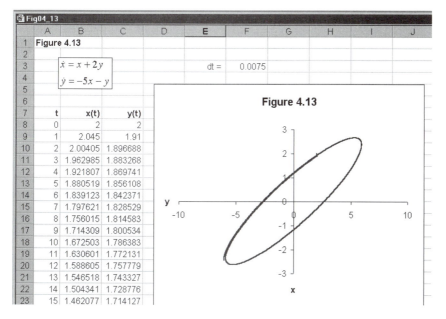

Figure 4.13

and the reader is encouraged to set this up in exactly the same way as the previous one. Take a point very close to the origin, say (0.5,0.5), and what will emerge is a clockwise spiral *away* from the origin. Also try the initial point (−0.5,−0.5), the same explosive clockwise spiral emerges.

Our final example illustrates a **centre**, and is shown in figure 4.13. Consider the model

$$\dot{x} = x + 2y$$
$$\dot{y} = -5x - y$$

(4.17)

Set this model up in exactly the same way as earlier models, with two differences. Let the time interval taken be very small, with a value around 0.0075 and plot for between 1000 and 2000 periods. The plot illustrated has 1100 periods. The trajectory forms a closed curve. In this example, the trajectory moves in a clockwise direction. It was necessary to take a very small time interval, since this is strictly a continuous model, and it is a centre for the continuous model only. By taking a very small time interval, and using over 1000 periods, we can obtain a reasonable approximation of the closed trajectory.[2]

Had we been considering the model

$$\dot{x} = 2x - 5y$$
$$\dot{y} = x - 2y$$

(4.18)

with the same small time interval and over 1000 periods, then we would observe once again a closed curve, but the trajectory would now take a counterclockwise motion from the initial point.

4.8 Limit cycles

In systems (4.17) and (4.18) of section 4.7, we considered a closed-curve trajectory. It did not matter what the initial value was, a closed curve passing through this value would result. A different situation can arise where the trajectory converges on a closed curve, and once on it remains on it. An example will help to clarify this. The example we shall discuss is referred to as the Van der Pol equations, which are

$$\dot{x} = f(x,y) = y$$
$$\dot{y} = g(x,y) = \mu(1 - x^2)y - x$$

(4.19)

Note that given the initial values $(x(0), y(0))$, then

$$x(1) = x(0) + f(x(0),y(0))\Delta t = x(0) + y(0)\Delta t$$
$$y(1) = y(0) + g(x(0),y(0))\Delta t = y(0) + [\mu(1 - x(0)^2)y(0) - x(0)]\Delta t$$

The first thing we note about these equations is that they are nonlinear. But setting the problem up on a spreadsheet, using the Euler approximation, is fundamentally no different from setting up a linear model. The model is shown in figure 4.14.

In cell F3 we place the value for the parameter μ, denoting this 'mu' and set equal to unity. In cell F4 we have the time interval, which we have set at 0.05. In cells B9 and C9 we have the initial values for x and y, respectively, which we have set at $(x(0), y(0)) = (2,4)$ in the phase space. We used the fill command to set the number of periods equal to 1000. Cells B10 and C10 have the following formulas entered

---

[2] Taking a time interval of 0.05 will lead to an explosive spiral.

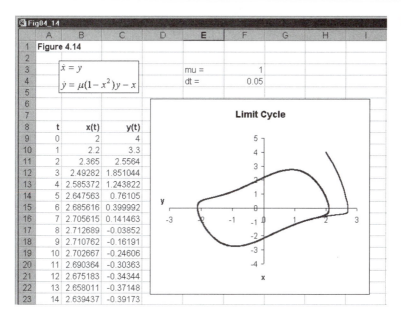

Figure 4.14

Cell B10	Cell C10
$= x(0) + f(x(0), y(0))\Delta t$	$= y(0) + g(x(0), y(0))\Delta t$
$= B9 + C9*\$F\$4$	$= C9 + (\$F\$3*(1 - B9^2)*C9 - B9)*\$F\$4$

which are then copied to the clipboard and pasted down up to period 1000. Finally, we block cells B9:C1009 and use the chart button to create the inserted chart. The chart shown in figure 4.14 has been annotated as before.

Figure 4.14 has the initial point outside the limit cycle that clearly emerges. But for a true limit cycle, then for points inside the same should also be true: that is, the trajectory should move outward until it blends into the limit cycle. To see if this is true, choose now an initial point close to the origin, say (0.5,0.5). It will be established that this is indeed the case.

In our investigation of the Van der Pol equations we set the value of the parameter μ to unity. Of course this need not be the only value for this parameter. You may wish to try a few values – both above and below unity. But we shall return to this set of equations and a discussion of the parameter μ in chapter 10.

4.9 Lorenz curves and strange attractors

It is already apparent that trajectories in the two-dimensional phase space can become very varied. An even stranger trajectory has been given much attention, and we shall present here a simple means of analysing the **Lorenz curves**. We introduce this to show that we can just as readily use our spreadsheet to

set up a three-equation model. The Lorenz curves, named after their origina-
tor, can be expressed

(4.20)
$$\dot{x} = \sigma(y - x)$$
$$\dot{y} = rx - y - xz$$
$$\dot{z} = xy - bz$$

where x, y and z are variables dependent on time, and σ, r and b are parameters. The model is set out in figure 4.15 in a slightly different way from the way
we have done it so far. In cells G3 to G6 we have the values of the three parameters and the interval set for time. Specifically, we have $\sigma = 10$, $r = 28$, $b = 8/3$
and $\Delta t = 0.01$. In cells A11 to A2011 we have numbered the 2000 time periods
that we shall use for plotting purposes. It is necessary to have a small time
interval and many time periods to see exactly what is happening in this model.
In columns B, C and D we set out the computations for dx/dt, dy/dt and dz/dt,
while in columns E, F and G we have the computations for x, y and z. Cells
E11, F11 and G11 contain our initial values for each of the three variables. In
this example, our initial point is $(x(0), y(0), z(0)) = (5,0,0)$. Cells B11, C11 and
D11 are simply the equations above. Thus

B11	$= \$G\$3*(F11 - E11)$
C11	$= \$G\$4*E11 - F11 - E11*G11$
D11	$= E11*F11 - \$G\$5*G11$

Next we compute cells E12, F12 and G12 as follows

E12	$= E11 + B11*\$G\$6$
F12	$= F11 + C11*\$G\$6$
G12	$= G11 + D11*\$G\$6$

Now copy cells B11, C11 and D11 to the clipboard and paste in B12, C12 and
D12. Now that all computations are complete for cells B12 to G12, these are
copied to the clipboard and pasted down for up to period 2000. This completes all the computations for this model.

It is now time to plot the trajectories. Spreadsheets do not allow three-
dimensional plots but we can obtain some idea of the system's behaviour by
plotting trajectories in three different phase planes, namely plane-(x,z), plane-
(x,y) and plane-(y,z). The three resulting charts are shown in figure 4.16. It is
difficult to draw trajectories in more than two dimensions, and so it can be
difficult to understand the complex phenomena that can, and do, occur in such
systems. Although the trajectories in figure 4.16 appear to cross over each
other, this does not occur in the three-dimensional space. What the graphs in
figure 4.16 show is a set of two-dimensional projections of *the* three-
dimensional trajectory. Changing the values of the parameters leads to some
very different patterns, but the general nature of the attracting points tend to
remain. We shall return to this model again in chapter 10 when we discuss
chaos theory.

Figure 4.15

Fig04_15

	A	B	C	D	E	F	G	H
1	Lorenz curve							
2								
3		$\dfrac{dx}{dt} = \sigma(y - x)$				$\sigma =$	10	
4						$r =$	28	
5		$\dfrac{dy}{dt} = rx - y - xz$				$b =$	2.666667	
6						$dt =$	0.01	
7								
8		$\dfrac{dz}{dt} = xy - bz$						
9								
10	t	dx/dt	dy/dt	dz/dt	x	y	z	
11	0	-50	140	0	5	0	0	
12	1	-31	124.6	6.3	4.5	1.4	0	
13	2	-15.44	114.41	10.91874	4.19	2.646	0.063	
14	3	-2.455	108.5118	14.83616	4.0356	3.7901	0.172187	
15	4	8.641685	106.1484	18.69995	4.01105	4.875219	0.320549	
16	5	18.39236	106.7127	22.97198	4.097467	5.936703	0.507549	
17	6	27.2244	109.7186	28.02008	4.28139	7.00383	0.737268	
18	7	35.47381	114.7676	34.17581	4.553634	8.101016	1.017469	
19	8	43.40319	121.5141	41.77142	4.908373	9.248691	1.359227	
20	9	51.21428	129.6304	51.16352	5.342404	10.46383	1.776941	
21	10	59.05589	138.7686	62.7474	5.854547	11.76014	2.288577	
22	11	67.02716	148.5209	76.96298	6.445106	13.14782	2.916051	
23	12	75.17654	158.3725	94.29107	7.115378	14.63303	3.68568	

4.10 Conclusion

In this chapter we considered just two interrelated markets in which the equations were autonomous. This emphasis is justified because the majority of dynamic models encountered in economics are of this type. Given this assumption of autonomous equations, a system involving two variables x and y moves through the (x,y)-plane over time starting from some initial point. This is called a **trajectory**, and for autonomous systems there is only *one* trajectory through any given initial point.

The more complex the equations describing a system, the more difficult it is to obtain trajectories. Two methods were outlined in this chapter. The first was purely qualitative and involves establishing vector forces. The first step is to derive an isocline for each variable (often each market). This is where there is no change in the variable, and therefore denotes the relationship between y and x for which each market is in equilibrium. In continuous models we have $\dot{x} = 0$ and $\dot{y} = 0$ denoting the two isoclines, while for discrete models, we have $\Delta x(t+1) = 0$ and $\Delta y(t+1) = 0$. If these isoclines are different, then we can identify four quadrants, and the forces that exist in each quadrant. Such vector forces give some useful qualitative information on the nature of the trajectories of the system. The second procedure was to use Euler's approximation. For any given initial condition, and taking small increments in time, it is possible to plot the solution path. The smaller the time interval, the better the plot. This procedure applies only to continuous systems. For discrete models,

Figure 4.16

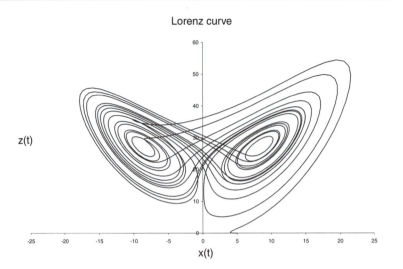

Lorenz curve

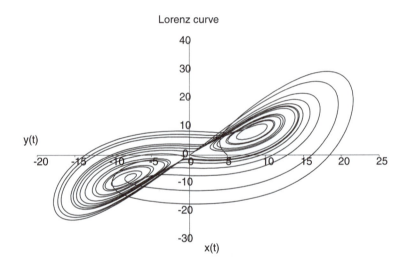

Lorenz curve

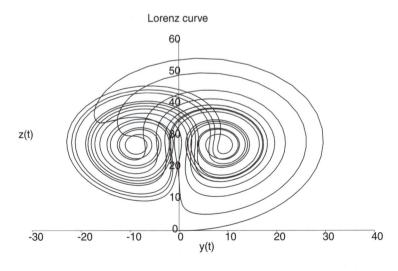

Lorenz curve

the difference equations specifying the systems dynamics are readily converted to recursive equations. These can be immediately plotted with the help of a spreadsheet. Using these two procedures, we considered a number of dynamic systems – both discrete and continuous. We finished by considering some special dynamic systems: namely, limit cycles and Lorenz curves.

Exercises

(1)   Construct diagrams showing isoclines and vector forces for the following systems

   (i) $\dot{x} = 3x$
         $\dot{y} = \frac{1}{2}y$

   (ii) $\dot{x} = x - 3y$
          $\dot{y} = -2x + y$

(2)   (i)   Use a spreadsheet and Euler's approximation to construct the trajectory for the following system. Use 0.05 for the time interval and $t = 0$ to 200

   $\dot{x} = -3x + y$
   $\dot{y} = x - 3y$
   $(x(0), y(0)) = (2, 10)$

   (ii)   Verify that this trajectory is consistent with the vector forces

(3)   (i)   Use a spreadsheet and Euler's approximation to construct the trajectory for the following system. Use 0.05 for the time interval and $t = 0$ to 200

   $\dot{x} = 2x + 3y$
   $\dot{y} = 3x + 2y$
   $(x(0), y(0)) = (1, 0)$

   (ii)   Verify that this trajectory is consistent with the vector forces.

   (iii)   Show that the trajectory for the system through the point $(1, -1)$ is different.

(4)   (i)   Establish the trajectory of the following discrete system

   $x(t + 1) = -8 - x(t) + y(t)$
   $y(t + 1) = 4 - 0.3x(t) + 0.9y(t)$
   $(x(0), y(0)) = (2, 8)$

   (ii)   What is the equilibrium value of the system and does the trajectory converge on this equilibrium?

(iii) Plot the path of $x(t)$ and $y(t)$ for $t=0$ to 20. What do you observe?

(5)   (i)   Establish the trajectory of the following discrete system

$$x(t+1)=-2+0.25x(t)+0.4y(t)$$
$$y(t+1)=10-2x(t)+0.5y(t)$$
$$(x(0),y(0))=(2.5,15)$$

(ii)   What is the fixed point of the system and does the trajectory converge on this value?

(iii) Plot $x(t)$ and $y(t)$ for $t=0$ to 20. What do you observe?

Chapter 5

IS-LM dynamics

5.1 The static model

Let us first outline briefly the static version of the IS-LM model. The model comprises a set of equations that denote behavioural relationships for expenditures, along with an equilibrium condition. These together comprise the goods market. An important difference in this version of the model from the one we discussed in chapter 3 is that investment is considered inversely related to the rate of interest. This is important in a number of respects, as we shall see. As in chapter 3, we have consumers' expenditure related to disposable income, which is defined as income *less* direct taxes. We assume a closed economy and so total expenditure is the sum of consumers' expenditure, investment expenditure and government expenditure. We treat government expenditure as the only exogenous variable in this model. The equilibrium condition for the goods market is that income is equal to total expenditure. The goods market equations are set out algebraically in the upper section of table 5.1.

The terms a, Tx_0 and I_0, denote autonomous expenditures; the parameter b denotes the marginal propensity to consume and tx denotes the marginal rate of tax. The equation $Y = C + I + G$ denotes the equilibrium condition in the goods market.

Carrying out substitutions, we arrive at the following condition for goods market equilibrium

$$Y = (a - bTx_0 + I_0 + G) + b(1 - tx)Y - hr$$

$$r = \frac{(a - bTx_0 + I_0 + G)}{h} - \frac{1 - b(1 - tx)Y}{h} \tag{5.1}$$

This is just a linear equation that we can write more simply as

$$r = A_0 - A_1 Y$$

$$A_0 = \frac{(a - bTx_0 + I_0 + G)}{h}, \quad A_1 = \frac{1 - b(1 - tx)}{h} \tag{5.2}$$

Generally this will have a positive intercept and a negative slope when drawn in (Y,r)-space, with Y on the horizontal axis and r on the vertical axis.

Now consider the money market. The money supply is assumed exogenous, and set at M. Substituting this into the equilibrium condition we have

$$M_0 + kY - ur = M$$

Table 5.1 *Goods market equations*

Goods market	Definitions
$C = a + b\,Yd \quad 0 \leq b \leq 1$	C = consumers' expenditure
$Yd = Y - Tx$	Yd = disposable income
$Tx = Tx_0 + tx\,Y \quad 0 \leq tx \leq 1$	Tx = total taxes
$I = I_0 - hr \quad h > 0$	r = interest rate
$Y = C + I + G$	I = investment expenditure
	G = government expenditure

Money market	Definitions
$Md = M_0 + kY - ur \quad k > 0, u > 0$	Md = demand for money
$Ms = M$	
$Md = Ms$	Ms = supply of money

or

(5.3)
$$r = \frac{M_0 - M}{u} + \frac{kY}{u}$$

This is just a linear equation that we can write more simply as

$$r = B_0 + B_1 Y$$

(5.4)
$$B_0 = \frac{M_0 - M}{u}, \; B_1 = \frac{k}{u}$$

This will have a positive slope when drawn in (Y, r)-space, because of our assumptions about the sign of the parameters k and u. The intercept can be positive, zero or negative.

Of course, what we have now is two equations

(5.5)
$$r = A_0 - A_1 Y$$
$$r = B_0 + B_1 Y$$

in two unknowns, which are Y and r. The situation is shown graphically in figure 5.1. The goods market equilibrium is labelled IS and the money market equilibrium is labelled LM.[1] All-round equilibrium is therefore where the two lines intersect, which is at point E in figure 5.1, leading to equilibrium levels Y^* and r^*.

Let us consider a numerical example, which we shall use in the early part of this chapter

$$C = 110 + 0.75\,Yd$$
$$Yd = Y - Tx$$
$$Tx = -80 + 0.2\,Y$$
$$I = 320 - 4r$$

---

[1] These designations for goods market equilibrium and money market equilibrium are historical. In a simple model with no trade and no government, equilibrium in the goods market can be shown to satisfy the condition that investment is equal to saving, $I = S$. The money market refers to the demand for money as the liquidity preference and so equilibrium in the money market is where liquidity preference, denoted L, is equal to the money supply, denoted M. Hence LM denotes money market equilibrium.

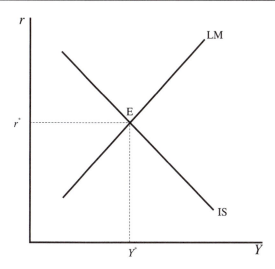

Figure 5.1

$G = 330$
$Y = C + I + G$
$Md = 20 + 0.25\,Y - 10r$
$Ms = 470$
$Md = Ms$ (5.6)

Carrying out the same substitutions as we described above, we arrive at the following two equations

> *IS curve*: $r = 205 - 0.1\,Y$
> *LM curve*: $r = -45 + 0.025\,Y$ (5.7)

and solving we obtain the equilibrium values $(Y^*, r^*) = (2000, 5)$.

All this is the standard IS-LM model found in most elementary or intermediate macroeconomics textbooks. Analysis proceeds by changing various items in the model. Here we shall just consider two since our real interest is in the dynamics. A rise in government spending raises the intercept A_0 and so shifts the IS curve to the right. In figure 5.2 this is shown by the shift in the IS curve from IS_0 to IS_1. Similarly, a rise in the money supply *reduces* the intercept B_0 (see (5.4)) and so shifts the LM curve down (or to the right). This results in equilibrium point E_2. In each case there is a rise in the level of national income; but for a fiscal expansion there is a rise in the rate of interest and in the case of a monetary expansion there is a fall in the rate of interest. For example, using the numerical example, a rise in government spending to 350 raises equilibrium income to 2040 and the interest rate to 6. A rise in the money supply from 470 to 500 leads to a higher equilibrium level of income of 2024 and to a fall in the interest rate to 2.6

All this is a comparative static argument. We simply begin with the equilibrium point E_0, then undertake either a fiscal expansion or a monetary expansion and the economy moves to point E_1 or E_2, respectively. But how do we know that the economy actually does move from one equilibrium to the other? To establish this requires a dynamic process to be specified. Even if the

Figure 5.2

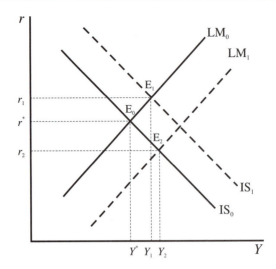

economy does move to the new equilibrium, what trajectory does it take to get there? This, too, is a dynamic consideration.

5.2 Instantaneous money market adjustment

As a way into the dynamics of the IS-LM model let us consider first an extreme case in which the money market adjusts immediately and the goods market takes time, i.e. is sluggish in its adjustment. This is not too unreasonable. Interest rates can adjust quickly as information spreads around the market. On the other hand, for the goods market to adjust, firms have to take on more labour, and output needs to be raised. This takes time. If the money market adjusts immediately, then the money market is *always* in equilibrium. Because the goods market is sluggish, this is not necessarily the case in this market. Geometrically, this means that the economy at any moment of time is *always* on the LM curve (since this denotes money market equilibrium) but not necessarily on the IS curve.

Under this assumption let us consider the trajectory of the economy in each of the two expansions mentioned in section 5.1. Take first the goods market expansion. We already know that this shifts the IS curve to the right. In the first round national income will rise by the rise in government spending. We know from our discussion in chapter 3 that this is only the beginning of the adjustment process. As income rises by this amount, this will raise the demand for money, and with a constant money supply the rate of interest will rise. On round number two, consumption rises because of the rise in income. This further increases income but by less than before (recall that the marginal propensity to consume lies between zero and one). Once again this will raise interest rates, but by not as much as in the first round. Income continues to rise by smaller and smaller amounts until the new equilibrium level of income is reached. Interest rates adjust by smaller and smaller amounts until the new equilibrium level of interest rate is reached. Geometrically, the economy is

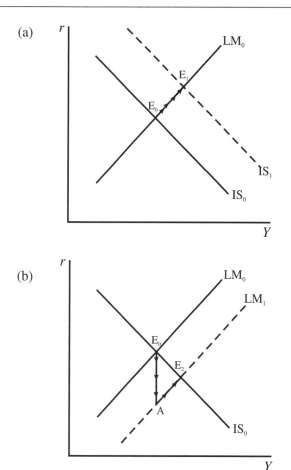

Figure 5.3

moving along the LM curve as shown in figure 5.3(a). The economy's trajectory is the path from E_0 to E_1 along the LM curve, shown by the arrows.

Now consider a monetary expansion. The economy's trajectory is quite different. We know this shifts the LM curve down (to the right), to LM_1 shown in figure 5.3(b). The rise in the money supply, with the demand for money constant, leads to an immediate fall in the rate of interest. The fall is shown by point A in figure 5.3(b). Point A must be immediately below E_0 since this change can virtually happen overnight, while income has not yet had a chance to change. Also note that point A is *off* the IS curve. But this fall in the rate of interest stimulates investment, and with a rise in investment income begins to increase. However, as income increases so does the demand for money. This puts pressure on the rate of interest to rise. As it rises, the money market remains in equilibrium. The economy now traverses a path along the *new* LM curve from point A to point E_2. For a monetary expansion, therefore, the economy's trajectory is the path $E_0 \to A \to E_2$, as shown by the arrows in figure 5.3(b). Notice, too, that although after the initial fall in interest rates they begin to rise, the rise never completely swamps the initial fall, so overall there is a fall in the equilibrium rate of interest. What we also observe here is the phenomenon of **overshooting**. The interest rate initially goes in the direction it will eventually go: that is, it falls. But the initial fall is too large, going beyond the eventual equilibrium value, and so has to rise for part of the period. This is important. An economist predicting the impact of monetary expansion on interest rates would predict a fall if considering only the comparative statics, but would predict an initial dramatic fall followed by a rise when considering the dynamics!

Let us use the numerical example to illustrate the dynamics implied by an instantaneous adjustment in the money market and a sluggish adjustment in the goods market. We do this by assuming a lag in consumption, i.e. consumption in time t depends on disposable income in time $t-1$. Because of instantaneous adjustment in the money market, all variables in the money market are at time t. Our model is then

$$C(t) = 110 + 0.75\,Yd(t-1)$$
$$Yd(t) = Y(t) - Tx(t)$$
$$Tx(t) = -80 + 0.2\,Y(t)$$
$$I(t) = 320 - 4r(t)$$
$$G = 330$$
$$Y(t) = C(t) + I(t) + G$$
$$Md(t) = 20 + 0.25\,Y(t) - 10r(t)$$
$$Ms(t) = 470$$
(5.8) $$Md(t) = Ms(t)$$

Lagging disposable income 1 period and substituting this into the consumption function, and then substituting this along with investment and government spending into the goods market equilibrium condition, we obtain an expression for the IS curve

(5.9) $$Y(t) = 820 + 0.6\,Y(t-1) - 4r(t)$$

Substituting the demand and supply for money into the money market equilibrium we obtain an expression for the LM curve

(5.10) $$r(t) = -45 + 0.025\,Y(t)$$

Notice that it is only the goods market that involves any lagged terms. This is picking up the sluggishness in the goods market. The fact that the money market clears in time period t indicates instantaneous adjustment in this market. We can now substitute the expression for the rate of interest derived in the money market, (5.10), into the goods market equation, (5.9), and solve for income in time period t. We obtain the following recursive equation

(5.11) $$Y(t) = 909.0909 + 0.54545\,Y(t-1)$$

We can first check this by setting $Y(t) = Y(t-1) = Y^*$ and solving for Y^*. Doing so gives a value for Y^* of 2000. Substituting this for income in the money market allows us to solve for the equilibrium interest rate, which is 5. Both these results are the same as before.

Before we set this up on a spreadsheet we need to take account of the increase in the money supply. We are considering a rise in the money supply from 470 to 500. This affects directly only the money market. In the money market we now have

$$500 = 20 + 0.25\,Y(t) - 10r(t)$$
$$r(t) = -48 + 0.025\,Y(t)$$

The goods market remains unchanged with

$$Y(t) = 820 + 0.6\,Y(t-1) - 4r(t)$$

Substituting the previous result for $r(t)$ into this expression, we arrive at

$$Y(t) = 820 + 0.6\,Y(t-1) - 4(-48 + 0.025\,Y(t))$$
$$Y(t) = 920 + 0.54545\,Y(t-1)$$

We are now in a position to set up our spreadsheet.

The spreadsheet is illustrated in figure 5.4. We have inserted at the top of the spreadsheet the dynamic representation of the goods market and the money market as a reminder. In cell B7 we have the initial level of income. Here we set it equal to 2000, the equilibrium level of income. In cell C7 we have

$$= -45 + 0.025\,Y(t)$$
$$= -45 + 0.025*\ B7$$

In cell B8 we retain income at level 2000 since the money supply affects the money market only in this period, i.e. we assume the change in the money supply takes place in period 1. In cell C8 we place the new expression for the LM curve

$$= -48 + 0.025\,Y(t)$$
$$= -48 + 0.025*\ B8$$

The impact from the money market now makes itself felt in the goods market. So in cell B9 we place our revised formula for $Y(t)$, i.e.

$$= 920 + 0.54545\,Y(t-1)$$
$$= 920 + 0.54545*\ B8$$

For C9 we simply copy C8 and paste in C9. Cells B9 and C9 are now copied to the clipboard and pasted down.

With all the computations now complete, we can block cells B7:C27 and invoke the chart wizard. This allows us to insert the chart with the trajectory in the (Y,r)-space. What is clearly shown by the inserted chart is just the trajectory we outlined above. The interest rate drops immediately from 5 to 2 and then over time rises to the eventual equilibrium value of 2.6 while income rises to 2024. It is also clear from the inserted chart that the trajectory follows the *new* LM curve. This must be so, since in each period the money market always clears. It is income that adjusts slowly. As income adjusts, this alters consumption, taxes *and* the demand for money. The demand for money alters the interest rate, which in turn alters the level of investment. In fact, the resulting rise in interest rates curbs the rise in investment resulting from the initial fall in the interest rate. The eventual result, however, is a fall in the equilibrium rate of interest and a rise in the level of equilibrium income.

The reader should undertake a number of experiments with this model, such as:

Figure 5.4

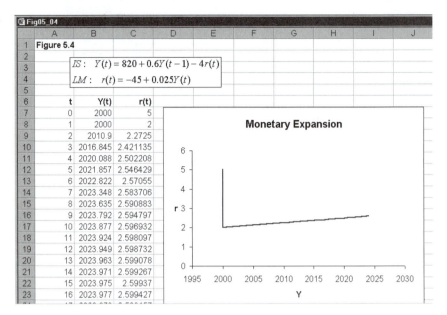

(i)   A rise in *G* from 330 to 350
(ii)   A fall in *tx* from 0.2 to 0.175
(iii)   A rise in *b* from 0.75 to 0.8
(iv)   A fall in *k* (a rise in the income velocity of money) from 0.25 to 0.3
(v)   A fall in *u* (a fall in the interest sensitivity of money demand) to 7 (or even zero)
(vi)   A fall in *h* (a fall in the interest sensitivity of investment) from 4 to 2 (or even zero).

5.3 A continuous model

We shall now consider a continuous model and also allow differential adjustments in both the money market and the goods market, neither of which is instantaneous. However, we shall assume in line with our previous analysis that the money market is quicker to adjust than the goods market. In setting out this continuous model we identify these adjustment coefficients in terms of two adjustment equations. In the goods market we assume that income rises over time if there is excess demand and falls if there is excess supply. More specifically

(5.12) $$\dot{Y}(t) = \alpha(E(t) - Y(t)) \quad \alpha > 0$$

where $E(t) = C(t) + I(t) + G$. In the money market we assume that the interest rate rises if there is excess demand in this market and falls if there is excess supply. More specifically

(5.13) $$\dot{r}(t) = \beta(Md - Ms) \quad \beta > \alpha > 0$$

In general terms our full model is then

$$C(t) = a + b\,Yd(t)$$
$$Yd(t) = Y(t) - Tx(t)$$
$$Tx(t) = Tx_0 + tx\,Y(t)$$
$$I(t) = I_0 - hr(t)$$
$$E(t) = C(t) + I(t) + G$$
$$\dot{Y}(t) = \alpha(E(t) - Y(t)) \quad \alpha > 0$$
$$Md(t) = M_0 + k\,Y(t) - ur(t)$$
$$Ms(t) = M$$
$$\dot{r}(t) = \beta(Md(t) - Ms(t)) \quad \beta > 0 \tag{5.14}$$

Notice that this is consistent with our earlier analysis. In equilibrium $\dot{Y}(t) = 0$, which implies $Y(t) = C(t) + I(t) + G$; and $\dot{r}(t) = 0$, which implies $Md(t) = Ms(t) = M$. Furthermore, the adjustment coefficients α and β have no bearing on these equilibrium values.

What we now wish to show is that we can set up this model in (Y,r)-phase space and show that the IS and LM curves are no more than isoclines. More importantly, we can then consider the four quadrants and the vector forces in those quadrants. Although the algebra is a little tedious, it takes the same form as we have done already, so we shall simply give the results here. They are derived by substituting all the relationships in each of the adjustment equations in turn. They are

$$\text{IS:} \quad \dot{Y}(t) = \alpha(a - bTx_0 + I_0 + G) - \alpha(1 - b(1 - tx))Y(t) - \alpha hr(t)$$
$$\text{LM:} \quad \dot{r}(t) = \beta(M_0 - M) + \beta k\,Y(t) - \beta ur(t) \tag{5.15}$$

It immediately follows from these equations that the IS curve is the isocline $\dot{Y} = 0$ and the LM curve is the isocline $\dot{r} = 0$. These are appropriately labelled in figure 5.5. For the moment, we shall assume that $(1 - b(1 - tx)) > 0$ or $b(1 - tx) < 1$. This means that the IS curve is negatively sloped. We are assuming k and u are positive, so the LM curve is positively sloped.

Let us now turn to the four quadrants and consider the vector forces. Consider first the goods market. If $\dot{Y}(t) > 0$ then $Y(t)$ is rising. This will be so when

$$\alpha(a - bTx_0 + I_0 + G) - \alpha(1 - b(1 - tx))Y(t) - \alpha hr(t) > 0$$
$$r(t) < \frac{(a - bTx_0 + I_0 + G)}{h} - \frac{(1 - b(1 - tx))Y(t)}{h}$$

Given our assumptions about the negatively sloped IS curve, then this refers to points below the IS curve. Hence, for points below the IS curve there is pressure for income to rise. It also follows that above the IS curve there is pressure for income to fall. These forces are indicated by the right and left arrows below and above the IS curve, respectively.

Now turn to the money market. If $r(t) > 0$ then $r(t)$ is rising and

$$\beta(M_0 - M) + \beta k\,Y(t) - \beta ur(t) > 0$$
$$r(t) < \frac{M_0 - M}{u} + \frac{k\,Y(t)}{u}$$

Figure 5.5

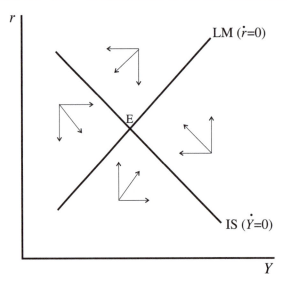

Figure 5.6

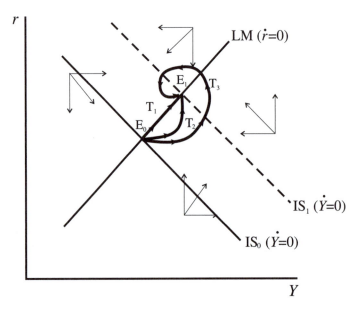

So below the LM curve there is pressure on interest rates to rise, while above the LM curve there is pressure on interest rates to fall. These forces are shown by the up and down arrows below and above the LM curve, respectively.

The dynamics is more clearly illustrated by considering some change, such as a rise in government spending. This is shown in figure 5.6. The initial equilibrium is E_0 and the new equilibrium is E_1. When the rise in government spending occurs, point E_0 is no longer an equilibrium point of the system. This is now E_1. The vector forces shown in figure 5.6 are with respect to the new equilibrium E_1 and *not* the initial equilibrium E_0. Under the assumption of instantaneous adjustment in the money market, the economy traverses the trajectory marked T_1, which lies along the LM curve. This is a counterclockwise movement. But if we relax the assumption of instantaneous adjustment in the money market, it is possible for the economy to traverse paths T_2 and T_3. What determines the trajectory of the economy in such circumstances? We investigate this by considering another numerical example, and set the problem up on a spreadsheet using the Euler approximation for continuous models that we outlined in chapter 4.

5.4 Continuous IS-LM on a spreadsheet

Return to the two differential equations representing the IS curve and the LM curve

$$IS: \ \dot{Y}(t) = f(Y,r) = \alpha(a - bTx_0 + I_0 + G) - \alpha(1 - b(1 - tx))Y(t) - \alpha hr(t)$$
$$LM: \ \dot{r}(t) = g(Y,r) = \beta(M_0 - M) + \beta k Y(t) - \beta ur(t) \tag{5.16}$$

Then given $(Y(0),r(0))$ we compute $Y(1)$ and $r(1)$ as follows

$$Y(1) = Y(0) + f(Y(0),r(0))\Delta t$$
$$r(1) = r(0) + g(Y(0),r(0))\Delta t$$

To see this in operation, consider the following numerical model, where we have included values for the adjustment coefficients. In particular, we have assumed $\alpha = 0.05$ and $\beta = 0.8$, which satisfies the condition that $\beta > \alpha > 0$

$$C(t) = 15 + 0.75\,Yd(t)$$
$$Yd(t) = Y(t) - Tx(t)$$
$$Tx(t) = 0.25\,Y(t)$$
$$I(t) = 10 - 1.525r(t)$$
$$G = 25$$
$$E(t) = C(t) + I(t) + G$$
$$\dot{Y}(t) = 0.05(E(t) - Y(t))$$
$$Md(t) = 0.25\,Y(t) - 0.5r(t)$$
$$Ms(t) = 8$$
$$\dot{r}(t) = 0.8(Md(t) - Ms(t)) \tag{5.17}$$

The equilibrium of this system, the fixed point, is $(Y^*, r^*) = (62, 15)$. The two differential equations, leaving α and β unspecified, are

$$\dot{Y} = f(Y,r) = 50\alpha - 0.4375\alpha Y - 1.525\alpha r$$
$$\dot{r} = g(Y,r) = -8\beta + 0.25\beta Y - 0.5\beta r \tag{5.18}$$

The fixed points are readily verified by setting $\dot{Y} = 0$ and $\dot{r} = 0$.

5.4.1 Monetary expansion

The example is set out in figure 5.7. First we set our time period from 0 to 1500 in column A. In cells G3, G4 and G5 we place the values of α and β and the value for the time interval. Next we place our initial equilibrium values in cells B8 and C8, namely 62 for Y and 15 for r. Since we are about to consider a rise in the money supply from 8 to 12 we need to re-specify the second differential

Figure 5.7

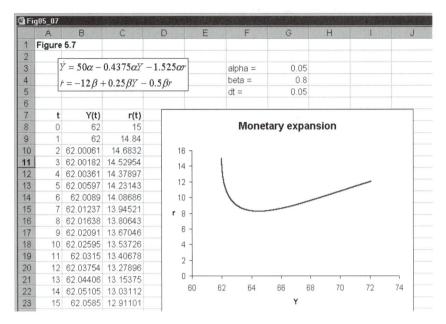

equation to take account of this. The new equation has -12β rather than -8β. The equations, then, which we shall use for computing the new values of Y and r are

$$\dot{Y}=f(Y,r)=50\alpha-0.4375\alpha Y-1.525\alpha r$$
$$\dot{r}=g(Y,r)=-12\beta+0.25\beta Y-0.5\beta r$$

(5.19)

which are shown on the spreadsheet. These lead to the new equilibrium point $(Y^*, r^*)=(72.1667, 12.0833)$. We accordingly enter the following in cells B9 and C9

B9	$= Y(0)+f(Y(0),r(0))\Delta t$ $= B8 + (50*\$G\$3 - 0.4375*\$G\$3*B8 - 1.525*\$G\$3*C8)*\$G\$5$
C9	$=r(0)+g(Y(0),r(0))\Delta t$ $= C8 +(-12*\$G\$4+0.25*\$G\$4*B8 - 0.5*\$G\$4*C8)*\$G\$5$

These are then copied to the clipboard and pasted down. The data in cells B8:C1508 is then used to create the chart with the chart wizard. The resulting trajectory is shown in the inserted chart. Not only does it show a counterclockwise movement, but also it shows the typical overshooting of the interest rate that we eluded to above. What we do not observe is any spiralling motion.

In section 5.3 we had instantaneous movement of the system with regard to the money market. This means that the parameter β is infinite. Increase the size of β in the spreadsheet and see the result. Try 1.5, 5, 10 and 20. What you will observe is that the trajectory gets closer to our extreme of figure 5.3(b). Think of it in a different way, the greater the adjustment in the money market

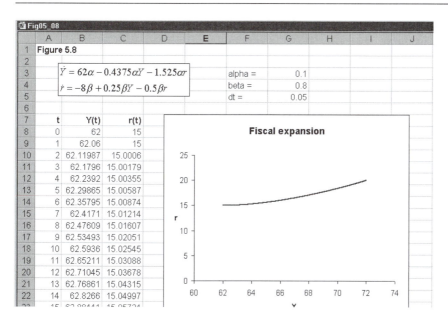

Figure 5.8

the more the trajectory is pulled towards the LM curve. Now leave the value of β at 0.8 and reduce the size of the parameter α. As you do so, a similar result occurs: namely, the trajectory gets closer to that of figure 5.3(b). What matters is the *differential* in the speeds of adjustment.

With β at 0.8 increase the value of α, first to 0.1 and then to 0.5. This still satisfies the condition $\beta > \alpha > 0$, but considers the result of the goods market being *less* sluggish. When $\alpha = 0.1$ the system still exhibits a counterclockwise movement directly towards the fixed point. Now, however, it does not follow the LM curve so directly. In fact it is further away from the LM curve. When $\alpha = 0.5$ the system exhibits a counterclockwise *spiral* to the fixed point. When a spiral occurs, both markets overshoot their equilibrium values. What this exercise illustrates, however, is that the goods market needs to be quick to adjust to disequilibrium states for a spiral path to occur. The conclusion we draw from this analysis is that overshooting of interest rates is inevitable, but overshooting of national income is highly unlikely to be observed within this particular model. National income will just steadily rise to its new equilibrium level.

5.4.2 Fiscal expansion

Next let us consider a fiscal expansion. The analysis is very much the same so we shall be brief. Suppose government spending rises from 25 to 37 (a rise of 12), then our differential equations (5.18) take the form

$$\dot{Y} = f(Y,r) = 62\alpha - 0.4375\alpha Y - 1.525\alpha r$$
$$\dot{r} = g(Y,r) = -8\beta + 0.25\beta Y - 0.5\beta r \tag{5.20}$$

with equilibrium values $(Y^*, r^*) = (72, 20)$. The model is illustrated in figure 5.8.

Other than the inserted equations, the only difference is cells B9 and C9. These now have formulas

B9	$= Y(0) + f(Y(0),r(0))\Delta t$ $= B8 + (62*\$G\$3 - 0.4375*\$G\$3*B8 - 1.525*\$G\$3*C8)*\$G\$5$
C9	$= r(0) + g(Y(0),r(0))\Delta t$ $= C8 + (-8*\$G\$4 + 0.25*\$G\$4*B8 - 0.5*\$G\$4*C8)*\$G\$5$

The resulting chart is shown in figure 5.8, which shows a gradual counter-clockwise movement to the new equilibrium. Income and interest rates rise steadily (but rather slowly in this example) to the new equilibrium. In the case of a fiscal expansion there is no overshooting.

A spiral counterclockwise path can occur if the goods market is quick to adjust – even if still less quick than the money market. Set the value of α to 0.5 and a spiral counterclockwise path will result. But such a path is highly unlikely within this particular model. What we observe in capitalist economies is a speedily adjusting money market and a slow adjusting goods market.

5.4.3 Combined fiscal and monetary policy

Of course, economies will have combined fiscal and monetary policy and the trajectory of the economy in such circumstances can be quite varied. Here we shall consider just one example, leaving other scenarios to be considered by the reader in terms of the exercises.

We shall consider a fiscal and monetary expansion. We know that each separately raises the level of equilibrium income, so we certainly know such a combined policy will raise the level of national income. However, the result on the equilibrium interest rate is less certain. A fiscal expansion raises the rate of interest while a monetary expansion lowers it.

Let us simply use our previous expansions. We shall let the money supply rise from 8 to 12 and government spending rise from 25 to 37. Our resulting differential equations are then

$$\dot{Y} = f(Y,r) = 62\alpha - 0.4375\alpha Y - 1.525\alpha r$$

(5.21)

$$\dot{r} = g(Y,r) = -12\beta + 0.25\beta Y - 0.5\beta r$$

The new equilibrium of the system is $(Y^*, r^*) = (82.0667, 17.0833)$, and the result is shown in figure 5.9.

Again the only real difference is in cells B9 and C9

B9	$= Y(0) + f(Y(0),r(0))\Delta t$ $= B8 + (62*\$G\$3 - 0.4375*\$G\$3*B8 - 1.525*\$G\$3*C8)*\$G\$5$
C9	$= r(0) + g(Y(0),r(0))\Delta t$ $= C8 + (-12*\$G\$4 + 0.25*\$G\$4*B8 - 0.5*\$G\$4*C8)*\$G\$5$

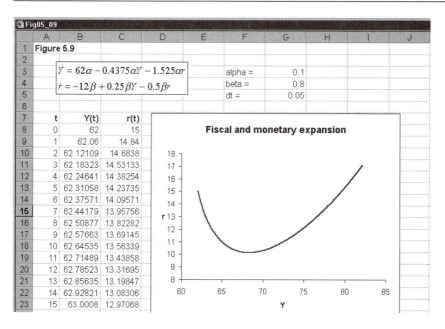

Figure 5.9

These new equations and the low adjustment coefficient in the goods market and the relatively high coefficient in the money market lead the system in the usual counterclockwise direction, with marked overshooting of the interest rate. The only time a spiral path is likely is if the adjustment in the goods market is high, which is not likely.

5.5 A discrete version of the IS-LM model

One may consider that a continuous form of the IS-LM model is not quite appropriate when modelling an economy, and that a discrete model is more appropriate. Such a model may take the following form

$$C(t) = a + b\,Yd(t)$$
$$Yd(t) = Y(t) - Tx(t)$$
$$Tx(t) = Tx_0 + tx\,Y(t)$$
$$I(t) = I_0 - hr(t)$$
$$E(t) = C(t) + I(t) + G$$
$$\Delta Y(t+1) = \alpha(E(t) - Y(t))$$
$$Md(t) = M_0 + k\,Y(t) - ur(t)$$
$$Ms(t) = M$$
$$\Delta r(t+1) = \beta(Md(t) - Ms(t)) \tag{5.22}$$

Substituting leads to the following difference equations

$$IS: \ \Delta Y(t+1) = \alpha(a - bTx_0 + I_0 + G) - \alpha(1 - b(1-tx))\,Y(t) - \alpha hr(t)$$
$$LM: \ \Delta r(t+1) = \beta(M_0 - M) + \beta k\,Y(t) - \beta ur(t) \tag{5.23}$$

Figure 5.10

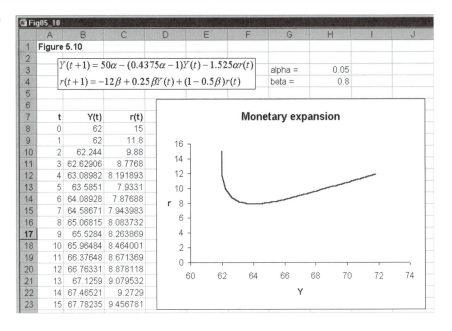

We can, as with the continuous model, show this in the (Y,r)-phase space with isoclines $\Delta Y(t+1)=0$ and $\Delta r(t+1)=0$. These, of course, lead to the same equilibrium (fixed point) as in the continuous model. Furthermore, the vector forces are the same as those shown in figure 5.5. What path the trajectory follows, however, needs to be established.

We can establish the trajectories by considering the recursive form of the model. These are

$$IS: \ Y(t+1)=\alpha(a-bTx_0+I_0+G)-[\alpha(1-b(1-tx))-1]\,Y(t)-\alpha hr(t)$$

(5.24)

$$LM: \ r(t+1)=\beta(M_0-M)+\beta k\,Y(t)+(1-\beta u)r(t)$$

Let us pursue this with our numerical example. Once again we leave α and β unspecified

$$IS: \ Y(t+1)=50\alpha-(0.4375\alpha-1)\,Y(t)-1.525\alpha r(t)$$

(5.25)

$$LM: \ r(t+1)=-8\beta+0.25\beta\,Y(t)+(1-0.5\beta)r(t)$$

Setting $Y(t+1)=Y(t)=Y^*$ and $r(t+1)=r(t)=r^*$ we establish the same equilibrium values of $Y^*=62$ and $r^*=15$.

Now let the money supply rise from 8 to 12. The situation is shown in Figure 5.10. The new equilibrium point, as before, is $(Y^*,\,r^*)=(72.1667,\,12.0833)$ and the trajectory is virtually the same as we established in figure 5.6. Increasing the money market adjustment coefficient moves the trajectory towards the LM curve as in the continuous model. However, we did make the point in chapter 4 that the discrete model can sometimes give rise to unusual behaviour patterns that are not shown in the continuous counterpart. Raise the parameter β to 2 and the trajectory moves close to that in figure 5.3(b). But raising the value of β to 3 begins to introduce cyclical behaviour in the earlier period, which then settles down to a movement along the LM curve. A rise in β to 4 leads to even more cyclical movement!

Figure 5.11

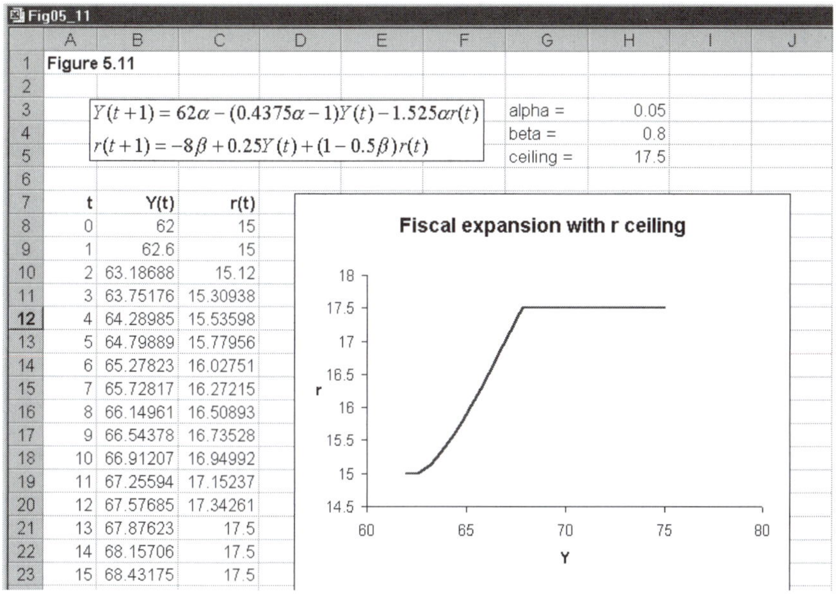

t	Y(t)	r(t)
0	62	15
1	62.6	15
2	63.18688	15.12
3	63.75176	15.30938
4	64.28985	15.53598
5	64.79889	15.77956
6	65.27823	16.02751
7	65.72817	16.27215
8	66.14961	16.50893
9	66.54378	16.73528
10	66.91207	16.94992
11	67.25594	17.15237
12	67.57685	17.34261
13	67.87623	17.5
14	68.15706	17.5
15	68.43175	17.5

A fiscal expansion shows a similar general movement to the new equilibrium without any overshooting – unless the adjustment coefficient in the goods market is particularly large. The reader can undertake all the same policy adjustments as we did before and establish similar results. We suggest some of these in the exercises.

5.6 Interest rate ceiling

Let us use the present numerical model to consider the trajectory of an economy experiencing a fiscal expansion and a ceiling imposed on interest rates. We again use the discrete model and raise government spending from 25 to 37. We have already established that this raises equilibrium income to 72 and interest rates to 20 with no market restrictions. But suppose a ceiling of 17.5 is placed on the rate of interest. We include the ceiling in the spreadsheet in cell H5, as shown in figure 5.11. The only other change is to cell C9, which now reads

C9	$= MIN(-8\beta + 0.25\beta Y(t) + (1-0.5\beta)r(t), 17.5)$ $= MIN(-8\$H\$4 + 0.25\$H\$4{*}B8 + (1-0.5{*}\$H\$4){*}C8,\ \$H\$5)$

Cells B9 and C9 are then copied to the clipboard and pasted down. The inserted graph clearly shows the trajectory rising at first, and once the ceiling is reached moving horizontally. In fact, with a ceiling of 17.5 on the rate of interest, the new equilibrium is at income level

$$\Delta Y(t+1) = 0 = 62\alpha - 0.4375\alpha Y^* - 1.525(17.5)$$
$$Y^* = 80.7143$$

which is not reached on this diagram.

5.7 Conclusion

In this chapter we have reconsidered the traditional closed economy IS-LM model but highlighted adjustment behaviour. The trajectory of the economy from one equilibrium to the next was very dependent on the assumptions about adjustment behaviour in the goods market and the money market. Of special importance was our *asymmetric* assumption: that the money market is quick to adjust (sometimes instantaneously), while the goods market takes time. We concentrated on the traditional slopes for the IS and LM curves. Having shown these represent isoclines, the four quadrants and their vector forces suggest a counterclockwise adjustment on the part of the economy. The precise nature of this counterclockwise movement, and the possibility and extent of overshooting, is dependent on the *relative difference* between the adjustment coefficients.

A typical observation of dynamic adjustments is overshooting of interest rates. This possibility is far less likely in income, given the models of this chapter. Any overshooting of income would require a high degree of adjustment in the goods market.

It must be emphasised that these dynamic adjustments are for a *closed* economy. An open economy can exhibit quite different adjustment paths.

Exercises

(1)   Set up model (5.8) on a spreadsheet and assume instantaneous money market adjustment and sluggish goods market adjustment. Establish the new equilibrium and plot the trajectory of the economy in (Y,r)-space starting from the initial equilibrium for each of the following. Treat each one separately and assume the change takes place in period 1

   (i)   Fall in G from 330 to 250.

   (ii)   Fall in Ms from 470 to 400.

(2)   Set up a vector force diagram for model (5.14) and illustrate possible trajectories for the economy in (Y,r)-space for each of the following

   (i)   A fall in government spending.

   (ii)   A fall in the money supply.

(3)   Use model (5.17) to establish the new equilibrium and to construct trajectories for the following events

   (i)   A fall in the money supply from 8 to 5.

   (ii)   A fall in business expectations resulting in a fall in autonomous investment from 10 to 5.

(iii)   A rise in savings at all levels of income, resulting in a fall in autonomous consumption from 15 to 12.

(4)   Set up model (5.22) using the parameter values in model (5.17). What are the new equilibrium and the trajectory of the economy for the following events

(i)   A rise in autonomous taxes from 0 to 10?

(ii)   A fall in the money supply from 8 to 5?

(5)   Set up model (5.22) using the parameter values in model (5.17), except let $\beta = 3$. What is the new equilibrium and the trajectory of the economy for the following events

(i)   A fall in G from 25 to 22?

(ii)   A fall in M from 8 to 5?

Chapter 6
Inflation–unemployment dynamics

6.1 The Phillips curve

Most discussions of inflation begin with the Phillips curve, and we shall be no exception. We shall, however, concentrate on those aspects that are important for the dynamics of inflation and unemployment. There are basically two specifications for the Phillips curve: the basic one relating inflation to unemployment, and the expectations-augmented Phillips curve, which relates inflation to unemployment and expected inflation. In general terms these are

(6.1)
$$\pi = f(u)$$
$$\pi = f(u) + \pi^e$$

where π = inflation, π^e = expected inflation and u = unemployment. For the moment, we shall assume a simple inverse relationship between inflation and unemployment, i.e. we assume

(6.2)
$$\pi = a_0 - a_1 u \quad a_0, a_1 > 0$$

It is not our intention here to present a full discussion of the Phillips curve, and we simply state that the natural level of unemployment, u_n, is the value of unemployment which satisfies the condition $f(u_n) = 0$ and $\pi^e = \pi$. Given our linear Phillips curve, then u_n satisfies the condition

$$u_n = \frac{a_0}{a_1}$$

The situation is illustrated in figure 6.1, where we have drawn an expectations-augmented Phillips curve. Of course, to draw such a Phillips curve we must assume that expected inflation is given, which we shall do for the moment.

In more recent treatments of the Phillips curve it has been convenient to specify the relationship between inflation and the level of real income. This is because we need to include the Phillips curve into a broader model of the macroeconomy. This takes the form

(6.3)
$$\pi = \alpha(y - y_n) + \pi^e \quad \alpha > 0$$

where y is real income and y_n is the natural level of income associated with u_n. But underlying this relationship are two reaction functions, which are worth spelling out. The first is a slightly reformulated Phillips curve that relates inflation to the unemployment gap, i.e.

(6.4)
$$\pi = -\gamma_1(u - u_n) + \pi^e \quad \gamma_1 > 0$$

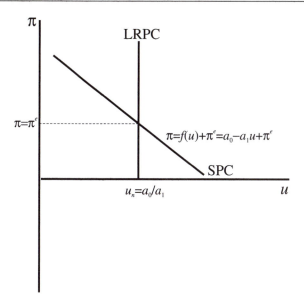

Figure 6.1

The second is Okun's law, which relates the unemployment gap to the income gap, i.e.

$$u - u_n = -\gamma_2(y - y_n) \quad \gamma_2 > 0 \tag{6.5}$$

Substituting (6.5) into (6.4) gives

$$\pi = \gamma_1\gamma_2(y - y_n) + \pi^e$$
$$\pi = \alpha(y - y_n) + \pi^e \quad \alpha > 0$$

which is our (6.3). The reason for labouring this point is that the coefficient α is seen to be composed of the product of two reaction coefficients, γ_1 and γ_2. For a given expected rate of inflation we have a positive relationship between π and y, the slope of which is (α/yn) (see figure 6.2, p. 116).

Note that when $\pi = \pi^e$ then $y = y_n$, and so when this occurs we have a vertical long-run aggregate supply curve at the natural level of real income.

6.2 A simple macroeconomic model of inflation

When modelling inflation within the context of a macroeconomic model, it is customary to set the model out as being linear in the logarithms, with the exception of inflation and interest rates, which are both percentages. We shall denote all real variables with lower-case letters. The model we are considering is set out in table 6.1.

Some remarks about this model are in order. First, the consumption function is similar to the one we have been using throughout this book; the only difference is that we are dealing with real consumers' expenditure. Investment is inversely related to the interest rate, but the interest rate relevant to investment decisions is the *real expected* rate of interest, $r - \pi^e$. We retain the

Table 6.1 *Macroeconomic model of inflation*

Goods market	Definitions of variables
$c = a + b(1 - tx)y$ $i = i_0 - h(r - \pi^e)$ $y = c + i + g$	y = real income c = real consumption i = real investment g = real government spending π^e = expected inflation
Money market	
$md = ky - ur$ $ms = m - p$ $md = ms$	r = nominal interest rate md = real money demand ms = real money supply m = nominal money stock p = price level

equilibrium condition, but now in real terms, as real income equalling the sum of real expenditures. Turning to the money market, the money demand equation is written as usual, except we are interpreting it as real money demand that is positively related to *real* income and negatively related to the *nominal* interest rate. The only unusual equation is the supply of real-money balances. But recall that the logarithm of the ratio of two numbers is the subtraction of the logarithms (see box 3), so

$$ms = \ln\left(\frac{M}{P}\right) = \ln M - \ln P = m - p$$

Box 3   Logarithms

Rules

In this box we highlight some properties of logarithms that we employ in this book. Let $\log_b(x)$ denote the logarithm of x to base b. If b is 10, then we have a *common logarithm*. In computer spreadsheets this has the designation LOG10(x). If b is the exponential value e, then we have *natural logarithms*. In computer spreadsheets this has the designation LN(x). There are three useful rules for logarithms:

Rule 1 (Product rule)

$$\log_b(xy) = \log_b(x) + \log_b(y)$$

Rule 2 (Quotient rule)

$$\log_b\left(\frac{x}{y}\right) = \log_b(x) - \log_b(y)$$

Rule 3 **(Power rule)**

$$log_b(x^k) = klog_b(x)$$

Two special cases will be used in this book

Case 1: $log_b b = 1$ e.g. $\ln(e) = 1$
Case 2: $log_b 1 = 0$ e.g. $\ln(1) = 0$

Application 1 **(Demand for money)**
Let the demand for money be expressed

$$\frac{Md}{P} = Y^k e^{-ur}$$

Taking natural logarithms, then

$$\ln\left(\frac{Md}{P}\right) = \ln(Y^k e^{-ur})$$

$$\ln Md - \ln P = k \ln Y - ur$$

This last line uses the fact that $\ln(e) = 1$. In modelling it is common to let lower-case letters denote the (natural) logarithm of variables. Thus, our demand for money equation can be expressed

$$md - p = ky - ur$$

or

$$md = p + ky - ur$$

Application 2 **(Purchasing power parity or PPP)**
Define the real exchange rate as

$$R = \frac{P}{SP^*}$$

where S is the spot exchange rate: defined as domestic currency units per unit of foreign currency. P and P^* are the price level at home and abroad, respectively. If purchasing power parity holds, the law of one price, then

$$P = SP^*   or   R = 1$$

Taking natural logarithms, then

$$\ln P = \ln S + \ln P^*$$

or in terms of lower-case letters

$$p = s + p^*$$

If P^* is constant and normalised at the value of unity, then $\ln P^* = 0$, and purchasing power parity (PPP) implies $p = s$.

Differentiation of logarithms and percentages

In this subsection we take only natural logarithms. Let $y = \ln(x)$, then

$$\frac{dy}{dx} = \frac{d\ln(x)}{dx} = \frac{1}{x}$$

Consider now its approximation

$$\frac{\Delta y}{\Delta x} = \frac{\Delta \ln(x)}{\Delta x} = \frac{1}{x}$$

Then

$$\Delta y = \Delta \ln(x) = \frac{\Delta x}{x}$$

We can therefore interpret the change in the logarithm of a variable, $\Delta \ln(x)$, to be approximately the percentage change in that variable, $\Delta x/x$.

Application 1 (**Inflation**)
Let P denote the price level. Then

$$\Delta \ln P = \frac{\Delta P}{P}$$

But $\Delta P/P$ is inflation, often denoted π, and so

$$\Delta \ln P = \pi$$

Application 2 (**Inflation in discrete time**)
Let $P(t)$ denote the price level at time t, then

$$\pi(t+1) = \frac{P(t+1) - P(t)}{P(t)} = \frac{\Delta P(t+1)}{P(t)}$$

But we can express this in the form

$$\frac{\Delta P(t+1)}{P(t)} = \Delta \ln P(t+1)$$

Using lower-case letters, define

$$p(t+1) = \ln P(t+1), \quad p(t) = \ln P(t)$$

Then

$$\Delta \ln P(t+1) = \ln P(t+1) - \ln P(t)$$
$$= p(t+1) - p(t)$$

Hence, inflation can be expressed

$$\pi(t+1) = p(t+1) - p(t)$$

We shall use this result frequently in our modelling of inflation.

Now substitute and simplify, with the results

$$y^* = \frac{(a + i_0 + g) + (h/u)(m - p) + h\pi^e}{1 - b(1 - tx) + (hk/u)}$$

$$r^* = \frac{ky^* - (m - p)}{u} \tag{6.6}$$

Our main concern here is with equilibrium income, and we can simplify this to a straightforward linear equation of the form

$$y = b_0 + b_1(m - p) + b_2\pi^e \quad b_1 > 0, b_2 > 0 \tag{6.7}$$

This represents the aggregate demand curve in the macroeconomic model of aggregate demand and aggregate supply. What we have done algebraically is solved for different intersection points of the IS-LM curves for different price levels. The resulting plot of price against real income is the **aggregate demand curve**. Notice especially that the nominal money stock is constant and so is the expected rate of inflation. Since it is traditional in economics to place price on the vertical axis and real income on the horizontal axis, it is useful to respecify this equation as an equation of p against y. Thus

$$p = \frac{b_0 + b_1 m}{b_1} - \left(\frac{1}{b_1}\right)y + \left(\frac{b_2}{b_1}\right)\pi^e$$

$$p = c_0 - c_1 y + c_2 \pi^e$$

where

$$c_0 = \frac{b_0 + b_1 m}{b_1}, \quad c_2 = \frac{1}{b_1}, \quad c_3 = \frac{b_2}{b_1}$$

The model is illustrated in terms of aggregate demand and the long-run aggregate supply in figure 6.2. Because this is a demand and supply model we must assume that all inflation rates are zero, i.e. $\pi = \pi^e = 0$, since how else in equilibrium could the price remain constant! If this is the case, as we pointed out at the end of section 6.1, this results in a vertical long-run Phillips curve at the natural level of income, which in turn implies a vertical long-run aggregate supply curve at $y = y_n$. Price is in equilibrium at level p^* and income is at its natural level.

6.3 The dynamics of the simple model

To see this model in operation, let expected inflation be zero. We do not make this assumption about actual inflation, because in the short run actual inflation can deviate from its expected value. Only in the long run will actual inflation equal expected inflation. So we need to show that the long-run result of this model satisfies this condition. Our numerical example is the following

$$y(t) = 9 + 0.2(m - p(t))$$
$$\pi(t + 1) = p(t + 1) - p(t) = 1.2(y(t) - y_n)$$
$$m = 5, y_n = 6 \tag{6.8}$$

Figure 6.2

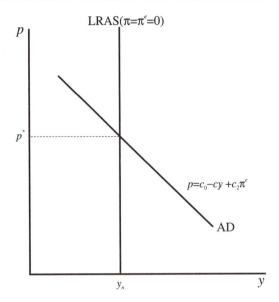

Note that inflation is defined as the difference in prices, since price is in logarithms (see box 3). Substituting we obtain the following recursive equation for the price level

$$p(t+1)=p(t)+1.2(y(t)-6)=p(t)+1.2(9+0.2(5-p(t)))-6)$$
$$p(t+1)=4.8+0.76p(t)$$

which is linear. First we solve for the equilibrium price by setting $p(t+1)=p(t)=p^*$, which leads to an equilibrium price of $p^*=20$. But is this fixed point stable?

We can answer this in a variety of ways. First we can set up the recursive equation in the form of a cobweb diagram and establish whether there is convergence to equilibrium. We show that this is indeed the case for an initial price of $p(0)=10$ in terms of figure 6.3. The price column in the spreadsheet shown in figure 6.4 also shows this. Turning to the spreadsheet, we have placed the values of the money stock and the natural level of income in cells G3 and G4, respectively. In cell B10 we place the initial price level, namely 10. Cell C10 has the formula

$$=9+0.2(m-p(0))$$
$$=9+0.2*(\$G\$3-B10)$$

while B11 has the formula

$$=4.8+0.76p(0)$$
$$=4.8+0.76*B10$$

C10 is copied to the clipboard and pasted into C11. Then B11 along with C11 is copied to the clipboard and pasted down, here to period 20. Finally, we used the chart wizard to construct the trajectory in the (y,p)-space. Notice in particular that this trajectory follows the path of the aggregate demand curve. Also notice from the spreadsheet that inflation falls continually until it reaches

Figure 6.3

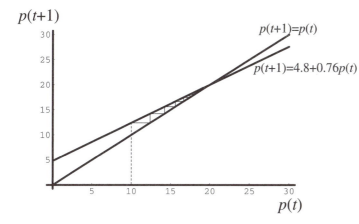

Figure 6.4

zero, which is identical to the expected rate of inflation. Only with actual and expected inflation at zero will the price level remain in equilibrium at the value $p^* = 20$.

This simple model illustrates a shortcoming of using the aggregate demand – aggregate supply model to discuss inflation. The model is an income–price determination model under the assumption of zero inflation! This is the only long-run acceptable solution to this model.

6.4 Dynamic model with positive inflation

Our previous model had the only acceptable solution as a zero rate of inflation (actual and expected). The problem is basically that the model is a comparative static model of price and income determination that has had a dynamic element added to it. In section 6.2 we developed the aggregate demand curve in terms of (6.7), here we include the time variable for clarity

(6.9) $$y(t+1) = b_0 + b_1(m(t) - p(t)) + b_2\pi^e(t+1)$$

Note that income in the next period is dependent on real-money balances in the previous period $(m(t) - p(t))$ and expected inflation in the next period. In period t we therefore have

$$y(t) = b_0 + b_1(m(t-1) - p(t-1)) + b_2\pi^e(t)$$

Subtracting this from (6.9) we obtain

$$
\begin{aligned}
y(t+1) - y(t) &= \Delta y(t+1) \\
&= b_1(m(t) - m(t-1)) - b_1(p(t) - p(t-1)) + b_2(\pi^e(t+1) - \pi^e(t))
\end{aligned}
$$

Because we are considering the model in logarithms, we note

$$m(t) - m(t-1) = \lambda = \text{the growth in the money supply}$$
$$p(t) - p(t-1) = \pi(t) = \text{inflation}$$
$$\pi^e(t+1) - \pi^e(t) = \Delta\pi^e(t+1) = \text{acceleration in the rate of expected inflation}$$

Therefore

(6.10) $$\Delta y(t+1) = b_1(\lambda - \pi(t)) + b_2\Delta\pi^e(t+1)$$

which is an expression for the **demand-pressure curve**.

Our model amounts to the following set of equations

$$\Delta y(t+1) = b_1(\lambda - \pi(t)) + b_2\Delta\pi^e(t+1) \quad b_1 > 0, \, b_2 > 0$$
$$\pi(t) = \alpha(y(t) - y_n) + \pi^e(t) \quad \alpha > 0$$
(6.11) $$\Delta\pi^e(t+1) = \beta(\pi(t) - \pi^e(t)) \quad \beta > 0$$

This model is composed of a demand-pressure curve, a Phillips curve and an expression for changing expectations. We shall pursue this model with a numerical example. The model is illustrated in figure 6.5.

Let $\lambda = 15$ and $y_n = 15$ with the numerical model

$$\Delta y(t+1) = 10(15 - \pi(t)) + 0.5\Delta\pi^e(t+1)$$
$$\pi(t) = 0.2(y(t) - 15) + \pi^e(t)$$
(6.12) $$\Delta\pi^e(t+1) = 1.5(\pi(t) - \pi^e(t))$$

Re-arranging the Phillips curve and substituting into the changing expectations formula, we have

$$\pi(t) - \pi^e(t) = 0.2(y(t) - 15)$$
$$\Delta\pi^e(t+1) = 1.5(0.2)(y(t) - 15) = 0.3(y(t) - 15)$$

This is our first fundamental equation. We now substitute this into the demand-pressure curve

$$
\begin{aligned}
\Delta y(t+1) &= 10(15 - \pi(t)) + 0.5(0.3)(y(t) - 15) \\
&= 150 - 10\pi(t) + 0.15y(t) - 2.25
\end{aligned}
$$

Finally we substitute the Phillips curve into this expression

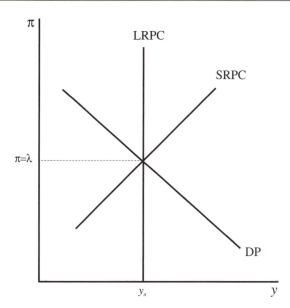

Figure 6.5

$$\Delta y(t+1) = 150 - 10[0.2(y(t)-15) + \pi^e(t)] + 0.15y(t) - 2.25$$
$$= 177.75 - 1.85y(t) - 10\pi^e(t)$$

which gives us our second fundamental equation.

To summarise, we have two difference equations

$$\Delta y(t+1) = 177.75 - 1.85y(t) - 10\pi^e(t)$$
$$\Delta \pi^e(t+1) = 0.3(y(t)-15) \tag{6.13}$$

which can be solved for y and π^e. Note that we are not solving for inflation, but rather for expected inflation. Once we have solved for expected inflation and income, we can solve for actual inflation from the Phillips curve, the second equation in (6.12).

Let us first establish any fixed points of the system. This is where $\Delta y(t+1) = 0$ *and* $\Delta \pi^e(t+1) = 0$, so we have

$$0 = 177.75 - 1.85y^* - 10\pi^{e*}$$
$$0 = 0.3(y^* - 15)$$

which gives the fixed point (y^*, π^{e*}). The situation is illustrated in figure 6.6. The fixed point is where the two isoclines $\Delta y(t+1) = 0$ and $\Delta \pi^e(t+1) = 0$ intersect. The isocline $\Delta \pi^e(t+1) = 0$ is clearly vertical at the natural level of income, $y^* = y_n = 15$. The isocline $\Delta y(t+1) = 0$ results in the equation

$$\pi^e = 17.775 - 0.185y \tag{6.14}$$

as shown in figure 6.6.

Turn now to the vector forces in the four quadrants of figure 6.6. If $\Delta \pi^e(t+1) > 0$ then $y > 15$ and so to the right of the $\Delta \pi^e(t+1) = 0$ isocline π^e is rising, and to the left, π^e is falling. These are shown by the up and down arrows, respectively. If $\Delta y(t+1) > 0$ then $\pi^e < 17.775 - 0.185y$ and so below the $\Delta y(t+1) = 0$ isocline y is rising while above y is falling, these are shown by

Figure 6.6

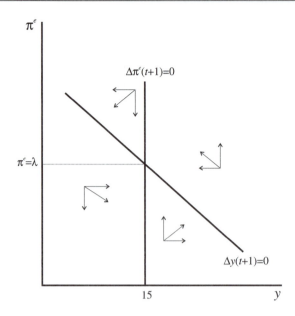

Figure 6.7

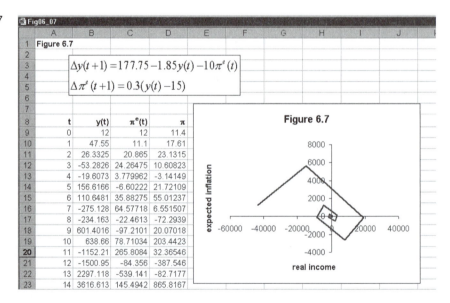

the right and left arrows, respectively. What we have established is an anti-clockwise movement. Whether this movement is directly towards the fixed point or spiralling we need to investigate further. We do this by means of the spreadsheet as shown in figure 6.7.

We enter the initial values for income and expected inflation, which are both 12. These are placed in cells B9 and C9, respectively. We next need to enter formulas in cell D9, for actual inflation, and cells B10, C10 and D10 to obtain values in period 1. These are

D9	$= 0.2(y(0) - 15) + \pi^e(0)$ $= 0.2*(B9 - 15) + C9$
B10	$= y(0) + 177.75 - 1.85y(0) - 10\pi^e(0)$ $= B9 + 177.75 - 1.85*B9 - 10*C9$
C10	$= \pi^e(0) + 0.3(y(0) - 15)$ $= C9 + 0.3*(B9 - 15)$
D10	$= 0.2(y(1) - 15) + \pi^e(1)$ $= 0.2*(B10 - 15) + C10$

Cells B10, C10 and D10 are then copied to the clipboard and pasted down. Finally we use the chart wizard to construct the trajectory of the economy in (y, π^e)-space. It is quite clear from the resulting trajectory that although the economy does have an anticlockwise movement, it is spiralling *away* from the fixed point. Even if we plot the trajectory in (y, π)-space, we still have an explosive anticlockwise spiral. The reader should verify this for himself or herself.

As another possibility, set up the following numerical model in exactly the same way

$$\Delta y(t+1) = 10(15 - \pi(t)) + 0.5\Delta\pi^e(t+1)$$
$$\pi(t) = 0.2(y(t) - 150) + \pi^e(t)$$
$$\Delta\pi^e(t+1) = 0.8(\pi(t) - \pi^e(t)) \tag{6.15}$$

Let $y(0) = 100$ and $\pi^e(0) = 10$, then what you should find is that this system has an anticlockwise spiral movement that *converges* on the fixed point $(y^*, \pi^{e*}) = (150,15)$.

6.4.1 Experimentation

In order to undertake experimentation with this model it is useful to set it out on a spreadsheet in general terms. Although this involves a little bit of algebraic substitution, it is well worth it for the insight it provides about the model's dynamics. Our model is

(1) $\Delta y(t+1) = b_1(\lambda - \pi(t)) + b_2\Delta\pi^e(t+1) \quad b_1 > 0, b_2 > 0$
(2) $\pi(t) = \alpha(y(t) - y_n) + \pi^e(t) \quad \alpha > 0$
(3) $\Delta\pi^e(t+1) = \beta(\pi(t) - \pi^e(t)) \quad \beta > 0$

Follow through the same substitutions as the numerical example. From (2) we have

$$\pi(t) - \pi^e(t) = \alpha(y(t) - y_n)$$

Substituting this into (3) and substituting this result into (1) gives

$$\Delta y(t+1) = b_1(\lambda - \pi(t)) + b_2\beta\alpha(y(t) - y_n)$$
$$= (\lambda b_1 - b_2\beta\alpha y_n) - b_1\pi(t) + b_2\beta\alpha y(t)$$

Now substitute (2) into this

$$\Delta y(t+1) = (\lambda b_1 - b_2 \beta \alpha y_n) - b_1[\alpha(y(t) - y_n) + \pi^e(t)] + b_2 \beta \alpha y(t)$$
$$= (\lambda b_1 - b_2 \beta \alpha y_n + b_1 \alpha y_n) - (b_1 \alpha - b_2 \beta \alpha)y(t) - b_1 \pi^e(t)$$

So our two difference equations are

$$\Delta y(t+1) = (\lambda b_1 - b_2 \beta \alpha y_n + b_1 \alpha y_n) - (b_1 \alpha - b_2 \beta \alpha)y(t) - b_1 \pi^e(t)$$

(6.16)

$$\Delta \pi^e(t) = \beta \alpha(y(t) - y_n)$$

In equilibrium

$$0 = (\lambda b_1 - b_2 \beta \alpha y_n + b_1 \alpha y_n) - (b_1 \alpha - b_2 \beta \alpha)y(t) - b_1 \pi^e(t)$$
$$0 = \beta \alpha(y(t) - y_n)$$

From this it immediately follows that $y^* = y_n$ and

$$b_1 \pi^e = (\lambda b_1 - b_2 \beta \alpha y_n + b_1 \alpha y_n) - (b_1 \alpha - b_2 \beta \alpha)y$$

$$\pi^e = \frac{\lambda b_1 - b_2 \beta \alpha y_n + b_1 \alpha y_n}{b_1} - \left(\frac{b_1 \alpha - b_2 \beta \alpha}{b_1} \right)$$

To check this result against our earlier numerical model, set

$$\lambda = 15, \quad y_n = 15, \quad b_1 = 10, \quad b_2 = 0.5, \quad \alpha = 0.2, \quad \beta = 0.3$$

This results in $y^* = 15$ and $\pi^{e*} = 15$.

In order to set this out on a spreadsheet for experimentation, let

$$\Delta y(t+1) = A_0 - A_1 y(t) - A_2 \pi^e(t)$$
$$A_0 = (\lambda b_1 - b_2 \beta \alpha y_n + b_1 \alpha y_n)$$
$$A_1 = (b_1 \alpha - b_2 \beta \alpha)$$
$$A_2 = b_1$$
$$\Delta \pi^e(t) = B_1(y(t) - y_n)$$
$$B_1 = \beta \alpha$$

All these values are placed in the spreadsheet shown in figure 6.8. The parameter values are placed in cells H3 to H8 and the derived parameters A_0, A_1 and A_2 are placed in cells H10, H11 and H12. The derived parameter B_1 is placed in cell J10. In cell J4 we place the equilibrium value y^*, which is cell H8 for y_n, while cell J5 has the formula

$$= ((\$H\$7*\$H\$3 - \$H\$4*\$H\$6*\$H\$5*\$H\$8 + \$H\$3*\$H\$5*\$H\$8)/$$
$$\$H\$3) - ((\$H\$3*\$H\$5 - \$H\$4*\$H\$6*\$H\$5)*\$H\$8)/\$H\$3$$

for π^{e*}. We now have everything in place to undertake experimentation.

First check the formulas have been entered correctly. Place the equilibrium values as the initial values for y and π^e. If the formulas are correct, all figures in columns B, C and D should all read 15. Next check the second example we gave above in which we changed the natural level of income to 150 and the parameter β to 0.8. Let $y(0) = 100$ and $\pi^e(0) = 10$. What you should find is an anticlockwise spiral to the fixed point $(y^*, \pi^*) = (150,15)$. Next retain this same example, but change the value of β from 0.8 to 0.3; what you should observe is a zigzag path converging on the same fixed point.

You should experiment with this model, changing some of the parameter values, especially the adjustment coefficient in the Phillips curve and the two

Figure 6.8

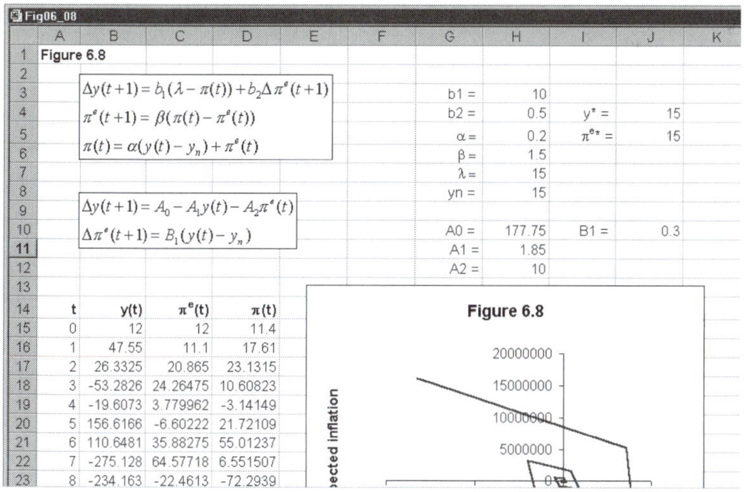

Fig06_08

Figure 6.8

$$\Delta y(t+1) = b_1(\lambda - \pi(t)) + b_2\Delta\pi^e(t+1)$$
$$\pi^e(t+1) = \beta(\pi(t) - \pi^e(t))$$
$$\pi(t) = \alpha(y(t) - y_n) + \pi^e(t)$$

$$\Delta y(t+1) = A_0 - A_1 y(t) - A_2\pi^e(t)$$
$$\Delta\pi^e(t+1) = B_1(y(t) - y_n)$$

b1 =	10		
b2 =	0.5	y* =	15
α =	0.2	π^{e*} =	15
β =	1.5		
λ =	15		
yn =	15		
A0 =	177.75	B1 =	0.3
A1 =	1.85		
A2 =	10		

t	y(t)	π^e(t)	π(t)
0	12	12	11.4
1	47.55	11.1	17.61
2	26.3325	20.865	23.1315
3	-53.2826	24.26475	10.60823
4	-19.6073	3.779962	-3.14149
5	156.6166	-6.60222	21.72109
6	110.6481	35.88275	55.01237
7	-275.128	64.57718	6.551507
8	-234.163	-22.4613	-72.2939

coefficients in the demand-pressure curve. Additional values for the parameter β should also be tried. In carrying out these experiments another consideration to bear in mind is that the parameter α is itself the product of two parameters. One denotes the reaction coefficient of inflation to the unemployment gap, (6.4); the second is the reaction coefficient relating the unemployment gap to the income gap, i.e. from Okun's law, (6.5). A rise in α can occur for either of these reasons.

6.5 A change in the money supply

We shall now use the second model of section 6.4, (6.15). Set the initial income and expected (equal to actual) inflation at 150 and 15, respectively. All values in column B should be 150 and all values in columns C and D should be 15. Now increase the growth in the money supply from 15 to 20. The result is an anticlockwise spiral of the economy converging on the new equilibrium of $(y^*, \pi^{e*}) = (150,15)$. The immediate impact is a rise in real-money balances. In the short run income rises above the natural level and inflation rises, which reduces real-money balances. The result is a converging anticlockwise spiral, with income and expected (also actual) inflation overshooting their long-run values.

Now reduce the money supply to 10. The result is an anticlockwise spiral converging on the new equilibrium $(y^*, \pi^{e*}) = (150,10)$. Show that in the first numerical model of section 6.4, (6.12), which had the explosive spiral, that this explosion still remains after a rise in monetary growth or a fall in monetary growth.

Return to (6.15) and begin again with the initial values being 150 and 15 for income and expected inflation, respectively. Now set the expectation's coefficient to 0.3. Let monetary growth fall from 15 to 10. What you will find is a zigzag path converging on the fixed point $(y^*, \pi^{e*}) = (150,10)$. This is shown in

Figure 6.9

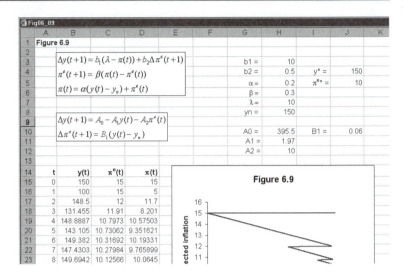

figure 6.9. A similar-looking path results if monetary growth is increased. You should verify this.

The conclusion one draws from this analysis is that a change in the growth of the money supply has no bearing on the convergent/divergent properties of the system, all it does is alter the equilibrium value (the fixed point). What matters for convergence are the various adjustment coefficients of the system.

6.6 A change in the natural level of unemployment

Suppose governments have implemented policies that are successful in raising the natural level of income, i.e. successful in reducing the natural rate of unemployment. Start with the model with parameter values

$$\lambda = 15, \quad y_n = 15, \quad b_1 = 10, \quad b_2 = 0.5, \quad \alpha = 0.2, \quad \beta = 1.5$$

which was our original model. Set the initial values for income and inflation expectations both to 15. Now consider a rise in the natural level of income to 20. The fixed point moves to $(y^*, \pi^{e*}) = (15,20)$, but the system never reaches this because it is explosive in just the same way it was earlier. The same is true for a fall in the natural level of income – a rise in the natural level of unemployment.

In the second numerical model we considered, (6.15), in which the system was convergent, the rise in the natural level of income from 150 to 180 leads to an anticlockwise spiral path from the initial equilibrium until the new fixed point of $(y^*, \pi^{e*}) = (180,15)$ is reached. This stability is retained even when the natural level of income falls – the natural level of unemployment rises.

If an economy has experienced a rise in the natural rate of unemployment, which many European countries have experienced in the 1980s and 1990s, then policies need to be directed towards two distinct aspects of the macroeconomy.

First, there need to be policies for reducing the natural rate of unemployment, which often means directing attention to policies towards the long-term unemployed and to the mis-match in skills, etc. But there also need to be policies directed towards the adjustment coefficients, since it is these which will change the speed and type of adjustment the economy is experiencing. It is most likely that the policies directed towards the former are different from those directed towards the latter.

6.7 Continuous model

Consider now a continuous version of our *original* model. This takes the form

$$\dot{y} = 10(15 - \pi) + 0.5\dot{\pi}^e$$
$$\pi = 0.2(y - 15) + \pi^e$$
$$\dot{\pi}^e = 1.5(\pi - \pi^e) \tag{6.17}$$

This leads to the same (continuous-form) isoclines

$$y = 15 \quad \dot{\pi}^e = 0$$
$$\pi^e = 17.775 - 0.185y \quad \dot{y} = 0$$

and fixed point $(y^*, \pi^{e*}) = (15,15)$. These results, along with the vector forces, have already been illustrated in figure 6.6. The only difference is that now the isoclines are for $\dot{\pi}^e = 0$ and $\dot{y} = 0$, and the variables are all continuous functions of time. Carrying out substitutions to those we did earlier, we can establish the following two differential equations

$$\dot{y} = f(y, \pi^e) = 177.75 - 1.85y - 10\pi^e$$
$$\dot{\pi}^e = g(y, \pi) = -4.5 + 0.3y \tag{6.18}$$

Although the qualitative properties are the same, we should observe an anti-clockwise movement around the equilibrium. However, do we observe similar trajectories? Interestingly, the answer is, no! To see this, let us construct the model on a spreadsheet, as shown in figure 6.10. Cell G3 contains the time difference we shall use for Euler's approximation. Cells B8 and C8 have the initial values of 12. Cell D8 can then be computed from the formula

$$= 0.2(y(0) - 15) + \pi^e$$
$$= 0.2*(B8 - 15) + C8$$

Cells B9, C9 and D9 are computed as follows

B9	$= y(0) + f(y(0), \pi^e(0))*\Delta t$
	$= B8 + (177.75 - 1.85*B8 - 10*C8)*\$G\$3$
C9	$= \pi^e(0) + g(y(0), \pi^e(0))*\Delta t$
	$= C8 + (-4.5 + 0.3*B8)*\$G\$3$
D9	$= 0.2(y(1) - 15) + \pi^e(1)$
	$= 0.2*(B9 - 15) + C9$

Figure 6.10

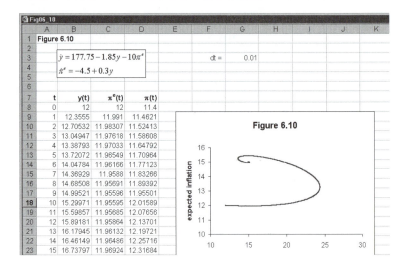

Cells B9, C9 and D9 are then copied to the clipboard and pasted down. Here we paste down to period 1000. Finally, we block the cells for the data in columns B and C to construct the inserted graph. What we immediately see is an anticlockwise *convergence* to the fixed point. This is in marked contrast to the anticlockwise *divergence* of the discrete model. This acts as a warning not to attribute the properties of one to the other without investigation.

Since the present model is basically similar to the discrete form, we can generalise the model as

$$\dot{y} = b_1(\lambda - \pi) + b_2\dot{\pi}^e \quad b_1 > 0, b_2 > 0$$
$$\pi = \alpha(y - y_n) + \pi^e \quad \alpha > 0$$
(6.19)
$$\dot{\pi}^e = \beta(\pi - \pi^e) \quad \beta > 0$$

which leads to the two differential equations

$$\dot{y} = A_0 - A_1 y - A_2 \pi^e$$
$$\dot{\pi}^e = B_1(y - y_n)$$

where

$$A_0 = (\lambda b_1 - b_2\beta\alpha y_n + b_1\alpha y_n)$$
$$A_1 = (b_1\alpha - b_2\beta\alpha)$$
$$A_2 = b_1$$
$$B_1 = \beta\alpha$$

We start by setting this up on the spreadsheet with exactly the same values as we have in the numerical example for figure 6.10, i.e. (6.17). To check that all formulas have been entered correctly, set the initial values equal to 15 for both income and expected inflation, and then all the figures in all three columns should be 15.

Now reduce the money supply growth from 15 to 10. The result is shown in figure 6.11. The fixed point moves to $(y^*, \pi^{e*}) = (15,10)$ and we observe an anticlockwise movement to the new fixed point.

Figure 6.11

	A	B	C	D	E	F	G	H	I	J	K
1	Figure 6.11										
2											
3		$\dot{y} = b_1(\lambda - \pi) + b_2\dot{\pi}^e$						b1 =	10			
4								b2 =	0.5	y* =	15	
5		$\pi = \alpha(y - y_n) + \pi^e$						α =	0.2	π^{e*} =	10	
6		$\dot{\pi}^e = \beta(\pi - \pi^e)$						β =	1.5			
7								λ =	10	dt =	0.01	
8								yn =	15			
9		$\dot{Y} = A_0 - A_1 y - A_2\pi^e$										
10		$\dot{\pi}^e = B_1(y - y_n)$						A0 =	127.75	B1 =	0.3	
11								A1 =	1.85			
12								A2 =	10	dt =	0.01	
13												
14	t	y(t)	π^e(t)	π(t)							
15	0	15	15	15							
16	1	14.5	15	14.9							
17	2	14.00925	14.9925	14.79435							
18	3	13.52833	14.97764	14.6833							
19	4	13.05779	14.95556	14.56712							
20	5	12.59817	14.92643	14.44606							
21	6	12.14996	14.8904	14.32039							
22	7	11.71364	14.84765	14.19038							
23	8	11.28967	14.79836	14.05629							

Figure 6.11

As we have indicated throughout, although the model solves for expected inflation, we can compute actual inflation from the Phillips curve. What is the difference between the path of $\pi(t)$ and the path of $\pi^e(t)$? In figure 6.12 we plot these paths that arise from a monetary growth contraction from 15 to 10. The figure also shows the path of income. What the lower diagram illustrates is not only the damped cyclical nature of actual and expected inflation, but that actual inflation is initially below expected inflation. This is because actual income initially falls short of the natural level of income and so dampens inflation, as shown in the upper diagram. When, however, income is above the natural level then actual inflation is above expected inflation, and so pushes up actual inflation.

6.8 Conclusion

In this chapter we introduced the Phillips curve in both its original form and in its augmented form – augmented for expected inflation. The typical aggregate demand and a vertical aggregate supply model determine only equilibrium prices and income. In this model, inflation in the long run must be zero. Such a model is sometimes used at the elementary level to discuss issues about inflation, but it is an unsuitable model for this purpose. As we have shown, inflation occurs only over the adjustment period. We then turned to a model that solves for income and a positive rate of inflation. This model is first set up generally with an explanation of the economy's vector forces. However, the model is in terms of income and *expected* inflation. There is no difficulty, however, deriving actual inflation once expected inflation is determined. This model is set out in both its discrete form and in continuous form. It is then used to establish the dynamic implications of a change in monetary growth and in the natural level of income (or the natural rate of unemployment). The

Figure 6.12

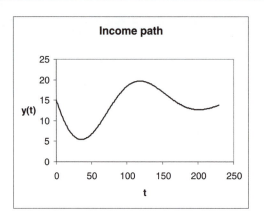

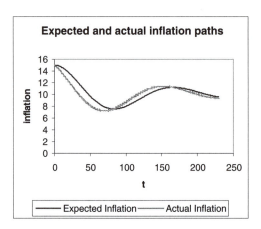

chapter also illustrated that discrete and continuous time models of the same structure can lead to quite different trajectories.

Exercises

(1)   Consider the following model in which expected inflation is zero

$$y(t) = 12 + 0.2(m - p(t))$$
$$p(t+1) - p(t) = 1.5(y(t) - y_n)$$
$$m = 10 \quad y_n = 8$$

(i)   What is the fixed point of this model and is it stable?

(ii)   If $p(0) = 15$, plot the inflation rate for $t = 1$ to 20.

(2)   Consider the following two models

Model A	Model B
$y(t) = 9 + 0.2(m - p(t))$	$y(t) = 9 + 0.2(m - p(t))$
$p(t+1) - p(t) = 1.2(y(t) - y_n)$	$p(t+1) - p(t) = 1.5(y(t) - y_n)$
$m = 5 \quad y_n = 6 \quad p(0) = 10$	$m = 5 \quad y_n = 6 \quad p(0) = 10$

(i) What are the recursive equations for each model and what is their fixed point?

(ii) Compare the adjustment of prices in each model.

(3) Consider the following model

$$\Delta y(t+1) = 10(20 - \pi(t)) + 0.75 \Delta \pi^e(t+1)$$
$$\pi(t) = 0.5(y(t) - 15) + \pi^e(t)$$
$$\Delta \pi^e(t+1) = 2(\pi(t) - \pi^e(t))$$

(i) Derive the two fundamental difference equations for this model.

(ii) What is the fixed point of the model?

(iii) Derive the two isoclines and the vector forces.

(iv) Set up the model on a spreadsheet, and construct the trajectory of the economy in (y, π^e)-space starting from the initial point $(15,15)$ for $t = 0$ to 9 only.

(4) Consider the following model

$$\Delta y(t+1) = 5(10 - \pi(t)) + 0.25 \Delta \pi^e(t+1)$$
$$\pi(t) = 0.25(y(t) - 60) + \pi^e(t)$$
$$\Delta \pi^e(t+1) = 0.5(\pi(t) - \pi^e(t))$$

(i) What is the equilibrium for this model?

(ii) Plot on the same diagram income against expected and actual inflation for $t = 0$ to 40 starting from point $(y(0), \pi^e(0)) = (40,15)$.

(iii) Now set the initial values at their equilibrium level. Derive the trajectory of the economy for a fall in the growth of the money supply from 10 to 5.

(5) Use the model in qu. 4, and set the initial values at their equilibrium level. What are the implications of a fall in the natural level of income (a rise in the natural rate of unemployment) from 60 to 50?

Chapter 7
Dynamics of the firm

7.1 Introduction

In this chapter we shall consider just some dynamic aspects of the theory of the firm. Surprisingly, little work has been done on dynamic aspects of firm behaviour. There has been some work on advertising, a dynamic consideration of diffusion of new products and a little more on the dynamics of oligopoly. We shall consider all three in this chapter.

7.2 Monopoly and advertising

Consider a monopolist who produces a single product that sells at a price p. It might be thought that a monopolist does not need to advertise since it is the sole supplier of a product. But even a monopolist needs to inform the public of its product. Furthermore, if the product is a consumer durable, then its sales will decline. Suppose we denote sales by $s(t)$, so that we are assuming sales are a continuous function of time. Furthermore, initial sales are $s(0) = s_0$. We assume that with no advertising sales decline at a constant rate r, which is proportional to the sales at that time. In other words, we have an initial value problem of the form

$$\frac{ds(t)}{dt} = -rs(t) \quad s(0) = s_0 \quad r > 0$$

or

(7.1)
$$\dot{s} = \frac{ds}{dt} = -rs \quad s(0) = s_0 \quad r > 0$$

To see what the path of sales looks like, we need to solve this equation. Solution methods are available for this (see Shone, 1997, ch.2), but here we shall use a spreadsheet to derive the path of sales. As in earlier chapters, we use Euler's approximation to do this. The model is set up in terms of figure 7.1.

First we insert in cells A8 to A1008 the periods for t using the **Fill** command. In cells F3 and F4 we place the values of r and Δt, respectively, where we use the label 'dt' for Δt. In this example we are assuming that sales decline at a constant rate of 5% continuously. In addition, we are using a value of $\Delta t = 0.05$ for our time interval. The initial value of sales is placed in cell B8, and we assume this is 100. Next, in cell B9, we place the formula for $s(1)$, i.e.

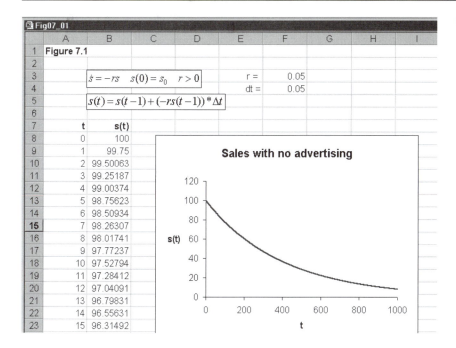

Figure 7.1

$$= s(0) - rs(0)\Delta t$$
$$= B8 - \$F\$3*B8*\$FS4$$

which is then copied to the clipboard and pasted down in cells B10 to B1008. Finally, we block cells A1:B1008 and activate the chart wizard. Using the X-Y chart, we create the chart that is shown in figure 7.1, after some suitable annotations. What we immediately see is that sales decline in a curvilinear fashion towards zero.

We know that it must be zero. Why? Consider the fixed point of this system. For a fixed point we know that $\dot{s} = 0$, which is true only for $s^* = 0$. Furthermore, since the differential has a negative slope, as we are assuming r is positive, then the system is globally stable. Note that since sales cannot be negative then we are considering only stability properties in the positive quadrant. No matter what the initial value of sales, they will over time decline to zero. The origin is an attractor of the system.

Now that we have established the time path of sales without advertising, we can consider the situation the company might face if it engages in some form of advertising. Of course, we must make some assumptions about the impact of advertising on this dynamic system. We make the following assumptions:

(1)   Advertising leads to an increase in sales directly proportional to the rate of advertising.

(2)   The increase in sales affected by advertising arises from the proportion of the market that has not already purchased the product.

(3)   The market has a maximum absorption m per period before the firm must lower its price.

If m is the maximum absorption per period, then in any period t, $m - s(t)$ denotes the part of the market which has not yet purchased the product, and so the proportion of the market which is not yet purchasing the product is

(7.2)
$$\frac{m - s(t)}{m}$$

Next let a denote the constant *rate* of advertising in thousands of pounds, and γ the proportion of sales improved by such advertising. If, then, sales rise directly in proportion to the rate of advertising, and this increase in turn can arise only from the proportion of the market that has not already purchased the product, then this increase is given by

(7.3)
$$\gamma a \left(\frac{m - s(t)}{m} \right)$$

Since this offsets the decline generally taking place, then in any period sales will be changing by the amount

$$\frac{ds(t)}{dt} = -rs(t) + \gamma a \left(\frac{m - s(t)}{m} \right)$$

or, more simply

(7.4)
$$\dot{s} = -rs + \gamma a \left(\frac{m - s}{m} \right) = -\left(r + \frac{\gamma a}{m} \right) s + \gamma a$$

First we need to establish the steady-state solution of our new model. Once again this is found by setting $\dot{s} = 0$. Doing this we readily establish that

$$0 = -\left(r + \frac{\gamma a}{m} \right) s^* + \gamma a$$

or

(7.5)
$$s^* = \frac{\gamma a m}{rm + \gamma a}$$

Not only is this no longer zero, but it is also a function of the amount of advertising. As the firm spends more on advertising, *equilibrium* sales rise. The rise, however, cannot be indefinite. As advertising expenditure increases indefinitely, sales cannot exceed the maximum absorptive capacity. This is readily established. First divide the numerator and the denominator by γa, and then take the limit as advertising expenditure rises indefinitely, i.e.

(7.6)
$$\lim_{a \to \infty} \left(\frac{m}{\dfrac{rm}{\gamma a} + 1} \right) = m$$

Return to our example shown in figure 7.1. We continue to let sales decline by a rate of 5% continuously, with initial sales at 100,000. The maximum absorption per period is 500,000. Now the firm engages in advertising at a rate of a, which we shall assume raises sales by a proportion 0.2. This means

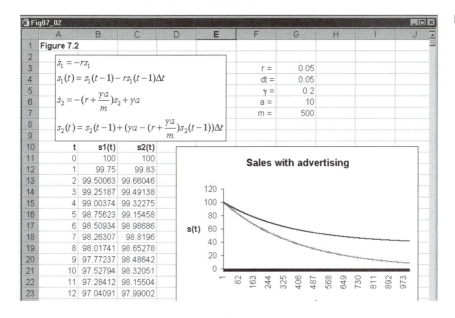

Figure 7.2

$$\dot{s}=-\left(0.05+\frac{0.2a}{500}\right)s+0.2a \qquad (7.7)$$

resulting in a steady state of

$$s^*=\frac{0.2a}{0.05+0.0004a}$$

Suppose the firm has an advertising rate of £10,000 then $s^*=37.037$ and (7.7) takes the form

$$\dot{s}=-\left(0.05+\frac{2}{500}\right)s+2=2-0.054s$$

The result is shown in figure 7.2. As we would expect, advertising curbs the decline in sales – in fact, preventing it from falling below 37,037.

7.3 Advertising model: discrete version

It could be considered that firms do not make decisions in continuous time and that a discrete model captures real-life decisions much more accurately. Consider, then, the model in section 7.2 in discrete time. We can be brief because we have explained the various ideas above. We assume that the change in sales over the period declines by a percentage r. Thus

$$\Delta s(t+1)=s(t+1)-s(t)=-rs(t) \qquad (7.8)$$

As a recursive equation this results in

$$s(t+1)=(1-r)s(t) \qquad (7.9)$$

Advertising is undertaken at a rate of a per period that raises sales by γ on the proportion of the market that is not yet purchasing the product. This is no more than (7.3), but now considered in discrete time. Consequently, the change in sales over the period is

(7.10)
$$\Delta s(t+1) = -rs(t) + \gamma a \left(\frac{m - s(t)}{m} \right)$$

or

(7.11)
$$s(t+1) = \left(1 - r - \frac{\gamma a}{m} \right) s(t) + \gamma a$$

Does the discrete model have the same fixed point as the continuous model? For a steady-state solution we have $s(t+1) = s(t) = s^*$ and so

$$s^* = \left(1 - r - \frac{\gamma a}{m} \right) s^* + \gamma a$$

$$s^* = \frac{\gamma a m}{rm + \gamma a}$$

which is the same as (7.5) above.

Return to the recursive equation (7.11) but now allow advertising to be different in the different periods, let the rate be denoted $a(t)$. Here we assume that advertising takes place from period 1 onwards. Then we can solve for the path of sales using the formula

(7.12)
$$s(t+1) = \left(1 - r - \frac{\gamma a(t+1)}{m} \right) s(t) + \gamma a(t+1)$$

which is very easy to set up on a spreadsheet. The reader is encouraged to do this for the problem we had above in which advertising in each period was constant with $a(t) = 2$ for all t. Here, however, we shall consider a slightly different problem. Suppose a monopolist has initial sales of 5 but faces declining sales at a rate of 1% per period, where maximum absorption per period is 20, and $\gamma = 0.6$. The monopolist decides on a constant amount for advertising over the next five years, and that this amount is spread evenly over this period. Let the total advertising budget, denoted A, be £10,000, amounting to

$$a(t) = \frac{A}{T} = \frac{£10,000}{5} = £2,000$$

in each of the next five years, and zero thereafter. The problem is set out in the spreadsheet shown in figure 7.3. This information is given in column C in cells C8 to C18, where we consider only up to time $t = 10$. Notice, that when $a(t+1) = 0$, (7.12) reduces to (7.9). The problem is shown in figure 7.3, with sales declining at a rate of 1% per period, given in cell G3; sales being offset by 0.6 of the proportion of the market that is not yet purchasing the product, given in cell G4; and the maximum absorption is 20, given in cell G5. In cell B8 we place the initial sales, set at 5. In cell B9 we insert the formula

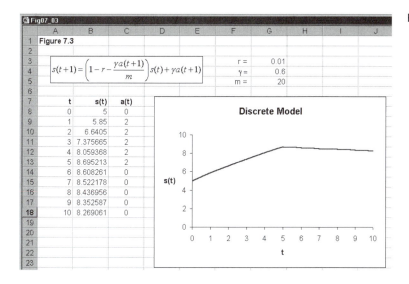

Figure 7.3

$$= \left(1 - r - \frac{\gamma a(0)}{m}\right) s(0) + \gamma a(1)$$

$$= (1 - \$G\$3 - (\$G\$4*C8/\$G\$5))*B8 + \$G\$4*C9$$

This is then copied to the clipboard and pasted down. Finally, we insert the graph as shown in figure 7.3.

For the first five years advertising leads to increased sales that offsets the natural decline. Once advertising stops, however, the natural decline begins to take effect.

7.4 Diffusion models

In recent years we have seen the widespread use of desktop computers, and more recently the increased use of the mobile phone. The process by which such innovations are communicated through society and the rate at which they are taken up is called **diffusion**. Innovations need not be products. They can just as easily be an idea or some contagious disease. Although a variety of models have been discussed in the literature the time path of the diffusion process most typically takes the form of the S-shaped (sigmoid) curve. The general nature of such a curve is shown in figure 7.4, where we have included some aspects of the curve. Considering the mobile phone, we would expect only a few adoptions in the early stages, possibly business people. The adoption begins to accelerate, diffusing to the public at large and even to youngsters. But then it begins to tail off as saturation of the market becomes closer. At the upper limit the market is saturated. Hence the S-shape that is depicted in figure 7.4.

Figure 7.4

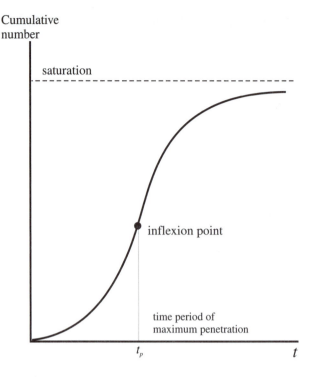

Although this is a verbal description of the diffusion process, and suggests an S-shaped mathematical formulation of the process, it supplies no exact information about the functional form – in particular, the slope, which indicates the speed of the diffusion, or the asymptote, which indicates the level of saturation. Furthermore, such diffusion processes may differ between products.

Let us begin by trying to describe the process in more algebraic terms. Here we shall consider a discrete modelling process. Let $N(t)$ denote the *cumulative* number of adopters at time t. Suppose there are m potential number of adopters, then at time t, there are $m - N(t)$ unadopted users. Furthermore let $g(t)$ denote the coefficient of diffusion. It is possible to think of $g(t)$ as the probability of adoption at time t, and so $g(t)(m - N(t))$ is the expected number of adopters at time t. Then the increase in adoption is given by

(7.13) $$\Delta N(t+1) = N(t+1) - N(t) = g(t)(m - N(t))$$

Turning to $g(t)$, the probability of adoption, this will depend on how many have already adopted the good. The more individuals already having a mobile phone makes it more attractive for another individual who does not have one to purchase one. In other cases, adoption has nothing to do with how many individuals already have a phone. We capture all this in simple terms by assuming

(7.14) $$g(t) = a + bN(t) \quad a>0, b>0$$

Of course, (7.14) is only one possible specification of $g(t)$. Our diffusion model now amounts to

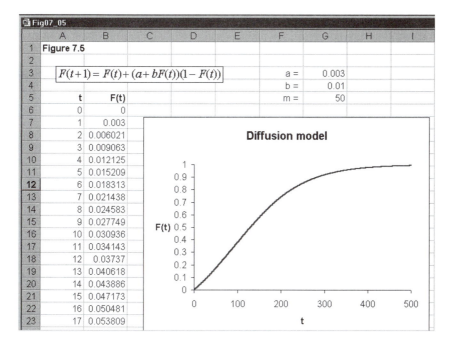

Figure 7.5

$$\Delta N(t+1) = (a+bN(t))(m-N(t)) \tag{7.15}$$

Equation (7.15) is clearly a nonlinear difference equation. This equation involves three parameters: a, b and m. It is possible to eliminate one of these by considering the cumulative number of users as a fraction of the potential number. Thus, we define $F(t) = N(t)/m$, which means $\Delta F(t+1) = \Delta N(t+1)/m$, so if we divide (7.15) throughout by m, we obtain

$$\Delta F(t+1) = (a+bF(t))(1-F(t)) \tag{7.16}$$

and it is this equation we shall analyse. To do this, however, we shall consider it in the form of a recursive equation, which is

$$F(t+1) = F(t) + (a+bF(t))(1-F(t)) \tag{7.17}$$

7.4.1 An example

Consider the diffusion model

$$F(t+1) = F(t) + (0.003 + 0.01F(t))(1-F(t)) \tag{7.18}$$

Our first task is to establish what this looks like. This model is shown in figure 7.5. Parameters a, b and m are placed in cells G3, G4 and G5, respectively. The model covers 500 time periods, with the initial level of cumulative adopters set at zero, which is placed in cell B6. Cell B7 has the formula

$$= F(0) + (a+bF(0))*(1-F(0))$$
$$= B6 + (\$G\$3 + \$G\$4*B6)*(1-B6)$$

This is then copied to the clipboard and pasted down. Finally cells A6:B506 is blocked and then the chart wizard is activated to create the chart shown in figure 7.5.

Consider the fixed points of this system. The fixed points are found by setting $\Delta F(t+1)=0$, so

$$0=(0.003+0.01F)(1-F)$$

where we have dropped the time dimension for simplicity. Clearly, there are two values for F

$$F_1^*=1 \quad \text{and} \quad F_2^*=-0.3$$

but in this model we are concerned only with positive F. But a useful feature to know about this model is the value of F when the rate of diffusion is at its greatest. Since the rate of diffusion is given by $\Delta F(t+1)$, then this is at its greatest when the rate of change of this value is zero; in other words, penetration of the market is then at its maximum rate. We need to differentiate $(0.003+0.01F)(F-1)$ with respect to F and set this value equal to zero, and then solve for F. Differentiating

$$(0.003-0.01)+2(0.01)F=0$$
$$F=0.35$$

To establish the time when maximum penetration of the market is established we need to find the value of t for which $F(t)=0.35$. From the spreadsheet we can establish that this is approximately period 93. There is a considerable literature on diffusion models, some of which are outlined in Mahajan and Peterson (1985).

7.5 Static theory of oligopoly

The model we shall consider in this chapter has a very simple linear demand curve and constant marginal costs. The model is as follows

$$\begin{aligned}
p &= 9 - Q \\
Q &= q_1 + q_2 \\
TC_1 &= 3q_1 \\
TC_2 &= 3q_2
\end{aligned}$$

(7.19)

Since our interest is with stability and the impact of increasing the number of firms in the industry, or changing the specification of marginal cost, we assume for simplicity that all firms are identical for any size n, where n represents the number of firms in the industry. Since this model of duopoly is dealt with in most intermediate microeconomic textbooks, we shall be brief.

Total revenue and profits for each firm are

$$\text{Firm 1 } TR_1=pq_1=(9-q_1-q_2)q_1 \quad \pi_1=(9-q_1-q_2)q_1-3q_1$$
$$\text{Firm 2 } TR_2=pq_2=(9-q_1-q_2)q_2 \quad \pi_2=(9-q_1-q_2)q_2-3q_2$$

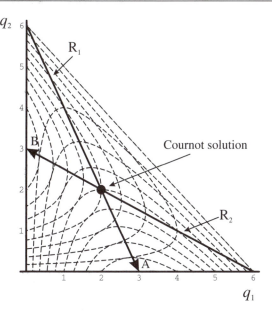

Figure 7.6

Since the **conjectural variation** is that firm 1 will maximise its profits under the assumption that firm 2 holds its output constant, then we can differentiate the profit function of firm 1 with respect to q_1, holding q_2 constant. The same conjectural variation holds for firm 2, so it will maximise its profits under the assumption that firm 1 will hold its output level constant, so here we differentiate the profit function of firm 2 with respect to q_2, holding q_1 constant. Doing this we obtain

$$\frac{\partial \pi_1}{\partial q_1} = 6 - 2q_1 - q_2 = 0$$

$$\frac{\partial \pi_2}{\partial q_2} = 6 - q_1 - 2q_2 = 0$$

Solving we obtain the two reaction functions

$$\text{Firm 1} \quad R_1 \quad q_1 = 3 - \tfrac{1}{2} q_2$$

$$\text{Firm 2} \quad R_2 \quad q_2 = 3 - \tfrac{1}{2} q_1$$

The Cournot solution, then, is where the two reaction curves intersect, i.e. where $(q_1, q_2) = (2, 2)$. The situation is shown in figure 7.6.

Notice that the isoprofit curves for firm 1 are at a maximum, for any given level of output for firm 2, at the point on the rection curve for firm 1. Furthermore, the preference direction is in the direction of the arrow on the reaction curve. The highest level of profits for firm 1 is at point A, where it is a monopolist. Similarly, the isoprofit curves for firm 2 are at a maximum, for any given level of output for firm 1, at the point on the reaction curve for firm 2. Firm 2's preference direction is in the direction of the arrow on its reaction curve, and the highest level of profits it can reach is indicated by point B, where firm 2 is a monopolist.

But how do we know whether from some arbitrary starting position the

Cournot solution will be achieved? In other words, is the Cournot solution stable? In order to answer this question we must set up the model in dynamic terms. Only then can we answer this question. Whatever the answer happens to be, the same question applies when we increase the number of firms in the industry. As we do so, we must move away from the diagrammatic formulation of the model and concentrate on its mathematical specification.

In section 7.6 we consider a discrete model with output adjusting completely and instantaneously. Our main concern is with the stability of oligopoly as the number of firms in the industry increases.

7.6 Discrete dynamic model with output adjusting instantaneously

In the static model the assumption was that firm 1 would maximise its profits under the assumption that firm 2 would hold its output level constant. A similar condition applies also to firm 2. Here we assume that in time period t its rivals will choose the same output level they chose in time period $t-1$, and choose its own output at time t so as to maximise its profits at time t. More specifically, $q_1(t)$ is chosen so as to maximise firm 1's profits in time period t, under the assumption that firm 2 has output in time period t the same level it was in time period $t-1$, so that $q_2(t)=q_2(t-1)$. For firm 2, $q_2(t)$ is chosen so as to maximise firm 2's profits in time period t, under the assumption that firm 1 has output in time period t the same level it was in time period $t-1$, so that $q_1(t)=q_1(t-1)$.

These dynamic specifications for each firm change the form of the total revenue function, and hence the profit functions. Total costs are unaffected. The profit function for each firm is

$$\text{Firm 1} \quad \pi_1(t)=(9-q_1(t)-q_2(t-1))q_1(t)-3q_1(t)$$

$$\text{Firm 2} \quad \pi_2(t)=(9-q_1(t-1)-q_2(t))q_2(t)-3q_2(t)$$

Again, in the spirit of Cournot, each firm is maximising its profits under the conjectural variation that the other firm is holding its output level constant. Therefore

$$\frac{\partial \pi_1(t)}{\partial q_1(t)}=6-2q_1(t)-q_2(t-1)=0$$

$$\frac{\partial \pi_2(t)}{\partial q_2(t)}=6-q_1(t-1)-2q_2(t)=0$$

which results in the following dynamic adjustments

$$q_1(t)=3-\tfrac{1}{2}q_2(t-1)$$

$$q_2(t)=3-\tfrac{1}{2}q_1(t-1)$$

First we need to establish the Cournot solution for this model. This is where $q_1(t)=q_1(t-1)=q_1$ and $q_2(t)=q_2(t-1)=q_2$. But inserting these values gives us

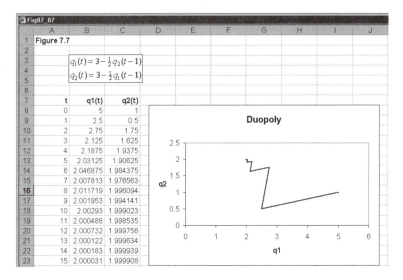

Figure 7.7

the same reaction curves of section 7.5, which intersect at the value $(q_1, q_2) = (2, 2)$.

We can now set out these two dynamic equations on a spreadsheet, supply some initial values for each firm's output, and see if the Cournot solution results as time passes. This is done in figure 7.7

Cells B8 and C8 supply initial values for each firm's output. Cells B9 and C9 have the formulas

B9	$=3-\frac{1}{2}q_2(0)$ $=3-(1/2)*C8$
C9	$=3-\frac{1}{2}q_1(0)$ $=3-(1/2)*B8$

These are then copied to the clipboard and pasted down for as many periods as you wish, here we have up to period 15. Cells B8 to C23 are then blocked and the chart wizard is initiated producing the inserted chart, as shown in figure 7.7. As in earlier chapters, you should check you have entered the formulas correctly by inserting in cells B8 and C8 the Cournot solution. Doing this gives all entries the value of 2.

Figure 7.7 shows this convergence for initial value $(q_1(0), q_2(0)) = (5, 1)$ and it is clear from the figure that it converges on the Cournot solution. Take the following two starting values

$(q_1(0), q_2(0)) = (3, 0)$, ie. where firm 1 begins from a monopoly position

$(q_1(0), q_2(0)) = (0, 3)$, ie. where firm 2 begins from a monopoly position

Once again the system converges on the Cournot solution. Finally consider the point $(q_1(0), q_2(0)) = (0, 0)$, which can be thought of as the position where both firms are deciding whether to enter the industry. Again the system converges on the Cournot solution. What is illustrated here is the general result that, for linear demand and constant marginal costs, Cournot duopoly is dynamically stable.

7.7 Dynamic oligopoly with three firms

Most elementary textbooks stop with the duopoly case. But it leaves the reader with the impression that such stability is quite general for oligopoly models. Is this in fact true? In order to consider this issue, we continue with our example, which assumes linear demand and constant marginal costs, and have three identical firms. Our model is now

(7.20)
$$p = 9 - Q$$
$$Q = q_1 + q_2 + q_3$$
$$TC_1 = 3q_1$$
$$TC_2 = 3q_2$$
$$TC_3 = 3q_3$$

Profits are readily found to be

$$\pi_1 = (9 - q_1 - q_2 - q_3)q_1 - 3q_1$$
$$\pi_2 = (9 - q_1 - q_2 - q_3)q_2 - 3q_2$$
$$\pi_3 = (9 - q_1 - q_2 - q_3)q_3 - 3q_3$$

resulting in three reaction **planes**

$$R_1 \quad q_1 = 3 - \tfrac{1}{2}(q_2 + q_3)$$
$$R_2 \quad q_2 = 3 - \tfrac{1}{2}(q_1 + q_3)$$
$$R_3 \quad q_3 = 3 - \tfrac{1}{2}(q_1 + q_2)$$

which intersect at the unique value $(q_1, q_2, q_3) = (\tfrac{3}{2}, \tfrac{3}{2}, \tfrac{3}{2})$, the static Cournot solution for a three-firm oligopoly, given the present model.

Given exactly the same assumptions about dynamic behaviour as we outlined above, then the profit for each firm is

Firm 1 $\pi_1(t) = (9 - q_1(t) - q_2(t-1) - q_3(t-1))q_1(t) - 3q_1(t)$

Firm 2 $\pi_2(t) = (9 - q_1(t-1) - q_2(t) - q_3(t-1))q_2(t) - 3q_2(t)$

Firm 3 $\pi_3(t) = (9 - q_1(t-1) - q_2(t-1) - q_3(t))q_3(t) - 3q_3(t)$

Again, in the spirit of Cournot, each firm is maximising its profits under the conjectural variation that the other firms are holding their output levels constant. Therefore

$$\frac{\partial \pi_1(t)}{\partial q_1(t)} = 6 - 2q_1(t) - q_2(t-1) - q_3(t-1) = 0$$

$$\frac{\partial \pi_2(t)}{\partial q_2(t)} = 6 - q_1(t-1) - 2q_2(t) - q_3(t-1) = 0$$

$$\frac{\partial \pi_3(t)}{\partial q_3(t)} = 6 - q_1(t-1) - q_2(t-1) - 2q_3(t) = 0$$

which result in the following dynamic adjustments

$$q_1(t) = 3 - \tfrac{1}{2} q_2(t-1) - \tfrac{1}{2} q_3(t-1)$$

$$q_2(t) = 3 - \tfrac{1}{2} q_1(t-1) - \tfrac{1}{2} q_3(t-1)$$

$$q_3(t) = 3 - \tfrac{1}{2} q_1(t-1) - \tfrac{1}{2} q_2(t-1)$$

What we have here is a simultaneous set of three recursive equations. The dynamics of this model are shown in figure 7.8. Cells B9, C9 and D9 contain the initial values. Here we have initial values (3,0,0) in which firm 1 is a monopolist. Cells B10, C10 and D10 have formulas

B10	$= 3 - \tfrac{1}{2} q_2(0) - \tfrac{1}{2} q_3(0)$ $= 3 - (1/2)*C9 - (1/2)*D9$
C10	$= 3 - \tfrac{1}{2} q_1(0) - \tfrac{1}{2} q_3(0)$ $= 3 - (1/2)*B9 - (1/2)*D9$
D10	$= 3 - \tfrac{1}{2} q_1(0) - \tfrac{1}{2} q_2(0)$ $= 3 - (1/2)*B9 - (1/2)*C9$

These values are then copied to the clipboard and pasted down, here up to period 15. Spreadsheet programmes cannot plot more than two variables. Using the chart wizard, we plot three graphs: (1) firm 1 against firm 2; (2) firm 2 against firm 3; and (3) firm 1 against firm 3. The graphs appear to show no obvious tendency towards the equilibrium. Firm 2 against firm 3 seems to show a direct path, but the trajectory itself is certainly not to the Cournot solution.

The problem is more clearly shown by plotting the path of output for each of the firms. Figure 7.9 provides the plot for all three firms. What is quite clear from this figure is that each firm exhibits oscillations in their output after a brief initial period. The Cournot solution is unstable. Is this result general? Try the initial values (1, 2, 3). It is readily observed that the same oscillatory behaviour results. Figure 7.9 in fact illustrates the general result that for *linear demand* with *constant marginal costs*, with *three* firms in the industry, the path of output for each firm will eventually give rise to a constant oscillation over time.

7.8 Partial-adjustment duopoly model

Return to the duopoly model with linear demand and constant marginal costs. Still in keeping with the Cournot spirit of dynamic adjustment, we now turn

Figure 7.8

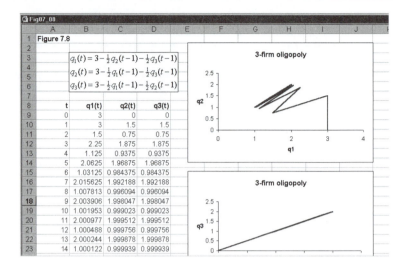

Figure 7.9

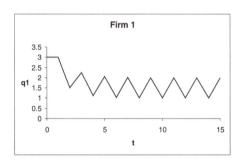

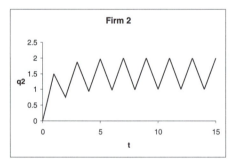

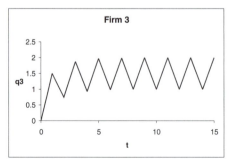

to incomplete and noninstantaneous adjustment. In particular, we assume that for each firm

$$\Delta q_1(t) = q_1(t) - q_1(t-1) = k_1(q_1^*(t) - q_1(t-1)) \quad k_1 > 0$$
$$\Delta q_2(t) = q_2(t) - q_2(t-1) = k_2(q_2^*(t) - q_2(t-1)) \quad k_2 > 0 \tag{7.21}$$

where $q_1^*(t)$ and $q_2^*(t)$ are the desired output levels for each firm. What these adjustment equations indicate is that each firm adjusts its previous period's output by a proportion of the discrepancy between its desired output level at time t and its output level in the previous period. Note also, however, that the optimal value at time t is adjusted according to the information at time $t-1$. Output at time t can therefore be considered a two-step procedure.

The desired output level on the part of each firm is given by their reaction function, so

$$q_1^*(t) = 3 - \tfrac{1}{2} q_2(t-1)$$

$$q_2^*(t) = 3 - \tfrac{1}{2} q_1(t-1) \tag{7.22}$$

Substituting (7.22) into (7.21) and simplifying we have

$$q_1(t) = 3k_1 + (1-k_1)q_1(t-1) - \tfrac{1}{2}k_1 q_2(t-1)$$

$$q_2(t) = 3k_2 - \tfrac{1}{2}k_2 q_1(t-1) + (1-k_2)q_2(t-1) \tag{7.23}$$

which is a set of two recursive equations involving the partial adjustment coefficients k_1 and k_2.

Equations (7.23) are set out in the spreadsheet shown in figure 7.10. In cells H3 and H4 we place the values of k_1 and k_2. Here we assume that they have the same value of 0.75. In cells B8 and C8 we have the initial values for the output of firms 1 and 2. We have an initial position with firm 1 a monopolist. In cells B9 and C9 we have the formulas

B9	$=3k_1 + (1-k_1)q_1(0) - \tfrac{1}{2}k_1 q_2(0)$
	$=3*\$H\$3 + (1-\$H\$3)*B8 - (1/2)*\$H\$3*C8$
C9	$=3k_2 - \tfrac{1}{2}k_2 q_1(0) + (1-k_2)q_2(0)$
	$=3*\$H\$4 - (1/2)*\$H\$4*B8 + (1-\$H\$4)*C8$

These values are then copied to the clipboard and pasted down. Finally, cells B8 to C28 are blocked and the chart wizard is initiated to produce the inserted chart in figure 7.10. Given the present model and the values of k_1 and k_2 given in the figure, the model exhibits stability, with output converging on the Cournot solution. But is this always true?

7.8.1 Experimentation

First check the formulas by placing the Cournot solution as the initial conditions. If all is correct, all entries in the table should have the value 2. Now return the initial values to the situation with firm 1 being a monopolist, with initial point (3,0). Consider the situation with firm 2 being the monopolist,

Figure 7.10

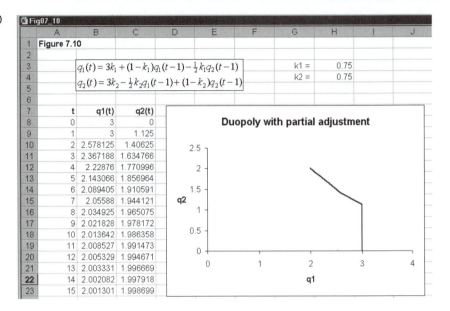

with initial point (0,3). Once again the system converges on the equilibrium. So far the results appear the same as our perfect adjustment. Return to the initial situation with firm 1 the monopolist and now let $k_1 = k_2 = 4/3$. The system after some time begins to settle down to an oscillatory behaviour. This is also true if the initial situation is with firm 2 being the monopolist. If firm 1 is the monopolist and $k_1 = k_2 = 1.5$ then the system is oscillatory and explosive. The same is true if firm 2 is initially the monopolist. Although the duopoly model with complete and instantaneous adjustment is stable, the same cannot be said of partial adjustment. In this instance, duopoly can exhibit stable, oscillatory or explosive adjustment paths, depending on the size of the adjustment coefficients.

Exercises

(1)   Consider the discrete advertising model of section 7.3. A product has present sales of 100,000 with sales declining at a rate of 2% per period. The maximum absorption per period is 250,000. £10,000 is to be spent on advertising over a five-year period or a ten-year period, in each case at a uniform rate. It is known that advertising raises sales by a proportion 0.25 of the advertising expenditure affecting the proportion of the market not yet already purchasing the product.

(i)   Derive the two time profiles and plot them on the same graph.

(ii)   If the choice is based on total sales over ten years, which expenditure policy will be implemented?

(2)   Consider the following diffusion model for a new product in which at the moment no sales have taken place

$$\Delta F(t+1) = (0.005 + 0.02F(t))(1 - F(t))$$

(i)   What are the fixed points of this system?

(ii)   At what time will the maximum penetration of the market occur?

(3)   Consider the following model of oligopoly in which total costs are different

$$p = 9 - Q$$
$$Q = q_1 + q_2$$
$$TC_1 = 3q_1$$
$$TC_2 = 1.5q_2$$

(i)   What is the Cournot solution?

(ii)   Assume firm 1 chooses $q_1(t)$ so as to maximise $\pi_1(t)$, assuming $q_2(t) = q_2(t-1)$; and firm 2 chooses $q_2(t)$ to maximise $\pi_2(t)$, assuming $q_1(t) = q_1(t-1)$. What are the dynamic adjustment equations?

(iii)   Assuming the initial values are where firm 1 is a monopolist, does the system converge on the Cournot solution?

(4)   Consider the following Cournot model with identical quadratic total costs

$$p = 9 - Q$$
$$Q = q_1 + q_2$$
$$TC_1 = 0.5q_1^2$$
$$TC_2 = 0.5q_2^2$$

(i)   What is the Cournot solution?

(ii)   Firm 1 chooses $q_1(t)$ so as to maximise $\pi_1(t)$, assuming $q_2(t) = q_2(t-1)$; and firm 2 chooses $q_2(t)$ to maximise $\pi_2(t)$, assuming $q_1(t) = q_1(t-1)$. What are the dynamic adjustment equations?

(iii)   Assuming the initial values are where firm 2 is a monopolist, does the system converge on the Cournot solution?

(5)   Consider the following three-firm oligopoly model

$$p = 20 - Q$$
$$Q = q_1 + q_2 + q_3$$
$$TC_1 = 2q_1$$
$$TC_2 = 2q_2$$
$$TC_3 = 2q_3$$

(i)   What is the Cournot solution?

(ii)   Firm i chooses $q_i(t)$ to maximise $\pi_i(t)$, assuming $q_j(t) = q_j(t-1)$ for all $j \neq i$. What are the dynamic adjustment equations?

(iii) Show that no matter which firm is the monopolist in period 0, the system moves to one of oscillations in which the Cournot solution is never reached.

Chapter 8
Saddles and rational expectations

8.1 What are saddles?

In chapter 4 we discussed a variety of trajectories in the phase plane. But the one trajectory we did not discuss was the one associated with a saddle-path solution. Saddle-path solutions have entered economics in a major way. They became most popular when rational expectations became a major specification of expectations formation. In earlier chapters we have considered adaptive expectations. The simplest one of all was that individuals expected the price in the current period to be equal to the price last period. Even the more complex expectations that base current prices on the trend in prices are *backward*-looking. In other words, the current expected price depends in some way on past prices. Not only are they backward-looking, but they also take no account of the modelling of the variable in question. Rational expectations theory takes quite a different approach. For the moment we shall simply say that in a rational expectations model, expected prices take account of all information, including the model under investigation, and based on that information attempts to minimise any errors. If successful in doing this, it is like having perfect foresight. In this chapter we shall use the assumption of perfect foresight as our means of analysing rational expectations.

Rational expectations modelling is more complex than the models we have discussed so far. So in this chapter we shall do two things only. First we will consider some simple examples so we can see how to derive saddle-point solutions and investigate their stability/instability. Second, we shall see how these concepts are applied to a model of the open economy in which prices and the exchange rate are flexible.

First it will be useful to consider the features of a saddle – an actual saddle! Figure 8.1 shows an idealised drawing of a saddle. The point of interest is the centre of the saddle. What are the characteristics of this point? It is both a maximum and a minimum simultaneously. When looked at from the point of view of the long length of the saddle it reaches a minimum at this point. When looked at from the narrow direction, it is a maximum. If we consider the saddle from the point of view of stability, then, in the long direction, it has features of stability. When looked at from the narrow direction, then it is unstable. It is this characteristic of a saddle-point which is of interest here. In simple terms, a saddle-point exhibits both stability and instability.

Figure 8.1

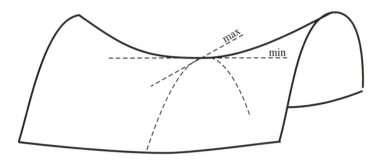

Figure 8.2

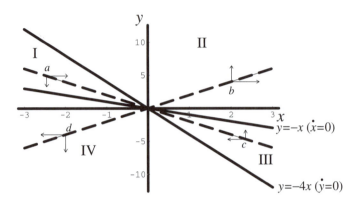

8.2 Two examples

In this section we shall simply concentrate on exhibiting diagrammatically saddle-point solutions in the phase plane so that we can get a feel for what they are. In doing this we consider two interrelated markets represented by the variables x and y. In these examples we shall assume continuous functions of time.

8.2.1 Example 1

Consider the following continuous dynamical system

(8.1)
$$\dot{x} = x + y$$
$$\dot{y} = 4x + y$$

First consider the fixed point of the system. This is where $\dot{x} = 0$ and $\dot{y} = 0$. The only values of x and y which satisfy these conditions is for $x = 0$ and $y = 0$. Now turn to the two isoclines. When $\dot{x} = 0$ then $y = -x$. This isocline is shown in figure 8.2. When $\dot{x} > 0$ then $y > -x$ and so above the line x is rising. Similarly, below the $\dot{x} = 0$ isocline x is falling. We have a similar situation for the second isocline. When $\dot{y} = 0$ then $y = -4x$. When $\dot{y} > 0$ then $y > -4x$ and so above the line y is rising. Similarly, below the $\dot{y} = 0$ isocline y is falling. All these vector forces are illustrated in figure 8.2. What these vector forces reveal is that in quadrants I and III the system appears to direct the solution path towards the origin, while in quadrant II and IV the system is directed away from the origin

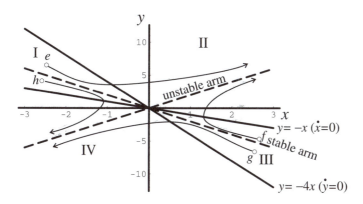

Figure 8.3

– where the origin is the fixed point of the system. The diagram shows four representative points: *a, b, c* and *d*. The central arrows *seem* to indicate the movements just alluded to.

We emphasised the word 'seem' because it is not obvious that the system if starting from a point in quadrant I will actually stay in quadrant I. We note in quadrant I that the system can be pulled in the positive direction towards quadrant II, while heading towards the fixed point. In fact there is nothing stopping the trajectory from passing from quadrant I into quadrant II. Once in quadrant II then any trajectory will start moving away from the fixed point. The situation is shown in figure 8.3, where our starting point is point *e* in quadrant I. Similarly, for a trajectory starting in quadrant III, such as point *f*, then the system begins by getting pulled towards the fixed point, then passes into quadrant II and gets pushed away from the fixed point. However, not all points in quadrant I get pulled into quadrant II. Depending on the initial point in quadrant I, the force acting on it may be greater in the downward direction. Take point *h* in quadrant I. Initially this moves towards the fixed point, the origin, but soon gets pulled into quadrant IV, and once there is moved away from the fixed point as shown by the trajectory emanating from point *h*. Similarly, the trajectory emanating from point *g*, which lies in quadrant III, starts to get pulled towards the origin, but then enters quadrant IV and moves away from the fixed point.

Let us establish these results by setting out the problem on a spreadsheet. In doing this we once again use the Euler approximation for the continuous system. We compute future values of *x* and *y* using the formulas

$$x(t+1) = x(t) + f(x(t),y(t))\Delta t$$
$$y(t+1) = y(t) + g(x(t),y(t))\Delta t \qquad (8.2)$$

where

$$\dot{x} = f(x,y) = x + y$$
$$\dot{y} = g(x,y) = 4x + y \qquad (8.3)$$

Plotting such (x,y)-values from some initial point will give us a particular trajectory.

The model is shown in figure 8.4. In cell E3 we place our time interval, which

Figure 8.4

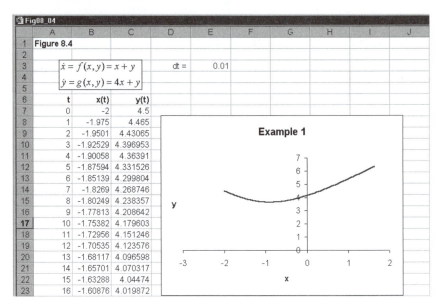

here we have at 0.01. Since this system can move rapidly away from the origin, we have *t* ranging only over 0 to 100, which are placed in cells A7 to A107. In cells B7 and C7 we insert our initial points for *x* and *y*, respectively. The figure illustrates point *e* from figure 8.3 with value $(-2,4.5)$. Having specified our initial point, then cells B8 and C8 have the formulas

B8	$= x(0) + f(x(0), y(0))*\Delta t$ $= B7 + (B7 + C7)*\$E\$3$
C8	$= y(0) + g(x(0), y(0))*\Delta t$ $= C7 + (4*B7 + C7)*\$E\$3$

Having computed cells B8 and C8, we copy these to the clipboard and paste down. This completes all our computations for constructing any trajectory in the phase plane. Finally, we block cells B7 to C107 and invoke the chart wizard, inserting the resulting chart as shown in figure 8.4. What we immediately see is the trajectory drawn in figure 8.3 emanating from point *e*. The trajectory only briefly gets drawn towards the origin, but soon enters quadrant II and gets directed away from the fixed point very rapidly and very forcibly!

The reader should verify the typical trajectories shown in figure 8.3 using the following initial values

$$\begin{array}{ll} \text{point } e & (-2,4.5) \\ \text{point } f & (2,-3) \\ \text{point } g & (2,-4.5) \\ \text{point } h & (-2,3) \end{array}$$

Trying a number of others will reveal that the trajectories seem to head towards a particular path in quadrants II and III.

In figure 8.3 we identified two special paths, which are labelled the **stable arm** in sectors I and III and the **unstable arm** in sectors II and IV. Deriving such arms is rather complex and a precise derivation is beyond the scope of this book. We shall, however, provide a method without proof. The proof of this technique can be obtained from my *Economic Dynamics* (Shone, 1997). The specific part without proof is to claim that we can replace the time derivatives with a product, i.e. $\dot{x} = \lambda x$ and $\dot{y} = \lambda y$. If we do this, then

$$\lambda x = x + y$$
$$\lambda y = 4x + y \tag{8.4}$$

Using the first equation of (8.4) to solve for y, and substituting this into the second equation, we obtain

$$4x - (1 - \lambda)^2 x = 0$$
$$\lambda^2 - 2\lambda - 3 = 0$$
$$(\lambda + 1)(\lambda - 3) = 0$$

Hence, the characteristic roots are $r = -1$ and $s = 3$. These are referred to as the *characteristic roots* of the system (also see box 4). Now return to the equations given in (8.4). If $\lambda = r = 3$, then, from the first equation we have

$$3x = x + y$$
$$y - 2x = 0 \tag{8.5}$$

Box 4   Computing characteristic roots of two-equation autonomous systems

Given the continuous dynamic system

$$\dot{x} = a_1 x + a_2 y$$
$$\dot{y} = b_1 x + b_2 y$$

or the discrete dynamic system

$$\Delta x(t + 1) = a_1 x(t) + a_2 y(t)$$
$$\Delta y(t + 1) = b_1 x(t) + b_2 y(t)$$

then it is possible to show that the resulting characteristic roots of the system are

$$r = \frac{(a_1 + b_2) - \sqrt{(a_1 + b_2)^2 - 4(a_1 b_2 - a_2 b_1)}}{2}$$

$$s = \frac{(a_1 + b_2) + \sqrt{(a_1 + b_2)^2 - 4(a_1 b_2 - a_2 b_1)}}{2}$$

Now set up a spreadsheet with parameters a_1, a_2, b_1 and b_2. Let their values be placed in cells C14, C15, C16 and C17, respectively. (Above we insert the equation and formulas as a reminder.) Then in cells E14 and E15 place the values of the characteristic roots, i.e.

E14 $= \dfrac{(a_1 + b_2) - \sqrt{(a_1 + b_2)^2 - 4(a_1 b_2 - a_2 b_1)}}{2}$

$= \dfrac{(\$C\$14 + \$C\$17) - \sqrt{(\$C\$14 + \$C\$17)^2 - 4(\$C\$14 * \$C\$17 - \$C\$15 * \$C\$16)}}{2}$

E15 $= \dfrac{(a_1 + b_2) + \sqrt{(a_1 + b_2)^2 - 4(a_1 b_2 - a_2 b_1)}}{2}$

$= \dfrac{(\$C\$14 + \$C\$17) - \sqrt{(\$C\$14 + \$C\$17)^2 - 4(\$C\$14 * \$C\$17 - \$C\$15 * \$C\$16)}}{2}$

Save the spreadsheet. We now show the resulting spreadsheet.

Box_4

	A	B	C	D	E	F
1	Solving roots of dynamical systems					
2						
3		$\dot{x} = a_1 x + a_2 y$				
4		$\dot{y} = b_1 x + b_2 y$				
5						
6						
7		$r = \dfrac{(a_1 + b_2) - \sqrt{(a_1 + b_2)^2 - 4(a_1 b_2 - a_2 b_1)}}{2}$				
8						
9						
10		$s = \dfrac{(a_1 + b_2) + \sqrt{(a_1 + b_2)^2 - 4(a_1 b_2 - a_2 b_1)}}{2}$				
11						
12						
13						
14		a1 =	1	r =	-1	
15		a2 =	1	s =	3	
16		b1 =	4			
17		b2 =	1			
18						

This spreadsheet can now be used to compute the characteristic roots of any two (homogeneous) autonomous equation system.

In fact, this result occurs no matter which of the two equations we choose. (Check that substituting 3 into the second equation results in the same relationship.) We know the system emanates to or from the fixed point, which is here the origin, so if we arbitrarily set $x = 1$, then from result (8.5) y has a value 2. Put more simply, we have an arm emanating from the fixed point with the formula $y = 2x$. This arm passes through quadrants II and IV, and we have already shown that in these quadrants the system tends towards plus or minus ($\pm$) infinity. Consequently the relationship $y = 2x$ denotes the unstable arm.

The analysis so far used the value of $r = 3$ for the parameter λ. Suppose now we take the other value which it can take, namely $s = -1$. Doing this we follow exactly the same analysis. Letting $\lambda = s = -1$ then from the first or second equation of (8.4) we obtain

$$-x = x + y$$
$$y + 2x = 0$$

which gives us an arm with the formula $y = -2x$. This arm passes through quadrants I and III, respectively. To summarise our results so far

> *Unstable arm* $y = 2x$ Quadrants II and IV
> *Stable arm* $y = -2x$ Quadrants I and III

It is now time to verify these results with the aid of our spreadsheet. If our results are correct, then the trajectories should be straight lines either tending away from the fixed point along the unstable arm, or towards the fixed point along the stable arm. Consider the unstable arm first. If this does move away from the origin, we need to take our initial point close to it. If $x = 0.5$ then $y = 1$. So let the initial point in the spreadsheet be $(0.5, 1)$. The path is seen to be a straight line moving away from the origin along the path given by $y = 2x$. Now take a point in quadrant IV, say $(-0.5, -1)$. Once again the system moves in a straight-line trajectory away from the fixed point towards infinity along the line denoted by $y = 2x$.

Next take a point in quadrant I. If $x = -2$, then $y = 4$ along the arm denoted by the formula $y = -2x$. Taking such an initial point leads to a straight-line trajectory towards the origin. The same is true for a point in quadrant III, such as $(2, -4)$. So we have indeed verified that the unstable arm has the formula $y = 2x$ while the stable arm has the formula $y = -2x$, and that these conform to the indicated markings in figure 8.3. These arms pass through the fixed point, and so we refer to such a fixed point as a **saddle-point solution**. The saddle-point solution exhibits both stability and instability simultaneously; it has trajectories moving towards it and away from it. Another way to identify that a model has a saddle-point solution is to show that the two characteristic roots are real and have opposite signs. Both the present example and the next in section 8.2.2 satisfy this condition. We shall utilise this feature of saddle-point solutions frequently, especially in the exercises.

8.2.2 *Example 2*

Consider the dynamical system

$$\dot{x} = 3x - 2y$$
$$\dot{y} = 2x - 2y \tag{8.6}$$

We shall analyse this system in exactly the same way as we did with example 1. Since the analysis follows the same pattern we can be brief.

Setting $\dot{x} = 0$ and $\dot{y} = 0$ readily gives the origin as the only fixed point of this system. The four quadrants are determined from the two isoclines

$$y = \frac{3x}{2} \quad \dot{x} = 0$$

$$y = x \quad \dot{y} = 0 \tag{8.7}$$

Figure 8.5

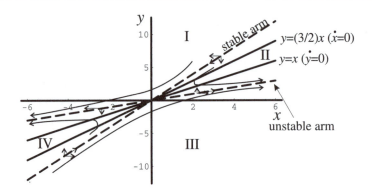

and have trajectories shown in figure 8.5. (The reader should verify the vector forces indicated in this diagram.)

The system moves quite differently from the example in section 8.2.2, but it still has an unstable arm and a stable arm passing through the fixed point. Once again we set up this model on a spreadsheet in order to investigate its trajectories. The situation is shown in figure 8.6. Everything is fundamentally the same as the previous example. The only item of note is that cells B8 and C8 now have the formulas

B8	$= x(0) + f(x(0),\, y(0)) * \Delta t$
	$= B7 + (3*B7 - 2*C7) * \$E\$3$
C8	$= y(0) + g(x(0),\, y(0)) * \Delta t$
	$= C7 + (2*B7 - 2*C7) * \$E\$3$

The reader should establish the trajectories shown in figure 8.5 by considering the following initial points

$$(2,6)\quad (3,5)\quad (-2,-6)\quad\quad (-3,-5)$$

Again set $\dot{x} = \lambda x$ and $\dot{y} = \lambda y$. Then

(8.8)
$$\lambda x = 3x - 2y$$
$$\lambda y = 2x - 2y$$

Using the value of y from the first equation of (8.8) and substituting this into the second we obtain

$$(2+\lambda)\left[\tfrac{1}{2}(3-\lambda)\right]x = 2x$$
$$\lambda^2 - \lambda - 2 = 0$$
$$(\lambda + 1)(\lambda - 2) = 0$$

So λ has values $r = -1$ and $s = 2$. If $\lambda = r = -1$ then

$$-x = 3x - 2y$$
$$y = 2x$$

which gives us one arm. The second arm is derived by setting $\lambda = s = 2$

Figure 8.6

	A	B	C	D	E	F	G	H	I	J
1	Figure 8.6									
2										
3	$\dot{x}=f(x,y)=3x-2y$			dt =		0.01				
4	$\dot{y}=g(x,y)=2x-2y$									
5										
6	t	x(t)	y(t)							
7	0	2	6							
8	1	1.94	5.92							
9	2	1.8798	5.8404							
10	3	1.819386	5.761188							
11	4	1.758744	5.682352							
12	5	1.697859	5.60388							
13	6	1.636717	5.525759							
14	7	1.575304	5.447979							
15	8	1.513603	5.370525							
16	9	1.451601	5.293387							
17	10	1.389281	5.216551							
18	11	1.326628	5.140005							
19	12	1.263627	5.063738							
20	13	1.200261	4.987736							
21	14	1.136514	4.911986							
22	15	1.07237	4.836477							
23	16	1.007812	4.761195							

$$2x = 3x - 2y$$
$$y = \tfrac{1}{2}x$$

Both arms are positively sloped. With the help of figure 8.5 we establish that $y=\tfrac{1}{2}x$ is the unstable arm and $y=2x$ is the stable arm. The reader should verify this for various values of x and y. Note again that the characteristic roots of the system are real and have opposite signs.

8.3 The Dornbusch model under perfect foresight

We have dealt little with the open economy in this book, but a major insight into exchange rate behaviour is provided by a model set out by Dornbusch (1976). There are many variants of this model (see Shone, 1997, ch.11), but here we shall consider the one involving perfect foresight. This variant neatly illustrates a saddle-point solution.

The model is set out stripped of any complications, like tax. The model is in natural logarithms (see box 3, p. 112), which are denoted by lower-case letters. So $y = \ln Y$, etc. The only nominal variable is the rate of interest. The model is set out in table 8.1.

The first equation of the goods market is basically the expenditure function ($E = C + I + G + NX$, where $NX =$ net exports) written in logarithms. Net exports are a function of the real exchange rate, which is the nominal exchange rate adjusted for prices in both countries. It is useful to just clarify how the real exchange rate enters the model. Let R denote the real exchange rate, then

$$R = P/(SP^*)$$

Table 8.1 *The Dornbusch model under perfect foresight*

Goods market	
$e = cy + g + h(s-p)$ $0 < c < 1, h > 0$	e = total expenditure
$\dot{p} = \alpha(e-y)$ $\alpha > 0$	g = government expenditure
	s = spot exchange rate
	p = domestic price level
	$\dot{p}$ = inflation (since $p = \ln P$)
	y = real income (exogenous)
Money market	
$md = p + ky - ur$ $k > 0, u > 0$	md = demand for money
$ms = md = m$	r = domestic interest rate
$md = ms$	ms = supply of money
	m = money balances (exogenous)
International assets market	
$r = r^* + \dot{s}^e$	r^* = interest rate abroad
$\dot{s}^e = \dot{s}$	$\dot{s}^e$ = change in expected spot rate
	$\dot{s}$ = change in spot exchange rate

In other words, R is the ratio of the domestic price over the foreign price expressed in domestic currency, and S is the exchange rate expressed as the *domestic* price of foreign currency. Under the law of one price, $P = SP^*$ and $R = 1$, which is also the **purchasing power parity** (PPP) condition. This is supposed to hold *in the long run*. Taking natural logarithms, then

$$\ln R = \ln P - \ln S - \ln P^*$$

If $R = 1$, then its logarithm is zero. If we hold foreign prices constant, which we are doing, and set them equal to unity, then the logarithm of P^* is also zero. Hence

$$0 = \ln P - \ln S$$
$$0 = p - s$$

or

$$s - p = 0$$

A rise in s is a rise in foreign prices expressed in domestic currency, and so home goods become more competitive. (Note that a rise in s is a depreciation of the domestic currency; or, equivalently, an appreciation of the foreign currency.) Exports rise and imports fall, resulting in an improvement in net exports. In other words, expenditure rises by an amount h when $(s-p)$ rises.

The second equation in the goods market is our familiar continuous market adjustment model: with one major difference. In this model income is held constant at the natural level (the model is very monetarist). Hence, any excess demand in the goods market forces prices up rather than change the level of income. Certainly this would be the case in the long run.

The money market is similar to the one we have used already. The variable p enters the demand for money equation because we are considering real money balances. (*Note*: If Md/P denotes real-money balances, then $\ln(Md/P) = \ln Md - \ln P = md - p$.)

In the international asset market domestic interest rates diverge from foreign interest rates by the amount of the expected depreciation/appreciation of the currency. Implicit in this condition is the assumption of perfect capital mobility. This can be seen more clearly if the exchange rate were fixed, and so there would not expect to be any change in it, then $\dot{s}^e = 0$. In this circumstance domestic interest rates cannot diverge from those abroad. Under perfect foresight, the expected change in the spot exchange rate is equal to the actual change in the spot exchange rate.

The model basically establishes two relationships: a goods market equilibrium relationship and an asset market equilibrium relationship. Each relationship is a function of p and s, and so the two relationships are sufficient to determine p and s. This is the equilibrium, the fixed point, of the system. Let us begin with the goods market equilibrium. This is quite straightforward. Substituting the expenditure function into the price adjustment equation gives

$$\dot{p} = \alpha[cy + g + h(s-p) - y]$$

or

$$\dot{p} = \alpha[h(s-p) - (1-c)y + g] \tag{8.9}$$

Goods market equilibrium occurs when prices are unchanging, i.e. when $\dot{p} = 0$, and when this is true, we have

$$0 = \alpha[h(s-p) - (1-c)y + g]$$

$$p = s - \frac{(1-c)y}{h} + \frac{g}{h}$$

But in the long run we have PPP, and so the real exchange rate is equal to unity and this in turn implies $p = s$. If this is true, then the constant term in our previous result must be zero. Which means this goods market equilibrium line passes through the origin with a slope of unity. This is shown in figure 8.7, and marked GM.

If $\dot{p} > 0$ then

$$\alpha[h(s-p) - (1-c)y + g] > 0$$

$$p < s - \frac{(1-c)y}{h} + \frac{g}{h}$$

So below the GM line prices are rising and above prices are falling. This should not be surprising. When $\dot{p} > 0$ then expenditure exceeds income, and income is constant. So prices are pushed up. Another way to view this is to take a point on the GM line, say, point A, and then move horizontally to the right to point B (which is, of course, below GM). As we pointed out earlier, a rise in s is a depreciation of the domestic currency and this makes home goods

Figure 8.7

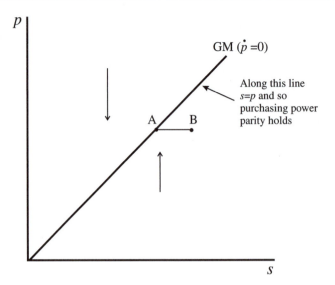

GM ($\dot{p}=0$)

Along this line
$s=p$ and so
purchasing power
parity holds

A   B

more competitive, so raising net exports. The rise in expenditure resulting from the rise in net exports leads expenditure to exceed the constant level of income, which in turn puts pressure on prices to rise.

Now turn to the asset market. First we substitute the perfect foresight assumption into the interest rate condition, and substitute this result into the money market equilibrium condition

$$m = p + ky - u(r^* + \dot{s})$$

or

(8.10) $$\dot{s} = \left(\frac{1}{u}\right)p + \left(\frac{1}{u}\right)(ky - m) - r^*$$

When $\dot{s} = 0$ then

$$0 = p + ky - m - ur^*$$

or

(8.11) $$p = m - ky + ur^*$$

which is a constant. This isocline is therefore horizontal and marked FX (for foreign exchange equilibrium)[1] in figure 8.8. When $\dot{s} = 0$ then

$$p + ky - m - ur^* > 0$$
$$p > m - ky + ur^*$$

and so above the FX line s is rising, while below the FX line s is falling.

To summarise our model so far, we have derived two differential equations in the form of (8.9) and (8.10), reproduced here slightly differently

$$\dot{p} = \alpha hs - \alpha hp + (g - (1 - c)y)$$

[1] Note that the FX line is *not* the asset market equilibrium line. This is, in fact, the stable arm of the saddle-point.

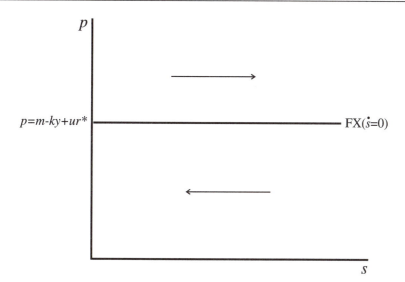

Figure 8.8

$$\dot{s}=\left(\frac{1}{u}\right)p+\left(\frac{1}{u}\right)(ky-m)-r^* \tag{8.12}$$

From these two equations we have two isoclines. The first denotes goods market equilibrium and we have labelled this isocline GM. It is a 45°-line through the origin. It also denotes the PPP condition. The second equation leads to asset market equilibrium, and specifically denotes no change in the exchange rate. This isocline is a horizontal line, and denoted FX. Given the vector forces we have already identified for each of the markets, then the combined vector forces are those illustrated in figure 8.9, which identifies a saddle-point solution.

8.4 A numerical example

Consider the following numerical example

$$\begin{aligned}
&e=0.8y+4+0.1(s-p)\\
&\dot{p}=0.1(e-y)\\
&md=p+0.5y-0.5r\\
&md=ms=105\\
&r=r^*+\dot{s}^e\\
&\dot{s}^e=\dot{s}\\
&y=20,\quad r^*=10
\end{aligned} \tag{8.13}$$

We know that the GM line leads to $s=p$, and from (8.11) we have

$$\begin{aligned}
p&=m-ky+ur^*\\
&=105-0.5(20)+0.5(10)=100
\end{aligned}$$

So we immediately have the fixed point of the system as[2] $(\bar{s},\bar{p})=(100,100)$. The differential equations of this system are

---

[2] We identify fixed points, equilibrium points, with bars rather than asterisks so that there is no confusion with variables abroad, which are identified with asterisks.

Figure 8.9

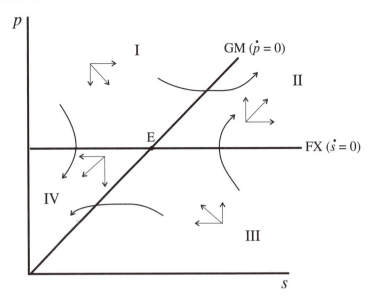

(8.14)
$$\dot{p} = -0.001p + 0.001s$$
$$\dot{s} = 2p - 200$$

which clearly leads to the same fixed point when we set $\dot{p} = 0$ and $\dot{s} = 0$.

It is now time to set this example up on a spreadsheet, as shown in figure 8.10. In line with the system of (8.12) we consider the model in the form

$$\dot{p} = A_1 p + A_2 s + A_3$$
$$\dot{s} = B_1 p + B_2$$

and set out the 'derived parameters' in cells I2 to I6. Notice that the appropriate signs are derived in the computations. In cells B9 and C9 we insert the initial values for s and p, respectively. In cells B10 and C10 we insert the following formulas (note that we calculate s first, which requires the B-parameters)

B10	$= s(0) + (B_1 p(0) + B_2)\Delta t$
	$= B9 + (\$I\$5 * C9 + \$I\$6) * \$G\$7$
C10	$= p(0) + (A_1 p(0) + A_2 s(0) + A_3)\Delta t$
	$= C9 + (\$I\$2 * C9 + \$I\$3 * B9 + \$I\$4) * \$G\$7$

B10 and C10 are then copied to the clipboard and pasted down. Here we have periods up to $t = 200$. Finally cells B9:C209 are blocked and the chart wizard is invoked to produce the chart shown in figure 8.10. (Check you have entered the formulas correctly by placing the equilibrium values in cells B9 and C9. Doing this should lead to all entries having the value of 100.)

Now try a variety of trajectories with initial points taken in each of the four quadrants. Six typical points for (s,p) are

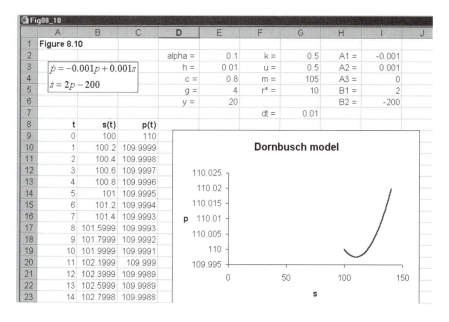

Figure 8.10

Quadrant I   (100,110) (50,100)
Quadrant II   (150,105)
Quadrant III   (150,100) (95,80)
Quadrant IV   (50,95)

All show the trajectories expected as indicated in figure 8.9.

We now need to establish the equations of the saddle-paths. In order to do this in the present model we need to consider the system in terms of deviations from the equilibrium. This eliminates the constant 200 in (8.14). Taking deviations from equilibrium for the system given in (8.14) we have

$$\dot{p} = -0.001(p - \bar{p}) + 0.001(s - \bar{s})$$
$$\dot{s} = 2(p - \bar{p}) \tag{8.15}$$

Now set $\dot{p} = \lambda(p - \bar{p})$ and $\dot{s} = \lambda(s - \bar{s})$. Substituting these into (8.15) gives

$$\lambda(p - \bar{p}) = -0.001(p - \bar{p}) + 0.001(s - \bar{s})$$
$$\lambda(s - \bar{s}) = 2(p - \bar{p}) \tag{8.16}$$

Re-arranging the first equation and solving for $s - \bar{s}$ and substituting this result into the second equation gives

$$s - \bar{s} = (1000\lambda + 1)(p - \bar{p})$$
$$\lambda(1000\lambda + 1)(p - \bar{p}) = 2(p - \bar{p})$$
$$1000\lambda^2 + \lambda - 2 = 0$$

Solving for λ we obtain the two solutions 0.04422 and -0.04522. (Note that these are real and opposite in sign.)

Now substitute the first root into the second equation in (8.16) (since it does not matter which one we choose, we have taken the simplest one). Then

$$0.04422(s - \bar{s}) = 2(p - \bar{p})$$
$$0.04422(s - 100) = 2(p - 100)$$
$$p = 97.789 + 0.0221s$$

We know from the vector forces in figure 8.9 that this represents the unstable arm of the saddle-point solution. We derive the equation of the stable arm in just the same way by substituting the second root. Thus

$$-0.04522(s - \bar{s}) = 2(p - \bar{p})$$
$$-0.04522(s - 100) = 2(p - 100)$$
$$p = 102.261 + 0.0226s$$

To verify these results take the value of s to be 105. On the unstable arm we have a value of p of 100.11. Setting the initial point at $(s(0), p(0)) = (105,100.11)$ we do indeed get a straight line trajectory away from the fixed point. Similarly, if we take $s = 120$ then the value of p on the stable arm is 99.564, so our initial point is $(s(0), p(0)) = (120,99.564)$. Taking this initial point we immediately obtain from the spreadsheet a linear trajectory towards the equilibrium. *The stable arm is what Dornbusch calls the asset market equilibrium line.*

At the moment all we have done is set up the model and established that the fixed point is a saddle-point solution. Furthermore, we have established the path of various trajectories in the phase plane – all of which conform to those indicated in figure 8.9. It is now time to consider some policy change.

8.5 A rise in the money supply

We assume a rise in the money supply takes place in period 1. A rise in the money supply has no bearing on the goods market equilibrium. So the GM line remains the same. A rise the money supply shifts the FX line vertically up by the change in the money supply. The situation is shown in figure 8.11. Let us use our numerical example to consider this problem. Let the money supply rise in period 1 by 5, to the new value of $m = 110$, so the new fixed point of the system is (105,105). Not only does the fixed point shift, but so do the two saddle-paths. More importantly, the vector forces *relative to the new equilibrium* point now dictate the movement of the system over time. How then does the system reach, if at all, the new equilibrium? What we certainly know is that the initial equilibrium is below the FX line and on the goods market line. We also know, however, that convergence on the new equilibrium will occur only if the system immediately moves to the *new* stable arm – to asset market equilibrium.

The roots of the system are unaffected by the change in the money supply, and so these remain 0.04422 and -0.04522. We are interested only in the stable arm, which is associated with root -0.04522. So the new equation of the stable arm can be found from

$$-0.04522(s - \bar{s}) = 2(p - \bar{p})$$
$$-0.04522(s - 105) = 2(p - 105)$$
$$p = 107.374 - 0.0226s$$

Figure 8.11

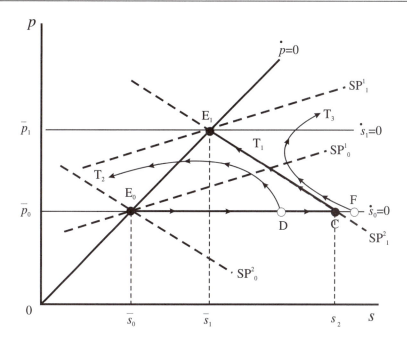

It is now we invoke the reasoning of rational expectations with perfect fore-sight. First we note that the exchange market can adjust extremely quickly, here instantaneously. With perfect foresight, market participants will know that the immediate impact is for the domestic currency to depreciate (a rise in s) to the point on the new stable arm at the existing price level. The idealised reasoning is illustrated in figure 8.11. The system will move immediately from point E_0 to point C, where C is a point on the stable arm passing through the new equilibrium point E_1. We establish point C by solving

$$100 = 107.374 - 0.0226s$$
$$s = 326.283$$

Using the same spreadsheet shown in figure 8.10, change the money supply to 110, and set the point for period 1 to $(s(1), p(1)) = (326.283, 100)$, i.e. point C. The situation is shown in figure 8.12. What is observed is exactly the trajec-tory shown in figure 8.11, and marked as trajectory T_1. The system will move first to point C, and then to the new equilibrium at point E_1. One of the most important predictions of this model is the characteristic of overshooting of the exchange rate. The exchange rate depreciates too far, rising initially to 326.283. As the system moves along trajectory T_1, the exchange rate appreciates (s falls), eventually settling down at the value of 105. The resulting equilibrium is still a depreciation, but it is nowhere near as large as we observe initially.

However, any lack of foresight (perfection!) on the part of market partici-pants will send the system either to plus infinity or minus infinity. If, for example, the system moved to point D, then it will eventually be pushed in a downward direction. Try this for yourself with the revised spreadsheet. Set the condition in period 1 at $(s(1), p(1)) = (300, 100)$, set the time interval to dt$= 0.1$ and extend the period to about $t = 500$. What your spreadsheet will reveal is the trajectory T_2 illustrated in figure 8.11. If the market overadjusted, moving

Figure 8.12

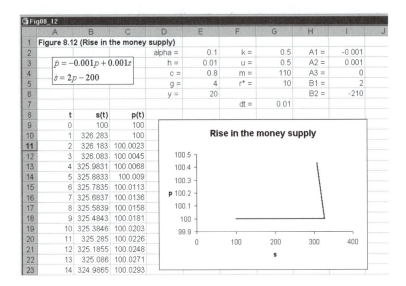

to point F, then the system eventually moves towards plus infinity. Establish this too by taking the condition in period 1 to be $(s(1), p(1)) = (350, 100)$. This is the trajectory T_3 illustrated in figure 8.11.

There is something unsatisfactory about this rational expectations modelling approach. The new equilibrium is reached for any disturbance only if the system moves immediately and directly to the new stable saddle-path. Anything short of this will send the system possibly towards the equilibrium for some time, but then away from it in either the positive or the negative direction. Another way to view this is that the system instantaneously achieves asset market equilibrium. This is a tall order for any economic system!

8.6 Announcement effects

One of the attractions of this model is being able to predict the likely consequences on the economic system of announcing, in advance, a policy change. One of the implications of rational expectations is the importance of policy makers to be transparent about their policies and to announce policies in advance. In the UK it became common, therefore, for the Chancellor of the Exchequer to announce movements in monetary growth for the coming few years. Consider, then, announcing a change in the money supply to take place some time in the future. Market participants, having perfect foresight, will know two things. They will know that in the long run the price level and the exchange rate will rise (and by the same amount). Second they will know that in the short run the domestic exchange rate will sharply depreciate, since it will overshoot its long-run value. Given this knowledge, transactors will attempt to move into real assets in order to preserve the value of their portfolio. They will also move out of domestic assets and into foreign assets. Although ideally this would take place just before the money supply is actually increased, in

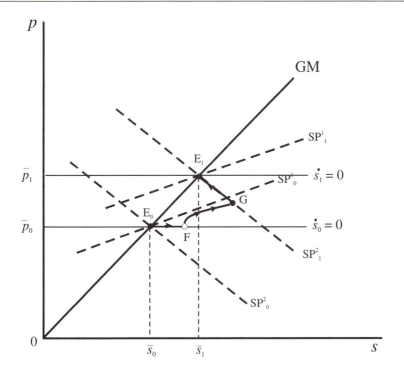

Figure 8.13

order to take advantage of the situation they would do it sooner. This line of reasoning will continue until the most sensible reaction is to move some funds immediately. This results in an immediate depreciation of the currency. In terms of figure 8.13, this moves the economy to point F. Notice that prices have not yet changed. The dynamics of the system is still governed by the initial equilibrium point, E_0, because as yet the policy has not taken place. Hence, the system will begin to diverge from point F towards the unstable arm, labelled SP_0^1. Under perfect foresight, however, the trajectory will coincide with the stable arm of the saddle-point at the moment the policy change takes place, denoted by point G. Once this happens the economy will move along this stable arm, labelled SP_1^2, until point E_1 is reached in the long run.

Let us establish such a path with our numerical example. The computations are set out in figure 8.14. The parameter values are given at the top of the sheet. The only difference here is that we distinguish two money supplies, labelled m1 and m2, and set in cells F3 and F4, respectively. This in turn leads to two derived parameters for B_2, labelled B21 and B22, and set in cells H5 and H6, respectively. Also we have set the time interval to dt $=0.1$ and the number of periods to 1000. We are assuming the immediate response takes place in period 1, so point F is given by $(s(1), p(1)) = (120,100)$, which is to the left of point C, which has coordinates $(s(1), p(1)) = (326.283,100)$.

Since we shall be doing quite a lot of copying and pasting, we shall set out all the formulas here for ease of reference. The change takes place in period 1, which is row 10 of the spreadsheet, and so a number of the formulas come into operation only in row 11, as indicated in the table overleaf.

Figure 8.14

	A	B	C	D	E	F	G	H	I	J
	Fig08_14									
1	Figure 8.14		alpha =	0.1	k =	0.5	A1 =	-0.001		
2			h =	0.01	u =	0.5	A2 =	0.001		
3			c =	0.8	m1 =	105	A3 =	0		
4			g =	4	m2 =	110	B1 =	2		
5			y =	20	r* =	10	B21 =	-200		
6					dt =	0.1	B22 =	-210		
7										
8	t	s(t)	p(t)	sp(t)	pp(t)	SPp(t)	diff	s1(t)	p1(t)	
9	0	100	100	100	100	105.114	5.114	100	100	
10	1	120	100	326.283	100	104.662	4.662	120	100	
11	2	120	100.002	325.283	100.0226	104.662	4.66	120	100.002	
12	3	120.0004	100.004	324.2875	100.0452	104.662	4.657991	120.0004	100.004	
13	4	120.0012	100.006	323.2966	100.0676	104.662	4.655973	120.0012	100.006	
14	5	120.0024	100.008	322.3101	100.0899	104.6619	4.653947	120.0024	100.008	
15	6	120.004	100.01	321.3281	100.1121	104.6619	4.651911	120.004	100.01	
16	7	120.006	100.012	320.3505	100.1342	104.6619	4.649867	120.006	100.012	
17	8	120.0084	100.014	319.3773	100.1563	104.6618	4.647813	120.0084	100.014	
18	9	120.0112	100.016	318.4086	100.1782	104.6617	4.64575	120.0112	100.016	
19	10	120.0144	100.018	317.4442	100.2	104.6617	4.643678	120.0144	100.018	
20	11	120.018	100.02	316.4842	100.2217	104.6616	4.641597	120.018	100.02	
21	12	120.022	100.022	315.5286	100.2434	104.6615	4.639507	120.022	100.022	
22	13	120.0264	100.024	314.5772	100.2649	104.6614	4.637408	120.0264	100.024	
23	14	120.0312	100.026	313.6302	100.2863	104.6613	4.635299	120.0312	100.026	

B10	120
C10	100
D10	326.283
E10	100
F10	107.374 − 0.0226*B10
G10	F10 − C10
H10	IF(G10>0.01,B10,D10)
I10	IF(G10>0.01,C10,E10)
B11	B10+($H$4*C10+$H$5)*$F$6
C11	C10+($H$1*C10+$H$2*B10+$H$3) *$F$6
D11	D10+($H$4*E10+$H$6) *$F$6
E11	E10+($H$1*D10+$H$2*E10+$H$3) *$F$6

Concentrate first on columns B and C. In cells B9 and C9 we have the original equilibrium values of s and p. In cells B10 and C10 we have the coordinates for point F. The trajectory the economy takes from this point is determined by the system's dynamics relative to the initial equilibrium point. The money supply is still 105, given in cell F3, and so the relevant B2-parameter is that given in cell H5. We then employ the Euler approximation to obtain the values in cells B11 and C11. These are then copied to the clipboard and pasted down.

We now place in cells D10 and E10 the values of s and p for point C. From point C, the trajectory the economy follows is with reference to the new equilibrium, and so we need to use money supply m2, given in cell F4, and the derived B2-parameter, given in cell H6. Having set these values, we once again employ Euler's approximation to obtain the values in cells D11 and E11. We already know from our earlier analysis that these observations will simply lie along the stable arm of the saddle-point associated with equilibrium E_2. Having derived cells D11 and E11, these are copied to the clipboard and pasted down.

Our problem now is to establish exactly the point when the trajectory followed by the economy in terms of columns B and C will hit the saddle-path. Once it hits this, then the economy will follow the trajectory given in terms of columns D and E. In order to establish this point we compute in column F the value of p, which is associated with the value of s given in column B. In other words, we utilise the formula

$$p = 107.374 - 0.0226s$$

which is the stable arm of the new saddle-point solution. (This we obtained in section 8.5.) Why do this? We need to establish exactly when the price on the trajectory emanating from F is exactly equal to the price emanating from C. It is not sensible to request the computer to find the exact match, because there never may be because of rounding. So we do this indirectly by considering the difference between column F and column C. When this difference is close to zero we have a match. So cell G10 simply computes the difference between F10 and C10. This is copied to the clipboard and pasted down. We now have the difference as our reference. As we have just said, there is little point requesting a condition on this difference to be zero. So we take a value of 0.01. If the difference is less than this then we can say that the price is the same. However, we consider here a statement in terms of a value greater than 0.01. Cell H10 therefore has the formula

IF(G10>0.01,B10,D10)

Exactly what does this mean? This is a conditional statement. It is read as follows: 'If the value in cell G10 is greater than 0.01, then enter the value in cell B10, else enter the value in D10.' Similarly, cell I10 has the formula

IF(G10>0.01,C10,E10)

which reads: 'If the value in cell G10 is greater than 0.01, then enter the value in cell C10, else enter the value in E10.' Having computed cells H10 and I10 these are copied to the clipboard and pasted down. The computations in columns H and I are exactly what we want. If the difference is greater than 0.01 then the economy is still on the trajectory emanating from point F, which are columns B and C. Once the difference is zero (less than 0.01), we want to plot the economy's trajectory as the stable arm through point E_2, but this is the trajectory defined by columns D and E. If you have set up your spreadsheet exactly as shown in figure 8.14, then you will observe the switch-over taking place at period 560.

Figure 8.15

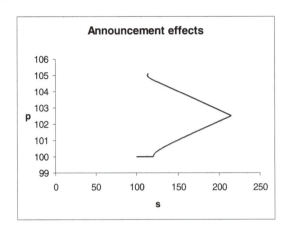

Having completed the computations, all that needs to be done now is to create a chart from the figures in columns H and I. Blocking cells H9:I1009 and invoking the chart wizard creates the economy's trajectory in the presence of announcements. We have placed this on sheet 2, and it is illustrated in figure 8.15. This is the path $(E_0 \rightarrow F \rightarrow G \rightarrow E_1)$ in figure 8.13.

There are a number of issues that can be considered with the aid of this spreadsheet, most especially a change in the announcement period. But we shall leave such considerations as exercises.

8.7 Discrete systems exhibiting saddle solutions

We discussed discrete systems of linear autonomous equations in chapter 4. In general these take the form

$$\Delta x(t+1) = a_1 x(t) + a_2 y(t) + a_3$$
$$\Delta y(t+1) = b_1 x(t) + b_2 y(t) + b_3$$

If $a_3 = b_3 = 0$, then we have a linear set of *homogeneous* autonomous equations. To illustrate the system's behaviour consider the following example

$$\Delta x(t+1) = x(t) + 2y(t)$$

$$\Delta y(t+1) = 3x(t) + \frac{7y(t)}{2}$$

The fixed point of the system, which requires $\Delta x(t+1) = \Delta y(t+1) = 0$ to be satisfied, is clearly the origin. The isoclines are given by

$$y = (-1/2)x \quad \Delta x(t+1) = 0$$
$$y = (-6/7)x \quad \Delta y(t+1) = 0$$

The situation is illustrated in figure 8.16.

If $\Delta x(t+1) > 0$ then $x(t)$ is rising, which occurs when

$$x + 2y > 0$$
$$y > -(1/2)x$$

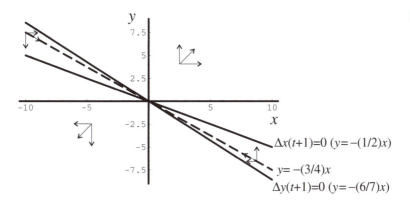

Figure 8.16

This occurs *above* the $\Delta x(t+1)=0$ isocline. Hence, the arrows above this isocline point to the right while those below point to the left.

Similarly, if $\Delta y(t+1)=0$, then $y(t)$ is rising, which occurs when

$$3x+(7/2)y>0$$
$$y>-(6/7)x$$

This occurs *above* the $\Delta y(t+1)=0$ isocline. Hence, above this isocline the arrows point upwards, and below the same isocline they point downwards. The vector forces shown in figure 8.16 suggest a saddle-point solution. But we need to be more specific.

Again we shall state without proof that we can investigate the stability of such systems by noting the following. Let

$$\Delta x(t+1)=\lambda x(t)$$
$$\Delta y(t+1)=\lambda y(t)$$

then

$$\lambda x(t)=x(t)+2y(t)$$

$$\lambda y(t)=3x(t)+\frac{7y(t)}{2}$$

Using the first equation we have

$$y(t)=\frac{(\lambda-1)x(t)}{2}$$

Substituting this into the second equation we have

$$\frac{\lambda(\lambda-1)x(t)}{2}=3x(t)+\frac{7(\lambda-1)x(t)}{2}$$

or

$$2\lambda^2-9\lambda-5=0$$

with characteristic roots $r=-0.5$ and $s=5$. (Note that these results could have been obtained using box 4 above on solving the roots of autonomous equation systems.)

The first thing we note is that the roots have opposite signs. This was a requirement in the continuous model for a saddle-point solution. But we require an *additional* condition in the present discrete case. We require the negative root to have an absolute value less than unity, i.e. $|r| < 1$, which is true for the present model. We shall refer to the root whose absolute value is less than unity as the *stable root*.

We can derive the stable arm by using the stable root. Thus

$$-0.5x = x + 2y$$
$$y = -(3/4)x$$

It is useful to set this model up on a spreadsheet to verify the saddle-point. This is left as an exercise. If a point satisfying $y = -(3/4)x$ is chosen, then the system moves towards the origin along the stable arm.

Exercises

(1)　For the system

$$\dot{x} = x + 2y$$
$$\dot{y} = 3x + y$$

(i)　Establish the fixed point.

(ii)　Derive the equations for the two isoclines and establish the vector of forces.

(iii)　Derive the equation for the stable and unstable arms.

(iv)　Take a point on the stable arm for $x = 2$, and show on a spreadsheet that the trajectory does indeed move towards the origin along the arm. Plot the trajectory from point $(2, -2)$, and show that this trajectory moves away from the stable arm.

(2)　For the system

$$\dot{x} = x + 3y$$
$$\dot{y} = 5x + 3y$$

(i)　What is the fixed point of the system?

(ii)　Set $\dot{x} = \lambda x$ and $\dot{y} = \lambda y$. What are the equations for the two arms of the saddle-point? Which is the stable arm and which the unstable arm?

(iii)　Use a spreadsheet to plot the trajectory of the system starting at the point $(3, -2.9)$. Include on the *same* diagram a plot of the two arms, and so verify that the trajectory approaches, but does not cross, the unstable arm.

(3)   Verify that the following two systems have saddle-point solutions at the origin

(i) $\dot{x} = 2x + y$
        $\dot{y} = 3x$

(ii) $\dot{x} = x + 4y$
        $\dot{y} = 4x - 7y$

Plot trajectories for initial point $(-2, 5)$.

(4)   For the system

$\dot{x} = x + y + 1$
$\dot{y} = 2x - y + 5$

(i)   Find the fixed point.

(ii)   Transform the system into deviations from the fixed point. What are the characteristic roots of this transformed system?

(iii)   Derive the equations for the stable and unstable arms.

(iv)   Set the model up on a spreadsheet and plot, on the same graph, the following trajectories:

        (a) The trajectory from initial point $(-2, 4)$.

        (b) The unstable arm passing through the point at which $x = 2$.

(5)   Consider the following Dornbusch model under perfect foresight

$e = 0.75y + 2.5 + 0.02(s - p)$
$\dot{p} = 0.2(e - y)$
$md = p + 0.75y - 0.2r$
$md = ms = 155$
$r = r^* + \dot{s}^e$
$\dot{s}^e = \dot{s}$
$y = 10, \quad r^* = 12.5$

(i)   What is the equilibrium exchange rate and price of this system?

(ii)   Set up the system on a spreadsheet.

(iii)   Let the money supply fall from 155 to 152 in period 1. Plot the trajectory of the economy.

Chapter 9

Fiscal dynamics and the Maastricht Treaty

9.1 Budgetary concepts

When the Maastricht Treaty first imposed fiscal conditions on Europe they were little understood. Elementary and intermediate textbooks in macroeconomics were, in large part, inadequate to consider the issues. Part of the reason for this was because they involved dynamics. Since dynamics were almost completely absent from their analysis, the reader had no foundation on which to discuss the issues sensibly. We have in this book supplied these foundations, and so it is possible, even at an elementary level, to consider the fiscal criteria of the Maastricht Treaty and its implications for Europe. These are important issues and so we shall consider the analysis in detail. In order to do this adequately, however, we do need to consider issues of government deficit financing. But these should be within the grasp of any undergraduate who has done an intermediate course in macroeconomics. As in previous chapters, we shall be concentrating on setting the problems up on a spreadsheet and then experimenting with them. The chapter does, however involve a little more algebraic manipulation than in other chapters. But the benefit derived in understanding the fiscal criteria of the Maastricht Treaty make it more than justified.

Our starting point is the budget deficit, which we shall denote BD. In setting out the dynamics of the budget deficit we need to be clear at all times between stocks and flows. A *stock* is a variable that is at a point in time. The amount of high-powered money (notes and coins) in the economy on 31 December 2000 is a stock. The amount of government debt at the end of the year is also a stock. National income, on the other hand, is a *flow*. It is the value of goods and services produced by an economy over some time period, say one year. Government spending on goods and services is also a flow. A flow requires a time *interval* to be specified. This distinction between stocks and flows is so important that we have set out the main variables we shall be discussing in figure 9.1. We highlight whether they are a stock, occurring at the end of period $t-1$ and/or the end of period t; or a flow, in which case they occur over the interval of time t. The diagram considers three time intervals: $t-1$, t and $t+1$; two end-of-period points in time, the end of period $t-1$ and the end of period t; and just one time interval, namely time *period t*. Figure 9.1 also includes a brief definition of most of the variables we shall be using in this chapter.

The budget deficit over time period t, $BD(t)$, comprises the excess of govern-

Figure 9.1

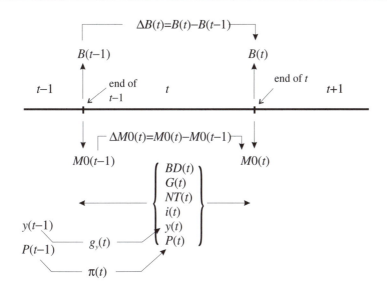

G	Government spending
NT	Net taxes
i	Nominal interest rate
r	Real interest rate $(= i\text{-}\pi)$
Y	Nominal GDP
y	Real GDP $(= Y/P)$
P	Price level
$M0$	Money base
B	Bonds (debt)
BD	Budget deficit
π	Inflation
g_y	Growth of real income

ment spending on goods and services, $G(t)$, *less* taxes net of transfers, $NT(t)$, *plus* the interest payments on outstanding debt. The outstanding debt is a stock, and occurs at the end of period $t-1$, which we designate $B(t-1)$, and denotes the value of government bonds at the end of time period $t-1$. However, the payment on that debt depends on the rate of interest, which is a flow. Let $i(t)$ denote the *nominal* interest rate over time period t. In fact, for our analysis we shall be assuming the rate of interest is constant, so we shall simply denote it by i. Given this rate of interest, then the interest payment on outstanding debt over period t is given by $iB(t)$. Another distinction of importance in this chapter is variables denominated in real terms as against those in nominal terms. At the moment we are considering all variables in *nominal* terms. Our (nominal) budget deficit is then

$$BD(t) = G(t) - NT(t) + iB(t-1) \tag{9.1}$$

The budget deficit, therefore, is government spending inclusive of interest payments *less* taxes net of transfers. This term is sometimes called the **official deficit** because it is in nominal terms and does not take account of inflation.

Over any time interval t, the budget deficit, $BD(t)$, must be financed. It can be financed in only two ways: either by printing more money or by borrowing. Let $M0$ denote money base (or high-powered money), which is basically notes and coins issued by the Central Bank. The money base is a stock. Let $M0(t-1)$ denote the money base at the end of period $t-1$ and $M0(t)$ the money base at the end of period t. Then $\Delta M0(t) = M0(t) - M0(t-1)$ is the amount of money created over period t to help finance the deficit. Of course, the other source of funds for the government is to borrow from the public. If $B(t)$ is the amount of bonds outstanding at the end of period t, and $B(t-1)$ is the amount of bonds outstanding at the end of period $t-1$, then $\Delta B(t) = B(t) - B(t-1)$ is the amount of new debt created over time period t which has been created to help finance the deficit. Considering the budget deficit from the point of view of financing it, then we have the important budget constraint

(9.2) $$G(t) - NT(t) + iB(t-1) = \Delta M0(t) + \Delta B(t)$$

which simply says the budget deficit must be financed either from printing more money or from borrowing from the public. A **pure money-financed budget deficit** means

(9.3) $$G(t) - NT(t) + iB(t-1) = \Delta M0(t)$$

while a **pure bond-financed budget deficit** means

(9.4) $$G(t) - NT(t) + iB(t-1) = \Delta B(t)$$

At this stage, we need to make one further distinction. The interest payment on outstanding debt can be considered to have arisen from borrowings made by all past governments, those presently in power and those in power over earlier periods. Such a payment is not necessarily the result of present policies. On the other hand, the excess of government spending on goods and services over net taxes *is* a result of present policies. To highlight this feature $G(t) - NT(t)$ is called the **primary deficit** (or **primary surplus** if net taxes is in excess of government spending).

9.2 Budget dynamics with no inflation and no monetary financing

We begin our analysis with a very simple case first. We shall assume no money financing of the budget deficit so $\Delta M0(t) = 0$, and we shall assume no inflation so all variables are both nominal and real. In this instance we do not need to consider the price level explicitly at all, which we shall do in a later section. From (9.4) we have

$$\Delta B(t) = G(t) - NT(t) + iB(t-1)$$
$$B(t) = G(t) - NT(t) + (1+i)B(t-1)$$

Since national income (gross domestic product or GDP), denoted $Y(t)$, is different in different periods, and also different for different countries, then it is much more usual to consider the situation relative to GDP in period t. Dividing our previous result throughout by $Y(t)$, we have

$$\frac{B(t)}{Y(t)} = \frac{G(t)}{Y(t)} - \frac{NT(t)}{Y(t)} + \frac{(1+i)B(t-1)}{Y(t)}$$

$$= \frac{G(t)}{Y(t)} - \frac{NT(t)}{Y(t)} + (1+i)\frac{Y(t-1)}{Y(t)}\frac{B(t-1)}{Y(t-1)}$$

or

$$b(t) = (g(t) - nt(t)) + (1+i)\left(\frac{Y(t-1)}{Y(t)}\right)b(t-1) \tag{9.5}$$

where

$$b(t) = \frac{B(t)}{Y(t)}, \ b(t-1) = \frac{B(t-1)}{Y(t-1)}, \ g(t) = \frac{G(t)}{Y(t)}, \ nt(t) = \frac{NT(t)}{Y(t)}$$

Notice that in deriving (9.5) we needed to be careful about our time periods. Now let GDP grow over time by a constant amount. Let the growth of income be denoted g_y, then

$$g_y = \frac{Y(t) - Y(t-1)}{Y(t-1)}$$

i.e. $\dfrac{Y(t-1)}{Y(t)} = \dfrac{1}{1+g_y}$

Substituting this result into (9.5) leads to the result

$$b(t) = (g(t) - nt(t)) + \left(\frac{1+i}{1+g_y}\right)b(t-1) \tag{9.6}$$

We could leave (9.6) as it is, but it will be much more convenient, especially later when we consider inflation and monetary financing, to use an approximation for the coefficient of $b(t-1)$. In fact, we shall be using four approximations in this chapter. Since we shall be using these approximations frequently throughout this chapter, let us take a minor digression (see box 5).

Box 5 Approximations

Consider any three variables x, y and z that are quite small. Since our variables will be percentages, then these will be something like 0.05 (for 5%). They therefore satisfy this condition of being quite small. If this is the case, then we can state here (without proof) that

(i) $\dfrac{x}{1+x} \simeq x$

(ii) $\dfrac{1+x}{1+y} \simeq 1 + x - y$

(iii) $\dfrac{x}{(1+y)(1+z)} \simeq x$

(iv) $\dfrac{1+x}{(1+y)(1+z)} \simeq 1+x-y-z$

The figure below shows these approximations set up on a spreadsheet, illustrating how close the true value and the approximate value are to one another if $x=0.01$, $y=0.02$ and $z=0.03$. It is observed that the approximations are quite good.

Return now to our dynamics. It will be noted that (9.6) involves the ratio in approximation (ii). So we can re-write this equation in the simpler form

$$b(t) = (g(t) - nt(t)) - (1 + i - g_y)b(t-1)$$

(9.7)

$$= (g(t) - nt(t)) - (g_y - i - 1)b(t-1)$$

Equation (9.7) is our first fundamental recursive equation. It is a recursive equation in terms of the variable b, i.e. the debt ratio. Considering (9.7) in its difference form, we have

(9.8) $$\Delta b(t) = (g(t) - nt(t)) - (g_y - i)b(t-1)$$

Notice first the fixed point of this system. This satisfies $\Delta b(t) = 0$ or

(9.9) $$b^* = \frac{g(t) - nt(t)}{g_y - i}$$

which can be positive or negative depending on whether there is a primary deficit or surplus, and whether GDP is growing faster than the nominal rate of interest or not. It can even be undefined if $g_y = i$.

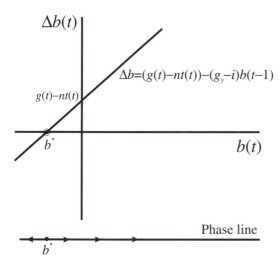

Figure 9.2

$\Delta b(t)$

$\Delta b = (g(t) - nt(t)) - (g_y - i)b(t-1)$

$g(t) - nt(t)$

b^*

$b(t)$

Phase line

b^*

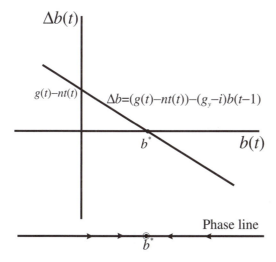

$\Delta b(t)$

$g(t) - nt(t)$

$\Delta b = (g(t) - nt(t)) - (g_y - i)b(t-1)$

b^*

$b(t)$

Phase line

b^*

Let us concentrate on the more usual situation of a primary deficit. Then two situations are shown in figure 9.2, one in which income growth is less than the nominal rate of interest ($g_y < i$), and a second in which income growth is greater than the nominal rate of interest ($g_y > i$). In the first instance the difference equation has a positive slope and a negative fixed point; in the second instance it has a negative slope and a positive fixed point. What is clear from figure 9.2, especially from the phase lines included in the diagram, is that the first has an unstable fixed point while the second has a stable fixed point.

The unstable situation is serious, and not untypical of European countries in the 1990s. If an economy begins with some outstanding debt/GDP ratio that is positive, a primary deficit/GDP ratio that is constant, a constant nominal interest and constant growth of income, then the economy's debt will continue to rise over time. Although many of these variables will not be constant over time, it does highlight the issue. Considering the unstable situation more carefully, it would appear that this is typical of a country with high inflation in which nominal interest rates are also high and one in which growth of GDP is low. Such an economy could find itself in a vicious circle of bond financing of the government budget and an ever-increasing debt. Stability requires a bringing down of the inflation rate and increasing the economy's growth of GDP. But we have yet to model inflation explicitly.

9.3 A numerical example

Consider a simple example. Suppose the primary deficit as a percentage of GDP is 1.2%, or 0.012, and that the difference between the nominal interest rate and the growth of GDP is 2%, or 0.02, i.e. we have a low-growth economy. Furthermore, we assume these will remain constant over the following periods. With an initial debt/GDP ratio of 50%, or 0.5, then there will be a continual growth of debt/GDP as shown in figure 9.3. In cells D3 and D4 we place the primary deficit as a percentage of GDP and the nominal interest rate *less* GDP growth, respectively. In cell B7 we have the initial debt/GDP ratio of 50%. In cell B8 we place the formula

B8	$= (g(0) - nt(0)) + (1 + i - g_y)b(0)$ $= \$D\$3 + (1 + \$D\$4)*B7$

In cells F3, F4 and F5 we place the equilibrium debt ratio, the debt ratio that the government wish to stabilise around, denoted bs, and the primary budget deficit which will stabilise the debt ratio at the chosen level, denoted PBDs. Finally, we block cells A7:B17 to create the inserted chart that plots the path of the debt/GDP ratio over time. It can be seen from figure 9.3 that by period 10 the situation is one in which the debt/GDP ratio is just under 75%! If left unchecked, it could even exceed 100%.

The equilibrium (fixed point) in this example is

$$b^* = \frac{g(t) - nt(t)}{g_y - i} = \frac{0.012}{-0.02} = -0.6$$

or –60%. This implies that *in equilibrium* this economy is a creditor. But it is not in equilibrium. The initial debt ratio is 50%, and as can be seen in figure 9.3, this will continue to grow over time.

Suppose we wish to stabilise the debt ratio at the initial value of 50%. What would need to be the primary deficit/surplus that would do this? If the debt ratio is to be stabilised at 50%, then $\Delta b(t)$ needs to be zero for $b = 0.5$. Hence

$$0 = (g(t) - nt(t)) + 0.02(0.5)$$
$$g(t) - nt(t) = -0.01$$

In other words, there needs to be a primary budget *surplus* relative to GDP of 1%. Put another way, the economy needs to implement a major deflationary

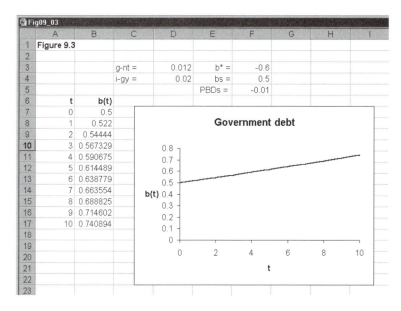

Figure 9.3

package and turn the country's primary budget deficit ratio into a primary budget surplus ratio of almost the same magnitude!

Before we consider any more numerical examples, we need to make the situation more realistic. It is now time to include money financing along with bond financing of the budget deficit, and we need to allow for inflation.

9.4 Budget dynamics with inflation and money plus bond financing

Our analysis is very much the same as in section 9.3, there are simply more terms to consider. We begin with the budget constraint in terms of (9.2), which we reproduce here

$$G(t) - NT(t) + iB(t-1) = \Delta M0(t) + \Delta B(t) \tag{9.10}$$

Next we make a distinction between real income at time t, $y(t)$, and nominal income at time t, namely $P(t)y(t)$, where $P(t)$ is the price level at time t. In terms of our analysis of section 9.3, $Y(t) = P(t)y(t)$. We now divide (9.10) by $P(t)y(t)$, giving

$$\frac{G(t)}{P(t)y(t)} - \frac{NT(t)}{P(t)y(t)} + \frac{iB(t-1)}{P(t)y(t)} = \frac{\Delta M0(t)}{P(t)y(t)} + \frac{\Delta B(t)}{P(t)y(t)}$$

It is important when carrying out this to keep the time periods clearly specified. First we rearrange this result

$$\frac{B(t)}{P(t)y(t)} = \left(\frac{G(t)}{P(t)y(t)} - \frac{NT(t)}{P(t)y(t)}\right) - \frac{\Delta M0(t)}{P(t)y(t)} + \frac{(1+i)B(t-1)}{P(t)y(t)}$$

$$\frac{B(t)}{P(t)y(t)} = \left(\frac{G(t)}{P(t)y(t)} - \frac{NT(t)}{P(t)y(t)}\right) -$$

$$\left(\frac{\Delta M0(t)}{M0(t-1)}\right)\left(\frac{M0(t)}{P(t)y(t)}\right)\left(\frac{M0(t-1)}{M0(t)}\right)$$

$$+(1+i)\left(\frac{P(t-1)y(t-1)}{P(t)y(t)}\right)\left(\frac{B(t-1)}{P(t-1)y(t-1)}\right)$$

We now make the following definitions

$$b(t)=\frac{B(t)}{P(t)y(t)}, \quad b(t-1)=\frac{B(t-1)}{P(t-1)y(t-1)},$$

$$g(t)=\frac{G(t)}{P(t)y(t)}, \quad nt(t)=\frac{NT(t)}{P(t)y(t)}$$

$$\lambda=\frac{\Delta M0(t)}{M0(t-1)}, \quad m=\frac{M0(t)}{P(t)y(t)}$$

Where we have assumed that λ and m are both constant. Using these definitions we have

$$b(t)=[(g(t)-nt(t))-\lambda m\left(\frac{M0(t-1)}{M0(t)}\right)]+$$

(9.11)

$$(1+i)\left(\frac{P(t-1)y(t-1)}{P(t)y(t)}\right)b(t-1)$$

Given the definitions for inflation, *real* income growth and monetary growth

$$\pi(t)=\frac{P(t)-P(t-1)}{P(t-1)}, \quad g_y=\frac{y(t)-y(t-1)}{y(t-1)}, \quad \lambda=\frac{M0(t)-M0(t-1)}{M0(t-1)}$$

then

$$\frac{P(t-1)}{P(t)}=\frac{1}{1+\pi}, \quad \frac{y(t-1)}{y(t)}=\frac{1}{1+g_y}, \quad \frac{M0(t-1)}{M0(t)}=\frac{1}{1+\lambda}$$

Substituting these into (9.11), we obtain

$$b(t)=[(g(t)-nt(t))-\left(\frac{\lambda}{1+\lambda}\right)m]+\frac{(1+i)}{(1+\pi)(1+g_y)}b(t-1)$$

Using approximations (i) and (iii) in box 5 (p. 177), we can simplify this expression to

$$b(t)=[(g(t)-nt(t))-\lambda m]+(1+i-\pi-g_y)b(t-1)$$

which is a recursive equation. We can do one final substitution. Let the real interest rate be defined, $r=i-\pi$ then our recursive equation becomes

(9.12)

$$b(t)=[(g(t)-nt(t))-\lambda m]+(1+r-g_y)b(t-1)$$

and the difference equation associated with this is

$$\Delta b(t)=[(g(t)-nt(t))-\lambda m]+(r-g_y)b(t-1)$$
(9.13)
$$=[(g(t)-nt(t))-\lambda m]-(g_y-r)b(t-1)$$

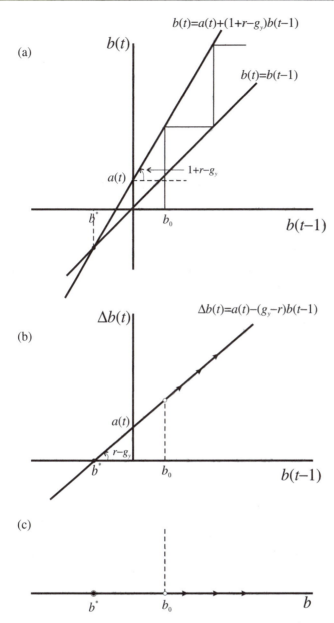

Figure 9.4

Sometimes it will be convenient for diagrammatic purposes to consider the term in square brackets as a single entity; this is because it will represent the intercept. We then define

$$a(t) = (g(t) - nt(t)) - \lambda m \qquad (9.14)$$

The fixed point of system (9.13) is

$$b^* = \frac{(g(t) - nt(t)) - \lambda m}{g_y - r}$$

The recursive equation can be illustrated with a cobweb diagram, figure 9.4(a); the difference equation shows the dynamics of b over time, figure 9.4(b); and finally the phase line, figure 9.4(c), shows the movement of b over time. In drawing figure 9.4 we have assumed the intercept, given by (9.14), is positive and so is the slope $r - g_y$, so the slope $1 + r - g_y$ exceeds unity.

There are, however, four possible cases, which we can summarise as follows

Case A	Primary deficit, high growth	Stable, $b^* > 0$
Case B	Primary surplus, high growth	Stable, $b^* < 0$
Case C	Primary deficit, low growth	Unstable, $b^* < 0$
Case D	Primary surplus, low growth	Unstable, $b^* > 0$

and which are illustrated in figure 9.5

In terms of the situations illustrated in figure 9.5, what appears to have happened for a number of European countries is that they have changed from case A in the 1960s into case C by the 1990s. Since for most European countries λm is generally very small, we shall ignore this for the moment. Considering the situation for France, Germany and the UK over the 1960s and 1990s we have figures in the order of (all figures in percentages)

| | $g(t) - nt(t)$ | | $(g_y - r)$ | |
	1960s	**1990s**	**1960s**	**1990s**
France	−0.8	1.8	4.07	−4.62
Germany	5.6	0.2	0.13	−1.42
UK	1.2	2.1	0.07	−3.79

For these three countries by the 1990s there was a primary deficit as a percentage of GDP and there was low growth relative to the real rate of interest. All three countries typified the situation in case C of figure 9.5. The situation was unstable, and given that all three countries have a positive debt/GDP ratio, then this will grow over time unless something is done.

9.5 Some numerical examples

Consider the case of the UK, first in the 1960s and then in the 1990s. We assume that in both periods $\lambda m = 0$. In the 1960s, the primary deficit as a percentage of GDP is 1.2%, or 0.012 and the growth of real income *less* the real rate of interest as a percentage of GDP is 0.07% or 0.0007. The equilibrium debt ratio is

$$b^* = \frac{g(t) - nt(t)}{g_y - r} = \frac{0.012}{0.0007} = 17.14$$

Figure 9.5

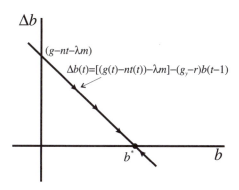

Case A
primary deficit ($>gnt$)
high growth ($g_y>r$)
b^* government debtor
b^* stable

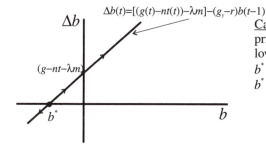

Case B
primary surplus ($g<nt$)
high growth ($g_y>r$)
b^* government creditor
b^* stable

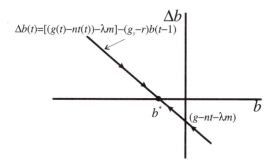

Case C
primary deficit ($>gnt$)
low growth ($g_y<r$)
b^* government creditor
b^* unstable

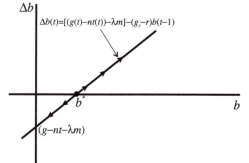

Case D
primary surplus ($g<nt$)
low growth ($g_y<r$)
b^* government debtor
b^* unstable

Figure 9.6

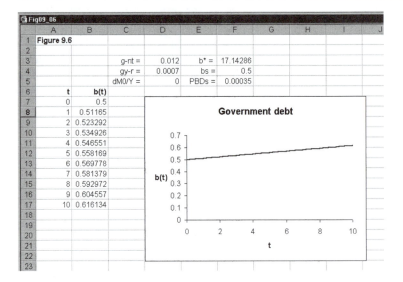

or 1714%. Although a large debt ratio for the equilibrium, the situation is stable. However, with such a large positive debt ratio, if the initial debt ratio is 50%, or 0.5, debt will still grow over time, as shown in figure 9.6.

By the 1990s, the primary deficit as a percentage of GDP had risen to 2.1%, or 0.021 and the growth of real income *less* the real rate of interest as a percentage of GDP had decreased markedly to –3.79% or –0.0379. The equilibrium debt ratio is

$$b^* = \frac{g(t) - nt(t)}{g_y - r} = \frac{0.021}{-0.0379} = -0.554$$

or –55.4%, which is a dramatic turn-around. The situation is unstable. Once again if the initial debt ratio were 50%, then by period 10 the debt ratio would be almost 100%!

If the government wished to stabilise the debt ratio at 50%, then what would it need to do about its budget deficit? To answer this question, once again we need to set $\Delta b(t)$ to zero at the level $b=0.5$. Thus

$$0 = (g(t) - nt(t)) + 0.0379(0.5)$$
$$g(t) - nt(t) = -0.019$$

i.e. a primary surplus/GDP ratio of 1.9%. But what if the government were prepared to let money grow at 0.5% of GDP, what would the surplus/deficit be in this instance? First we note that $\lambda m = 0.005$, and so

$$0 = (g(t) - nt(t)) - 0.005 + 0.0379(0.5)$$
$$g(t) - nt(t) = -0.014$$

In other words, the government can pursue a smaller primary surplus/GDP ratio, 1.4% as against 1.9%, so long as it is prepared to finance some of this deficit from creating high-powered money. Of course, such a policy will probably fuel future inflation.

Figure 9.7

	A	B	C	D	E	F	G	H	I	J
1	Figure 9.7									
2			bs =	50						
3			dM0/Y =	0						
4										
5			1960s				1990s			
6		g-nt	gy-r	b*	PBDs	g-nt	gy-r	b*	PBDs	
7	France	-0.8	4.07	-19.656	2.035	1.8	-4.62	-38.961	-2.31	
8	Germany	5.6	0.13	4307.692	0.065	0.2	-1.42	-14.0845	-0.71	
9	UK	1.2	0.07	1714.286	0.035	2.1	-3.79	-55.409	-1.895	
10										

The UK is not alone in this problem of explosive debt in the 1990s. France and Germany are just two other countries of Europe showing this typical explosive pattern. Just as for the UK, each country would need to run a budget surplus in order to stabilise the debt at, say, 50%. If we assume no monetary financing of the debt, France in particular would need to convert its 1.8% primary deficit/GDP ratio into a primary surplus/GDP ratio of the order of 2.3%, as illustrated in figure 9.7.

The spreadsheet illustrated in figure 9.7 is quite straightforward. The figures for the primary deficit/surplus as a percentage of GDP and the growth of real GDP *less* the real interest rate are as given above. It is to be noted that all figures are in percentages. In cell D2 we supply the desired deficit ratio as a percentage and in cell D3 we supply the increase in high-powered money relative to nominal income, again as a percentage. The equilibrium debt ratio for France is placed in cell D7, and is simply B7*100/C7 as a percentage figure. This is then copied to the clipboard and pasted into cells D8 and D9. Cells D7 to D9 are then copied to the clipboard and pasted into cells H7 to H9. The primary budget deficit/surplus figures that arise from stabilising the debt ratio to the figure in cell D2 need to be carefully constructed. They need to take account of the fact that all figures are in percentages. The entry for cell E7 is therefore

E7	$= \lambda m + (g_y - r)bs$ $= ((\$D\$3/100) + (D7/100)*(\$D\$2/100))*100$

where again the figure is supplied in percentage form. This is then copied to the clipboard and pasted into cells E8 and E9. Finally, cells E7 to E9 are copied to the clipboard and pasted into cells I7 to I9. This completes all the computations of figure 9.7. In figure 9.7 we have no money financing of the budget deficit, but it is easy to incorporate any amount of money financing. We leave this as an exercise.

We now have all the necessary analysis to discuss the budget criteria of the Maastricht Treaty.

9.6 Budget criteria of the Maastricht Treaty

The Maastricht Treaty imposed two fiscal constraints on member states:

(1)   Government debt must not exceed 60% of GDP.
(2)   The government budget deficit must not exceed 3% of GDP.

In terms of our modelling the first is quite straightforward. It implies that $b \leq 0.6$. The second is not so straightforward. From (9.4), if we divide throughout by nominal income, $P(t)y(t)$, then we have

$$\frac{\Delta B(t)}{P(t)y(t)} = \frac{G(t)}{P(t)y(t)} - \frac{NT(t)}{P(t)y(t)} + \frac{iB(t-1)}{P(t)y(t)}$$

In other words, if the government budget deficit is not to exceed 3%, then this means that

$$\frac{\Delta B(t)}{P(t)y(t)} \leq 0.03$$

But

$$\frac{\Delta B(t)}{P(t)y(t)} = \frac{G(t)}{P(t)y(t)} - \frac{NT(t)}{P(t)y(t)} + \frac{iB(t-1)}{P(t-1)y(t-1)}\left(\frac{P(t-1)y(t-1)}{P(t)y(t)}\right)$$

$$= (g(t) - nt(t)) + ib(t-1)\left(\frac{P(t-1)y(t-1)}{P(t)y(t)}\right)$$

But we already know that

$$\frac{P(t-1)}{P(t)} = \frac{1}{1+\pi}, \quad \frac{y(t-1)}{y(t)} = \frac{1}{1+g_y}$$

so

$$\frac{\Delta B(t)}{P(t)y(t)} = (g(t) - nt(t)) + \frac{ib(t-1)}{(1+\pi)(1+g_y)}$$

Using approximation (iii) in box 5 (p. 177), we have that the coefficient of $b(t-1)$ is simply i. Hence

(9.15)
$$\frac{\Delta B(t)}{P(t)y(t)} = (g(t) - nt(t)) + ib(t-1)$$

which must be less than or equal to 3%.

In considering the dynamics of the Maastricht Treaty, therefore, we have two crucial equations and their constraints

$$\Delta b(t) = (g(t) - nt(t)) - (g_y - r)b(t-1) \quad b(t) \leq 0.6$$

(9.16)
$$\frac{\Delta B(t)}{P(t)y(t)} = (g(t) - nt(t)) + ib(t-1) \leq 0.03$$

where we have assumed no monetisation of the debt. The situation is more clearly revealed in terms of figure 9.8. We are here assuming instability with a

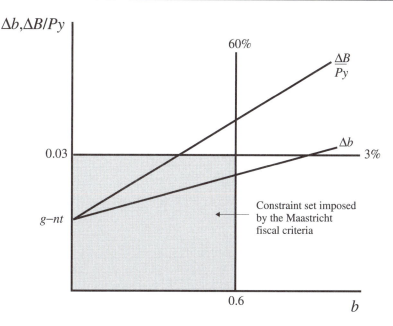

Figure 9.8

situation of a primary deficit as a percent of GDP and low growth. Since $r - g_y = i - \pi - g_y$ then the slope of the first equation will always be less than the slope of the second equation in (9.16). Furthermore, both lines emanate from the same value, the value of the primary deficit as a percent of GDP. The 60% criterion places an upper limit on the value along the horizontal axis of figure 9.8, while the 3% criterion places a limit along the vertical axis. In order to satisfy both constraints, therefore, an economy must lie within the rectangle formed by these two constraints.

Given the instability shown in figure 9.8, which we have already indicated is illustrative of the 1990s, then sooner or later either one or both of the criteria will be violated. Let us see the situation over time by considering two simple examples.

9.6.1 Example 1

First take the UK around the mid-1990s. We have the following information. The primary deficit as a percentage of GDP is 4.3%; nominal interest rates are 7.8%; inflation is 2.5%; and GDP is growing at a rate of 4%. Debt/GDP is initially 50%. The situation is shown in figure 9.9. The first observation is that at the initial debt/GDP ratio of 50%, the budget deficit/GDP ratio of no greater than 3% is violated in a major way. The budget deficit/GDP ratio stands at 8.2% since

$$\frac{\Delta B(t)}{P(t)y(t)} = (g(t) - nt(t)) + ib(t-1) = 0.043 + 0.078(0.5) = 0.082$$

However the initial debt ratio is below 60%. Using a spreadsheet similar to figure 9.9, we find that the 60% is reached by period 2, by which time the budget deficit/GDP ratio has risen to 8.6%.

Figure 9.9

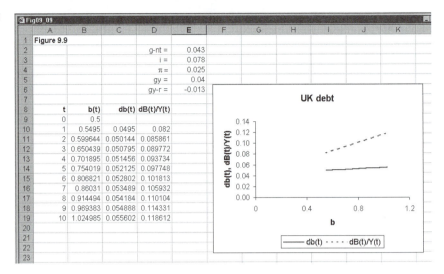

Suppose we ask the following qustion. 'What would have to be the size of the budget deficit/surplus as a percentage of GDP in order to stabilise the debt at the initial 50%?' We can answer this question simply by rearranging (9.13) after setting $\Delta b(t) = 0$ and $b = 0.5$, i.e.

$$0 = (g(t) - nt(t)) + (0.013)(0.5)$$
$$(g(t) - nt(t)) = -0.0065$$

In other words, a primary deficit/GDP of 4.3% needs to be turned into a primary surplus of just over 0.5%. If no corrective action is taken, and the debt/GDP ratio rises to 60% by period 2, then the corrective action on the part of the budget to stabilise the debt at this level would need to be

$$0 = (g(t) - nt(t)) + (0.013)(0.6)$$
$$(g(t) - nt(t)) = -0.0078$$

which is a larger surplus. Given the instability inherent in the economy, this result is quite general. The longer the delay to stabilise the budget the larger the adjustment has to be.

But there is another consideration worth noting. Even if the debt/GDP ratio were stabilised at 50% by means of a major deflation of the economy, the situation is still unstable! The debt ratio will continue to rise and yet further deflation will be necessary. This is not a reassuring prospect.

9.6.2 Example 2

Consider the following hypothetical situation. A country has a primary deficit/GDP of 0.5%; nominal interest rates are 7% with inflation at 2%; GDP is growing at a respectable 3.5%; and the initial debt/GDP ratio is 0.32. The initial budget deficit/GDP ratio is

$$\frac{\Delta B(t)}{P(t)y(t)} = (g(t) - nt(t)) + ib(t-1) = 0.005 + 0.07(0.32) = 0.0274$$

or 2.74%. This means both criteria of the Maastricht Treaty are satisfied. The situation is still, however, unstable. The debt ratio line has a slope of 0.015, and so the debt/GDP ratio will inevitably rise over time. Which of the Maastricht criteria will be violated first? It should not be surprising that it is the budget deficit/GDP ratio of 3% that will be violated first. Even at the initial debt ratio of 32%, the budget deficit/GDP ratio is already close to 3% at 2.74%. This is because of the high nominal interest rate as much as anything. If the economy carries on the same path, then it will hit the upper limit on the budget deficit/GDP ratio of 3% in period 5. On the other hand, it will take up to period 24 before the 60% limit on the debt/GDP ratio is hit. For this economy, the more serious problem is to do with the budget deficit/GDP ratio.

If it took immediate action to stabilise the debt/GDP ratio at 0.32, then

$$0 = (g(t) - nt(t)) + (0.015)(0.32)$$
$$(g(t) - nt(t)) = -0.0048$$

and so it would need to convert its primary deficit into a primary surplus of almost the same magnitude.

Of course we have been assuming in these examples that the real interest rate and the growth of real output remains constant, which is highly unlikely. The model as it stands, however, cannot endogenise these variables.

9.7 Some final observations on the Maastricht Treaty

In the above analysis we have noted that in order to satisfy the deficit ratio of the Maastricht Treaty a number of countries will need to convert a primary deficit/GDP ratio into a primary surplus/GDP ratio. This will require very deflationary policies on the part of many countries. But we ignored in our analysis monetary financing of the budget deficit. Any monetary financing of the budget deficit will reduce the size of the intercept on the vertical axis and so reduce the need for part of the deflationary package. But such monetary financing of the budget deficit is not considered prudent. Furthermore, this will require an increase in monetary growth that could fuel inflation. The rise in inflation in turn could raise the nominal rate of interest. The Maastricht Treaty therefore imposed two additional constraints: one on inflation and the other on nominal interest rates. These are:

(1)   Inflation must be less than the average inflation rate of the lowest three countries of the EU, *plus* 1.5%.
(2)   Nominal interest rates must be less than the average interest rates of the three countries referred to under (1) *plus* 2%.

Since money financing raises inflation, this is curbed by the first of these two additional criteria. The second curbs both the use of money financing, since a rise in inflation raises nominal interest rates, but also reduces the degree of bond financing because this, too, will raise the interest payment on the debt. What all this means is that there is even greater pressure on countries to adjust the primary deficit/GDP ratio.

An unstable situation could be converted to a stable situation if the growth in real income is raised relative to the real rate of interest. If this were to be achieved without raising inflation in the process, then economies will need to consider supply-side policies. These, however, take a long time to implement, and an even longer time to have an impact on growth. In the meantime the two main fiscal criteria set out in the Maastricht Treaty will be violated.

It has been very tempting for individual member states to satisfy the criteria by one-off events and a process of 'creative accounting.' These include such policies as telephone payments (as in France and Denmark), privatising government-owned businesses (Austria) and changes in the provision of pension funds (Portugal). Germany even tried to revalue its gold reserves. But most of these are one-off events. They cannot be sustained over periods of time. It is necessary, therefore, for member states to find ways to stabilise their budget dynamics.

Exercises

(1)   A country has no inflation, is growing at 2.5% and has a nominal interest of 4%. It is presently running a budget deficit as a proportion of GDP of 6%.

    (i)   What is the expression for $b(t)$ in terms of $b(t-1)$?

    (ii)   What is the equilibrium debt/income ratio? Is this country a creditor or debtor in equilibrium?

    (iii) If the initial debt/income ratio is 30%, will this rise or fall over time?

    (iv)   Draw Δb against b and the phase line for this model.

(2)   For the economy in the numerical example in section 9.3, where $b(0) = 50\%$

    (i)   At what time period does the debt/income ratio equal 100%?

    (ii)   If the nominal interest rate is higher so $i - g_y = 2.5\%$, at what time period does the debt/income ratio equal 100%?

    (iii) If the primary deficit/GDP is lower at 1%, at what time period does the debt/income ratio equal 100%?

(3)   A country is growing at 3% and has a debt/GDP ratio of 50%. Assuming no money financing, what is the primary budget deficit/surplus that keeps the debt/income ratio constant when

(i)   The real interest rate is 2%?

(ii)   The real interest rate is 5%?

(4)   A country has 2% inflation, is growing at 2.5% and has a nominal interest rate of 6% and a debt/income ratio of 40%. It presently has a budget deficit as a percentage of GDP of 3% and involves no money financing. This budget deficit exists for periods 0 to 5 and is then reduced to 1% for the next five years. Plot the debt/income ratio for $t = 0$ to 10.

(5)   Consider the numerical example in section 9.3.

(i)   Suppose the debt/income ratio was to be stabilised at $b = 55\%$. What is the level of the primary deficit/surplus to GDP that will achieve this?

(ii)   What is the primary deficit/surplus to GDP that will stabilise the debt/income ratio at 60%?

(iii) What do you conclude about a country's adjustment to its primary budget deficit/surplus if it waits until it reaches the debt/income ratio limit set under the Maastricht Treaty?

Chapter 10
A little bit of chaos

10.1 Introduction

One of the most recent advances in Mathematics has been the subject of chaos theory. One might recall in the Spielberg film, *Jurassic Park*, the mathematician trying to explain chaos with a drop of water over the back of the hand of one of the other scientists. The second drop, when dropped as close to the first as possible, would still very soon move off the hand in a different direction. This is a very useful account of the way dynamic systems can become drastically different from some very small change in the initial condition. What is important about this is that even if the system is deterministic it can still give the impression of being chaotic. Chaos does not require something to have a random nature. If something is purely random, then it is impossible to predict. A deterministic system, on the other hand, is completely predictable. However, if the system is very sensitive to the initial conditions, and moves quite differently for different initial conditions – even if these are extremely close together – then to all intents and purposes the system becomes unpredictable.

One may wonder why scientists have only just discovered such chaos. Part of the reason is that these chaotic systems occur only in the presence of nonlinearity, and scientists have only recently turned their attention to nonlinear systems. Even very simple nonlinear deterministic systems can exhibit chaos. In this chapter we shall consider just some of these. But it is worth recalling what a deterministic system is all about, and it may well be worth re-reading section 1.3. In highlighting the features of such a system, consider the logistic equation in the standard form

$$x(t+1) = \lambda x(t)(1 - x(t)) \quad 0 \le \lambda \le 4 \tag{10.1}$$

This equation is concerned with just one variable, x, which moves over time and one parameter, λ. We can generalise and think of the equation as simply $f(x,\lambda)$. Now in order to know the sequence of values for x, we need to know the initial condition, i.e. the value of x when $t = 0$, which we write $x(0)$. We also need to know the value of the parameter λ. Once we have the initial condition and the value of the parameter λ, we know everything about this series and can generate it quite readily on a spreadsheet. No matter what the series looks like, it will always be the same if the initial condition is the same and the value of the parameter is the same. In other words, given the same values, the series will be identical on different computers using different software packages, on a hand-held calculator, etc. It is in this sense that the system is deterministic.

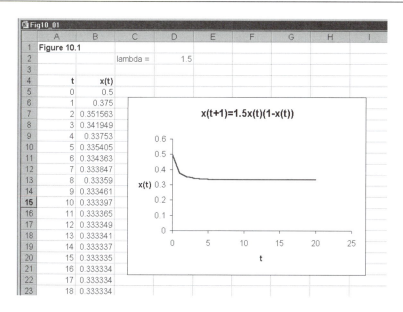

Let us set this problem up on a spreadsheet, which is quite straightforward, and shown in figure 10.1. In cell D2 we place the value of λ, and in cell B5 we place the initial condition, the initial value of x. Cell B6 simply has the formula

$$= \lambda x(0)(1 - x(0))$$
$$= \$D\$2*B5*(1 - B5)$$

which is then copied to the clipboard and pasted down. Here we have t running from 0 to 20. Finally, we block cells A5:B25 and generate the inserted graph. With $x(0) = 0.5$ and $\lambda = 1.5$ the series tends to a steady-state value of 0.3333. There appears nothing chaotic about this series. Now change the value of λ to 3.82, and lo the series is quite different! It exhibits peaks and troughs up to just beyond period 10, then settles down up to about period 17, and then for no apparent reason starts to cycle again. You may want to extend the series way beyond period 20, to, say, period 100, and see what the series looks like over this more extended range. What is clear, however, is that although the system is quite deterministic, it is far from predictable when $\lambda = 3.82$, and seems to be quite chaotic.

We shall return to this equation in detail later. Here all that is being demonstrated is that such a simple nonlinear equation can exhibit rather chaotic behaviour. We now need to investigate why this is so. To do this, we first discuss the topic of **bifurcation**. It is this concept that is at the heart of chaotic behaviour. Armed with this concept, we can discuss chaos theory in more concrete terms.

10.2 Defining bifurcations

In this section we shall consider a simple nonlinear equation of a single variable and a single parameter. This example is adapted from Sandefur (1990). The equation we want to investigate is

(10.2)
$$x(t+1)=f(x(t))=1.5x(t)(1-x(t))-\lambda$$

First let us define the term 'bifurcation'. Bifurcation theory is the study of points in a system at which the qualitative behaviour of the system changes as the value of a parameter is changed. We know that a fixed point of this system satisfies the condition

(10.3)
$$x^* = 1.5x^*(1-x^*)-\lambda$$

or solving

$$15x^{*2} - 5x^* + 10\lambda = 0$$

(10.4)
$$x^* = \frac{1 \pm \sqrt{1-24\lambda}}{6}$$

What we immediately discover from this result is that the equilibrium value of x depends on the precise value of the parameter λ. Furthermore, the stability properties of the equilibrium point will also depend on the precise value of this parameter. For instance, if $1-24\lambda < 0$, i.e. $\lambda > 1/24$, then no equilibrium exists. If $1-24\lambda > 0$, i.e. $\lambda < 1/24$, then two equilibria exist, namely

(10.5)
$$x_1^* = \frac{1 - \sqrt{1-24\lambda}}{6}, \quad x_2^* = \frac{1 + \sqrt{1-24\lambda}}{6}$$

At the value $\lambda = 1/24$ the characteristics of the system change. In other words, either side of this value the characteristics of the system are quite different. These points are called **bifurcation points**.

This particular bifurcation point is illustrated in the spreadsheet shown in figure 10.2. This spreadsheet calculates and plots the equilibrium values as the value of λ changes. The function and the formulas used are shown at the top of the spreadsheet. Consider first column A. In cell A10 we have placed the initial value of λ, namely unity. We now use the fill command. But this is the first time we have used it with a negative value, which is still allowed. Our step value is set at -0.02, which is quite small but we wish to have a 'clean' plot. The termination point is set at -1.00. In cells B10 and C10 we have the formulas

B10	$=(1-\sqrt{1-24\lambda})/6$
	$=(1-SQRT(1-24*A10))/6$
C10	$=(1+\sqrt{1-24\lambda})/6$
	$=(1+SQRT(1-24*A10))/6$

These formulas are then copied to the clipboard and pasted down. The first thing we note is the entry #NUM! in cells B10 to C57. Once $\lambda = 1/24 = 0.0417$, then we have real values. In terms of the spreadsheet, this occurs at the value 0.04 and beyond. Notice that we do have two different values for $\lambda = 0.04$ because this is not equal to the value of 1/24. Finally, we block cells A10:C110

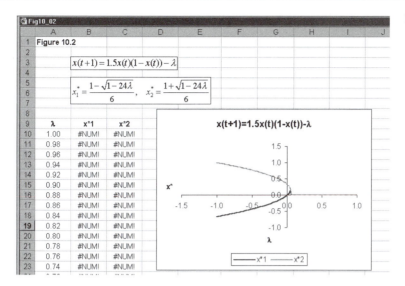

Figure 10.2

and produce the inserted graph. Notice that this is a multiple X-Y plot with the value on the *x*-axis remaining the same, which is simply the value of λ. The spreadsheet simply plots the value zero when it encounters the expression #NUM!, which is fine. What we clearly observe from the chart is the bifurcation that takes place around λ = 0.04 (and occurs at the value 0.0417, to four decimal places).

Turning now to the stability of the fixed points, we recall that stability must be defined locally when there is more than one fixed point. Also, the stability of a fixed point is determined by the first derivative of $f(x = x^*)$ given in (10.2), where the derivative is with respect to the variable *x* and x^* is replaced by the particular fixed point under consideration. Of course, the fixed point itself depends on the value of λ.

The first derivative is

$$f'(x^*) = 1.5 - 3x^* \tag{10.6}$$

Substituting the equilibrium values given in (10.5), we have for the lower fixed point, x_1^*

$$f'(x_1^*) = 1.5 - 3x_1^* =$$

$$1.5 - 3\left(\frac{1 - \sqrt{1 - 24\lambda}}{6}\right) = 1 + 0.5\sqrt{1 - 24\lambda} > 0 \quad \text{for } \lambda < 1/24 \tag{10.7}$$

Since the first derivative is positive around the fixed point x_1^*, then this fixed point is unstable or repelling.

Next consider the stability of x_2^*

$$f'(x_2^*) = 1.5 - 3x_2^* =$$

$$1.5 - 3\left(\frac{1 + \sqrt{1 - 24\lambda}}{6}\right) = 1 - 0.5\sqrt{1 - 24\lambda} \quad \text{for } \lambda < 1/24$$

However, this represents stability only if $-1<f'(x_2^*)<1$, i.e.

$$-1<1-0.5\sqrt{1-24\lambda}<1$$
$$-0.625<\lambda<0.0417$$

This system is stable or attracting, therefore, only for values of λ lying in the range $-0.625<\lambda<0.0417$.

The third and final situation is where $\lambda=1/24=0.0417$. In this case the two fixed points have the same value, namely 1/6. Furthermore

$$f'(x^*=1/6)=1$$

and so the stability of the fixed point is inconclusive or semistable. The value $x^*=1/6$ is the *bifurcation value* for this problem.

We can combine all this information about the equilibrium points and their attraction or repelling on a diagram which has the parameter λ on the horizontal axis, and the equilibrium point x^* on the vertical axis. Such a diagram is called a **bifurcation diagram**, and such a diagram is shown in figure 10.3 for the present problem. It is to be noted that this is a stylised version of the diagram we constructed in the spreadsheet shown in figure 10.2. The vertical arrows show the stability properties of the equilibria. Inside the curved area[1] the arrows point up while outside this area they point down. If $-0.625<\lambda<0.0417$ then there are two equilibrium points, the greater one of which is stable and the lower one unstable.

We have used this example to show what a bifurcation point looks like. But we can be a little more precise. We shall continue to use this example, however, to illustrate the additional concepts. Let N_λ denote the number of equilibrium values of a system when the parameter is equal to λ, then if for any interval $(\lambda_0-\varepsilon,\lambda_0+\varepsilon)$ N_λ is not constant, λ_0 is called a **bifurcation point** and the system is said to undergo a **bifurcation** as λ passes through λ_0. For the example we have been discussing, we have

$$N_\lambda=\begin{cases}2,\text{ for }\lambda<1/24\\1,\text{ for }\lambda=1/24\\0,\text{ for }\lambda>1/24\end{cases}$$

and so $\lambda=1/24$ is a bifurcation.

10.3 Saddle-node bifurcation

The type of bifurcations encountered in dynamic systems is often named according to the type of graph that they exhibit, e.g. **saddle-node bifurcation** and **pitchfork bifurcation**, to name just two. The example we discussed in section 10.2 is a saddle-node bifurcation. It is called this because at the value λ_0 the fixed points of the system form a U-shaped curve, which is open at one end. In this example it is open to the left. In this section we shall consider an alternative example, which is based on a continuous model.

---

[1] The curve relating x and λ in fact forms a parabola, with formula $(6x^*-1)^2=1-24\lambda$.

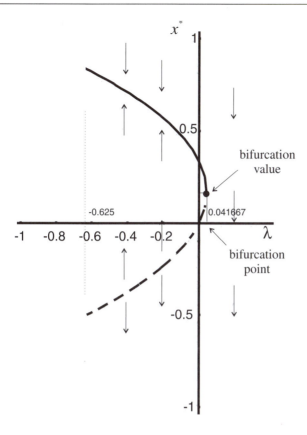

Let

$$\dot{x}(t) = f(x(t)) = \lambda - x^2(t) \tag{10.8}$$

First we need to establish the fixed points of the system. We certainly know there is more than one because we have a quadratic in terms of the variable x. For equilibrium we have

$$0 = \lambda - x^{*2}$$
$$x^* = \sqrt{\lambda} \tag{10.9}$$

If $\lambda < 0$, then, no equilibrium exists. For $\lambda > 0$ there are two fixed points, one for $+\sqrt{\lambda}$ and another for $-\sqrt{\lambda}$. This can be set up on a spreadsheet in exactly the same way as the previous example. The formulas entered are simply the negative and positive square root of the entry in column A, which gives the values of λ.

In order to consider the stability conditions for the continuous system we need to consider $f'(x^*)$ in the neighbourhood of the fixed point. If $f'(x^*) < 0$ then x^* is locally stable; and if $f'(x^*) > 0$, then x^* is locally unstable. Since

$$f'(x^*) = -2x^* \tag{10.10}$$

then

$$f'(x_1^*) = f'\left(-\sqrt{\lambda}\right) = +2\sqrt{\lambda} > 0 \text{ for } \lambda > 0$$

Figure 10.4

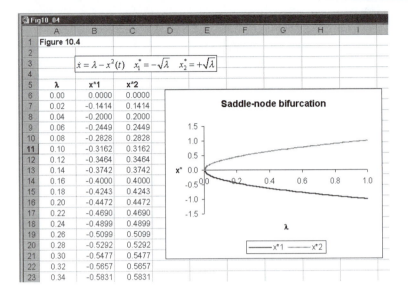

and so $x_1^* = -\sqrt{\lambda}$ is unstable. On the other hand

$$f'(x_2^*) = f'\left(+\sqrt{\lambda}\right) = -2\sqrt{\lambda} < 0 \text{ for } \lambda > 0$$

and so $x_1^* = +\sqrt{\lambda}$ is stable. At $\lambda = 0$ the two fixed points coincide and the fixed point is stable from above. The situation is shown in figure 10.4.

Summarising in the neighbourhood of the point $\lambda = 0$

$$N_\lambda = \begin{cases} 2, \text{ for } \lambda > 0 \\ 1, \text{ for } \lambda = 0 \\ 0, \text{ for } \lambda < 0 \end{cases}$$

(10.11)

and so $\lambda = 0$ is once again a saddle-node bifurcation.

10.4 A transcritical bifurcation and a pitchfork bifurcation

10.4.1 A transcritical bifurcation

Consider the following continuous nonlinear dynamical system

(10.12)
$$\dot{x}(t) = f(x(t)) = \lambda x - x^2 = x(\lambda - x)$$

The fixed points are clearly

$$x_1^* = 0 \text{ and } x_2^* = \lambda$$

Obviously, the two fixed points become identical if $\lambda = 0$. Summarising in the neighbourhood of $\lambda = 0$, we have

$$N_\lambda = \begin{cases} 2, \text{ for } \lambda > 0 \\ 1, \text{ for } \lambda = 0 \\ 0, \text{ for } \lambda < 0 \end{cases}$$

(10.13)

and so $\lambda = 0$ is a bifurcation value.

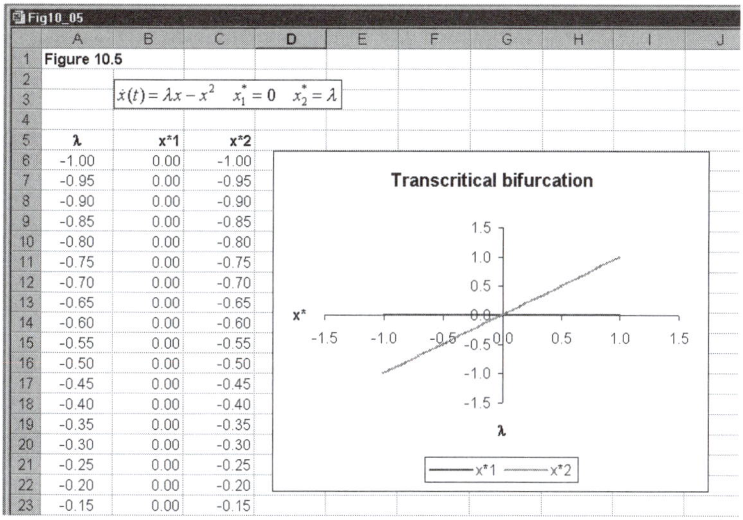

λ	x*1	x*2
-1.00	0.00	-1.00
-0.95	0.00	-0.95
-0.90	0.00	-0.90
-0.85	0.00	-0.85
-0.80	0.00	-0.80
-0.75	0.00	-0.75
-0.70	0.00	-0.70
-0.65	0.00	-0.65
-0.60	0.00	-0.60
-0.55	0.00	-0.55
-0.50	0.00	-0.50
-0.45	0.00	-0.45
-0.40	0.00	-0.40
-0.35	0.00	-0.35
-0.30	0.00	-0.30
-0.25	0.00	-0.25
-0.20	0.00	-0.20
-0.15	0.00	-0.15

Figure 10.5

This too is extremely easy to set up on a spreadsheet, as shown in figure 10.5. Column A has the values of λ, column B has the value of x_1^*, which is simply zero, and column C has the value of x_2^*, which is λ. The value of λ should be taken over a positive and negative range, say $-1<\lambda<1$.

Turning to the stability properties, we have

$$f'(x^*) = \lambda - 2x^* \tag{10.14}$$

and

$$f'(0) = \lambda \begin{cases} >0 \text{ for } \lambda>0 \text{ hence unstable} \\ <0 \text{ for } \lambda<0 \text{ hence stable} \end{cases}$$

For the second fixed point, we have

$$f'(\lambda) = -\lambda \begin{cases} <0 \text{ for } \lambda>0 \text{ hence stable} \\ >0 \text{ for } \lambda<0 \text{ hence unstable} \end{cases}$$

Another way to view this is to consider $x_1^*=0$ being represented by the horizontal axis in figure 10.5, and $x_2^*=\lambda$ being represented by the 45°-line. The two branches intersect at the origin and there takes place an *exchange of stability*. This is called a **transcritical bifurcation**. The characteristic feature of this bifurcation point is that the fixed points of the system lie on two intersecting curves, neither of which bends back on themselves (unlike the saddle-node bifurcation).

10.4.2 Pitchfork bifurcation

Consider the following continuous nonlinear dynamical system

$$\dot{x}(t) = f(x(t)) = \lambda x(t) - x^3(t) = x(t)(\lambda - x^2(t)) \tag{10.15}$$

This system has three critical points.

$$x_1^* = 0, \quad x_2^* = +\sqrt{\lambda}, \quad x_3^* = -\sqrt{\lambda} \tag{10.16}$$

Figure 10.6

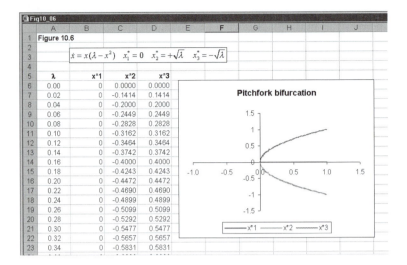

where the second and third fixed points are defined only for positive λ. Summarising in the neighbourhood of $\lambda = 0$, we have

(10.17)
$$N_\lambda = \begin{cases} 1 \text{ for } \lambda \leq 0 \\ 3 \text{ for } \lambda > 0 \end{cases}$$

and so $\lambda = 0$ is a bifurcation value.
Since

(10.18)
$$f'(x^*, \lambda) = \lambda - 3x^{*2}$$

then at each fixed point we have

$$f'(0) = \lambda \begin{cases} < 0 \text{ for } \lambda < 0 \text{ hence stable} \\ > 0 \text{ for } \lambda > 0 \text{ hence unstable} \end{cases}$$

$$f'\left(+\sqrt{\lambda}\right) = -2\lambda < 0 \text{ for } \lambda > 0 \text{ hence stable}$$

$$f'\left(-\sqrt{\lambda}\right) = -2\lambda < 0 \text{ for } \lambda > 0 \text{ hence stable}$$

The characteristic feature of this bifurcation is that at the origin we have a U-shaped curve, which is here open to the right, and another along the horizontal axis that crosses the vertex of the U. It forms the shape of a pitchfork, as shown in figure 10.6, and is therefore called a **pitchfork bifurcation**.

10.5 The logistic equation, periodic-doubling bifurcations and chaos

Return to the logistic equation, which we are considering in its discrete form

(10.19)
$$x(t+1) = f(x(t)) = \lambda x(t)(1 - x(t)) \quad 0 \leq \lambda \leq 4$$

Why λ ranges over zero to four we shall explain later. First, establish the equilibrium points where $x(t+1) = x(t) = x^*$ for all t. Then

$$x^* = \lambda x^*(1 - x^*)$$
$$\lambda x^{*2} + (1 - \lambda)x^* = 0$$
$$x^*[\lambda x^* + (1 - \lambda)] = 0$$

i.e. we have the two fixed points

$$x_1^* = 0, \quad x_2^* = \frac{\lambda - 1}{\lambda} \tag{10.20}$$

To investigate the stability of these solutions we need to employ a linear approximation around the fixed point. This is given by

$$x(t+1) = f(x^*) + f'(x^*)(x(t) - x^*)$$

But if x^* is an equilibrium point, then

$$f(x_1^*) = 0 \text{ and } \quad f(x_2^*) = \frac{\lambda - 1}{\lambda}$$

Furthermore

$$f'(x^*) = \lambda - 2\lambda x^*$$

and so

$$f'(x^*) = \begin{cases} \lambda \text{ for } x^* = 0 \\ 2 - \lambda \text{ for } x^* = \dfrac{\lambda - 1}{\lambda} \end{cases} \tag{10.21}$$

Consider $x_1^* = 0$ first. If $0 < \lambda < 1$ then the system in the neighbourhood of this fixed point is stable. Now consider $x_2^* = (\lambda - 1)/\lambda$, then

$$x(t+1) = x^* + (2 - \lambda)(x(t) - x^*)$$
$$\text{or } u(t+1) = (2 - \lambda)u(t)$$

where $u(t+1) = x(t+1) - x^*$ and $u(t) = x(t) - x^*$. So the system in the neighbourhood of this fixed point is stable if

$$|2 - \lambda| < 1$$
$$-1 < 2 - \lambda < 1$$
$$1 < \lambda < 3$$

So the system is stable around the second fixed point for $1 < \lambda < 3$.

What we observe is that for $0 \le \lambda < 1$ the only fixed point is $x_1^* = 0$ and this is locally stable. The point $x_1^* = 0$ is an **attractor**. For $1 < \lambda < 3$ we have an equilibrium solution $x_2^* = (\lambda - 1)/\lambda$, which varies with λ. The situation is shown in figure 10.7. At $\lambda = 1$, where the two solution curves intersect, there is an *exchange of stability* from one equilibrium solution to the other.

Of course, λ is not restricted to a range below 3. The question is: What happens to the solution values as λ is allowed to increase beyond 3? This is not straightforward to answer at the elementary level. We can, however, get some idea of the problem by considering the conditions for equilibrium more carefully. Given $f(x) = \lambda x(1 - x)$ then fixed points are established by finding the value a that satisfies $a = f(a)$. We did this above, where we used x^* rather than

Figure 10.7

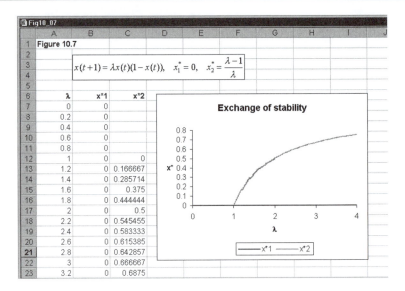

a. If a two-cycle occurs then this satisfies the condition that $a = f(f(a))$. In the first case we can find the value of a by finding where $f(a)$ cuts the 45°-line. Similarly, we can find the values of the two-cycle, if it exists, where $f(f(a))$ cuts the 45°-line. Of course, the situation will be different for different values of λ.

Let us set all this up on a spreadsheet. The computations are going to be placed on sheet 1 of the spreadsheet and the diagrams (since there will be more than one) will be placed on sheet 2. Figure 10.8 shows the computations sheet. In cells G2 to G5 we place four different values for λ, namely 0.8, 2.5, 3.0 and 3.4. In cells A9:A29 we place the different values of x, which range between 0 and 1. We have here used a step size of 0.05. In column B we place the values of $x(t+1)$ that occur along the 45°-line, which are no more than the values given in cells A9:A29. We therefore copy cells A9:A29 and place them into cells B9:B29. In cell C9 we enter the following formula

$$= \lambda_1 x(0)(1 - x(0))$$
$$= \$G\$2*A9*(1 - A9)$$

This is then copied to the clipboard and pasted down. Next we consider cell D9 which has the formula

$$= f(\lambda_1 x(0)(1 - x(0)))$$
$$= \$G\$2*C9*(1 - C9)$$

Notice here that we write out the formula again, but use the values already computed in cell C9, which itself uses the formula. Doing this means that the value in cell D9 is $f(f(x(0)))$. This is then copied to the clipboard and pasted down. To construct the first of our diagrams, we block cells A9:D29 invoke the X-Y plot, which plots multiple graphs on the same x-axis (column A) and insert this on sheet 2. The result is shown in figure 10.9(a).

To derive columns E and F, we simply copy cells C9 and D9 and paste them into cells E9 and F9, respectively. Then we change the cell for the value of the

Figure 10.8

	x	x(t+1)=x(t)	f1(x)	f1(f1(x))	f2(x)	f2(f2(x))	f3(x)	f3(f3(x))	f4(x)	f4(f4(x))
Figure 10.8						λ1 =	0.8			
$f(x) = \lambda x(1-x)$						λ2 =	2.5			
						λ3 =	3			
						λ4 =	3.4			
9	0.00	0.00	0.00	0.00	0.00	0.00	0.00	0.00	0.00	0.00
10	0.05	0.05	0.04	0.03	0.12	0.26	0.14	0.37	0.16	0.46
11	0.10	0.10	0.07	0.05	0.23	0.44	0.27	0.59	0.31	0.72
12	0.15	0.15	0.10	0.07	0.32	0.54	0.38	0.71	0.43	0.83
13	0.20	0.20	0.13	0.09	0.40	0.60	0.48	0.75	0.54	0.84
14	0.25	0.25	0.15	0.10	0.47	0.62	0.56	0.74	0.64	0.79
15	0.30	0.30	0.17	0.11	0.53	0.62	0.63	0.70	0.71	0.69
16	0.35	0.35	0.18	0.12	0.57	0.61	0.68	0.65	0.77	0.60
17	0.40	0.40	0.19	0.12	0.60	0.60	0.72	0.60	0.82	0.51
18	0.45	0.45	0.20	0.13	0.62	0.59	0.74	0.57	0.84	0.45
19	0.50	0.50	0.20	0.13	0.63	0.59	0.75	0.56	0.85	0.43
20	0.55	0.55	0.20	0.13	0.62	0.59	0.74	0.57	0.84	0.45
21	0.60	0.60	0.19	0.12	0.60	0.60	0.72	0.60	0.82	0.51
22	0.65	0.65	0.18	0.12	0.57	0.61	0.68	0.65	0.77	0.60
23	0.70	0.70	0.17	0.11	0.53	0.62	0.63	0.70	0.71	0.69

Figure 10.9

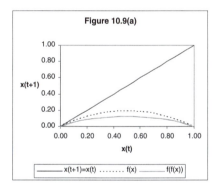

Figure 10.9(a)

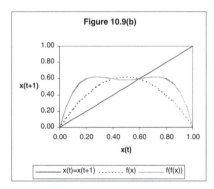

Figure 10.9(b)

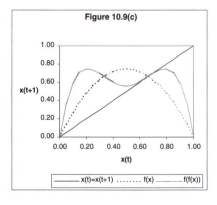

Figure 10.9(c)

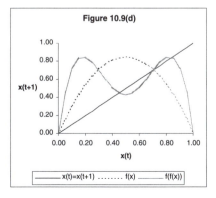

Figure 10.9(d)

parameter to $G$3 and ensure that the value of x is that in cell A9. The change to cell D9 is more straightforward. All we need to do is change the parameter designation to $G$3. The cell will already denote the value of x to be that in cell E9. To summarise these we have

E9	$= \lambda_2 x(0)(1 - x(0))$ $= \$G\$3*A9*(1 - A9)$
F9	$= f(\lambda_2 x(0)(1 - x(0)))$ $= \$G\$3*E9*(1 - E9)$

These are then copied to the clipboard and pasted down. In constructing the second diagram, however, we need to block non-contiguous cells. Block A9:B29 along with E9:F29 and invoke the chart wizard. Choose the X-Y chart. This will automatically assume the values in column A; denote the values on the x-axis and the other three columns will form three series to be plotted. The result, after some manipulation, is shown in figure 10.9(b).

Exactly the same procedure is followed to derive figures 10.9(c) and 10.9(d). We have now completed all the computations and the diagrams. It is now time to see what is happening.

From figure 10.9(a) we see that for a value of $\lambda = 0.8$ the only solution is $x_1^* = 0$ since this is the only value at which $f(x)$ cuts the 45°-line. In fact this is true for any value of λ lying between zero and unity. The reader should change the value of λ_1 in this range in the spreadsheet to verify this. You will also verify that $f(f(x))$ lies below the 45°-line. This means that no two-cycles occur for this range of λ. Hence, any initial value of x 'close to' zero will be attracted to the fixed point $x_1^* = 0$. Also notice from (10.21) that $f'(x_1^*) = 0.8 < 1$, and so $x_1^* = 0$ is locally stable. Turning to figure 10.9(b), with $\lambda = 2.5$, we have

$$x_1^* = \frac{\lambda - 1}{\lambda} = \frac{2.5 - 1}{2.5} = 0.6$$

Furthermore, from (10.21) we have $f'(x_1^* = 0.6) = 2 - 2.5 = -0.5$, and since the absolute value of this is between 0 and 1, then $x_1^* = 0.6$ is stable. Also notice in figure 10.9(b) that $f(f(x))$ cuts the 45°-line only once, and this is at the same value of $x_1^* = 0.6$. So once again no two-cycles occur. In fact, as we demonstrated above, there is only a single positive value when λ ranges over the interval $1 < \lambda < 3$. The reader should verify this by changing the value of λ_2 in the spreadsheet within this range. The situation begins to change when $\lambda = 3$. The change is highlighted in terms of figures 10.9(c) and 10.9(d). In figure 10.9(c) we have the situation in which $\lambda = 3$ precisely. In this case the $f(f(x))$ curve is *tangential* to the 45°-line at the fixed point. The value of the fixed point is

$$x_1^* = \frac{\lambda - 1}{\lambda} = \frac{3 - 1}{3} = \frac{2}{3}$$

Furthermore, from (10.21) we have $f'(x_1^* = 3) = 2 - 3 = -1$ and so $x_1^* = 2/3$ is semistable. Once λ goes beyond the value of 3, then the curve $f(f(x))$ cuts the 45°-line in three places. It is also clear from figure 10.9(d) that the curve $f(x)$

Table 10.1. *Patterns for the logistic equation*

Description	Value of λ
Exchange of stability	1
Fixed point becomes unstable (2-cycles appear)	3
2-cycle becomes unstable (4-cycles appear)	3.44949
4-cycles becomes unstable (8-cycles appear)	3.54409
Upper limit value on 2-cycles (chaos begins)	3.57
First odd-cycle appears	3.6786
Cycles with period 3 appears	3.8284
Chaotic regions ends	4

cuts the curve $f(f(x))$ on the 45°-line and that this is the central value of the three intersection points. This value is given by

$$x_1^* = \frac{\lambda - 1}{\lambda} = \frac{3.4 - 1}{3.4} = 0.70588$$

This is in fact unstable.[2] It is not easy to establish the intersection points precisely without some additional software. But it is apparent from the diagram that the lower value is approximately 0.45 and the upper value is approximately 0.84. These approximations can be verified from the data in the spreadsheet. At the value of $x = 0.45$ (row 18) the entry in cell J18 is also 0.45. For the upper value see rows 25 and 26 of the spreadsheet. In fact the values are $x_2^* = 0.451963$ and $x_3^* = 0.842154$ and it can be established that both these values are stable (see Shone, 1997, ch.6). However, once $\lambda = 3.449$ the two-cycle itself becomes unstable.

What one finds is that the two-cycle becomes unstable and bifurcates itself into a four-cycle. This in turn bifurcates into an eight-cycle, and so on. In addition, there are also odd-numbered cycles. As λ approaches approximately 3.65 there are no regular cycles at all and the whole picture is one of chaos. Table 10.1 summarises the patterns that have been found for the logistic equation.

10.6 Sensitivity to initial conditions and unusual patterns

We point out in table 10.1 that the two-cycle ends at the value of λ equalling approximately 3.57. We also pointed out right at the beginning of this chapter that a major difficulty encountered with chaotic systems is that they are very sensitive to initial conditions. This situation is illustrated in figure 10.10. Here

---

[2] This can be established by taking the derivative of $f(f(x))$ with respect to x, and then replacing x by the value 0.70588. The result is a value of 1.96 and since this is greater than unity, then the fixed point is unstable.

Figure 10.10

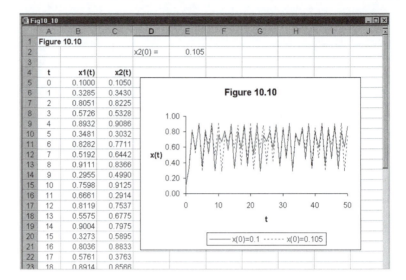

we have set the value of λ equal to 3.65 and have plotted the logistic equation for two different initial values, namely $x(0) = 0.1$ and $x(0) = 0.105$ which are pretty close together. The initial value for the second series we place first in cell E2, this is so we can change this value. The only other cells of any significance are

B5	0.1
B6	3.65*B5*(1 − B5)
C5	$E$2
C6	3.65*C5*(1 − C5)

We have then generated the two series and plotted $x(t)$ against t.

These starting values are very close to one another. The series themselves are close for about the first ten periods but then begin to diverge and very soon there is little comparison between them. The reader may wish to try the situation where the second series has the initial condition 0.1005, which is even closer still.

But another characteristic arises in the case of a series entering the chaotic region for its parameter value. Consider the following logistic equation

(10.22) $$x(t+1) = 3.94\,x(t)(1 − x(t)) \quad x(0) = 0.99$$

Although this series is chaotic, it does not appear purely random, and in particular exhibits sudden changes. As shown in figure 10.11, the series suddenly changes from showing oscillations to one that is almost horizontal, which it does for about ten periods, and then just as suddenly, and for no obvious reason, begins to oscillate once again. Recall that this system is deterministic. It is not like saying on three throws of a dice it is always a possibility that a six

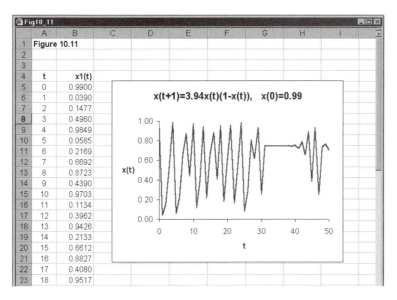

Figure 10.11

will come up each time.[3] This is because on the next three throws of the dice it is extremely unlikely this will happen (but there is always a small probability that it will). On the other hand, plotting this series will *always* give this change of behaviour around period 33 and *always* lead to a sudden change around period 43. This system is deterministic and not random. It just gives the impression of a random series. Even more, this series too is very sensitive to initial conditions. Change the initial value to 0.9905, which is very close to that in figure 10.11 and you will find a totally different pattern emerges – even for such a small change!

10.7 Van der Pol equations and a Hopf bifurcation

We introduced the Van der Pol equations in chapter 4 (section 4.8) when we discussed limit cycles. These equations involve two variables, x and y, each a function of time, and one parameter, denoted μ. The two equations are

$$\dot{x}(t) = y(t)$$
$$\dot{y}(t) = \mu(1 - x^2(t))y(t) - x(t)$$

or dropping the time variable for ease

$$\dot{x} = y$$
$$\dot{y} = \mu(1 - x^2)y - x \tag{10.23}$$

System (10.23) has only one unknown parameter, μ. We showed in chapter 4 how to use Euler's approximation to construct the series $\{x(t), y(t)\}$, which we did in terms of figure 4.14. In this figure we set the value of μ to unity. What

---

[3] This occurs with a probability of $(1/6)^3$.

Figure 10.12

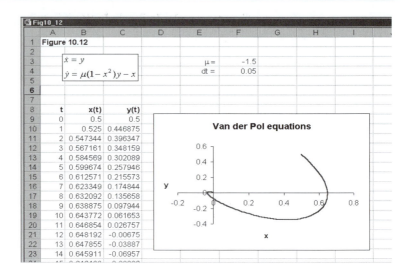

we are now concerned about is what the system looks like as we change the value of μ.

First let us establish the fixed point(s) of the system. We do this by setting $\dot{x} = 0$ and $\dot{y} = 0$. Thus

$$0 = y$$
$$0 = \mu(1 - x^2)y - x$$

From the first result we immediately have that y^* is equal to zero, and using this value in the second result, we immediately have that x^* is equal to zero. The fixed point of the system is therefore $P = (0,0)$. This is the only fixed point of the system, and it is independent of the value of μ.

The system is set up in figure 10.12, which reproduces figure 4.14 with some minor modifications. In this figure we have set the value of μ to -1.5, and set the initial values of x and y both at 0.5, i.e. close to zero, the fixed point of the system. Recall that we are using Euler's approximation and the dynamics of the system is in relation to the neighbourhood of the fixed point (0,0). This system is too complex to investigate in mathematical terms, but we can do some experimentation with our spreadsheet, shown in figure 10.12, to verify some properties of the system as we change the value of μ.

10.7.1 Experimentation

Throughout we shall leave the initial values at 0.5, respectively, for x and y. Now set the value of μ to less than -2, say -2.5. From the inserted graph it will be observed that the system moves clockwise and directly to the fixed point. This result holds for any value of μ less than or equal to -2. Point $P = (0,0)$ is here referred to as a *stable node*. Now take a value of μ a little higher than -2, say -1.5 (the value we have in the spreadsheet illustrated in

Figure 10.13

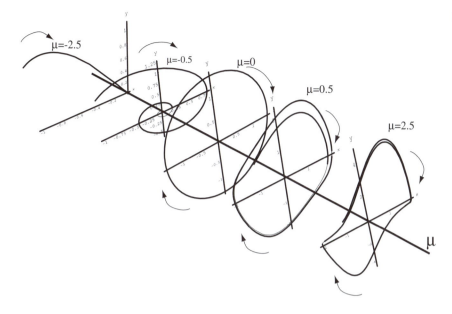

figure 10.12), then the system moves in a clockwise but spiral fashion to the fixed point. The spiral is even more marked if you set the value of μ to -0.5. This spiral path occurs for all values of μ in the range $-2<\mu<0$. For $\mu=0$ the system has a centre, but this is just revealed by our approximation. Notice that the path of the system is still clockwise. For $0<\mu<2$ the system exhibits an unstable focus but, as can be seen from the spreadsheet, tends to a limit cycle. It is unstable in the sense that it moves away from the fixed point $P=(0,0)$, in a clockwise direction; at the same time, however, it converges on a limit cycle. In fact, this feature of the limit cycle occurs for positive values of μ up to about 8, and then the system becomes totally unstable. Try a few values, such as $\mu=1.5, 2, 2.5, 3, 5, 7.5$ and 8.

If we concentrate on the equilibrium values for x and y, say x^* and y^*, then for $\mu<0$, $x^*=0$ and $y^*=0$ and the system moves along the μ-axis. At $\mu=0$ the system changes dramatically taking on the shape of a circle at this value. Then, as μ continues in the positive direction the system takes on a limit cycle in the x-y plane for any particular positive value of μ, the shape of which is no longer a circle – up to about the value of $\mu=8$. All of these are schematically illustrated in figure 10.13, which also shows the direction of movement of the system by means of arrows. It can be seen from the diagram that the system changes dramatically as the value of μ passes through zero. Hence the system exhibits a bifurcation at the value $\mu=0$. This is an example of a **Hopf bifurcation**.

10.8 Lorenz equations again

In section 4.9 of chapter 4 we outlined the Lorenz equations and how to plot them using Euler's approximation. The results are shown in figures 4.15 and 4.16. The Lorenz equations are

Figure 10.14

	A	B	C	D	E	F	G	H
1	Lorenz curve							
2								
3		$\dfrac{dx}{dt} = \sigma(y-x)$				$\sigma =$	10	
4						$r =$	20	
5		$\dfrac{dy}{dt} = rx - y - xz$				$b =$	2.666667	
6						$dt =$	0.01	
7								
8		$\dfrac{dz}{dt} = xy - bz$						
9								
10	t	dx/dt	dy/dt	dz/dt	x	y	z	
11	0	0.0000	9.2500	-1.0833	0.5000	0.5000	0.5000	
12	1	0.9250	9.1629	-1.0082	0.5000	0.5925	0.4892	
13	2	1.7488	9.2569	-0.9292	0.5093	0.6841	0.4791	
14	3	2.4996	9.5106	-0.8437	0.5267	0.7767	0.4698	
15	4	3.2007	9.9083	-0.7493	0.5517	0.8718	0.4614	
16	5	3.8715	10.4390	-0.6436	0.5837	0.9709	0.4539	
17	6	4.5282	11.0953	-0.5238	0.6225	1.0753	0.4474	
18	7	5.1849	11.8733	-0.3871	0.6677	1.1862	0.4422	
19	8	5.8538	12.7714	-0.2298	0.7196	1.3050	0.4383	
20	9	6.5455	13.7905	-0.0479	0.7781	1.4327	0.4360	
21	10	7.2700	14.9336	0.1635	0.8436	1.5706	0.4355	
22	11	8.0364	16.2051	0.4101	0.9163	1.7199	0.4372	
23	12	8.8533	17.6111	0.6989	0.9966	1.8820	0.4413	

$$\dot{x} = \sigma(y - x)$$
$$\dot{y} = rx - y - xz$$
(10.24)
$$\dot{z} = xy - bz$$

In this section, however, we intend to consider the system as the parameter r varies. We shall set the value of the other two parameters at $\sigma = 10$ and $b = 8/3$. In this instance we have the system

$$\dot{x} = 10(y - x)$$
$$\dot{y} = rx - y - xz$$
(10.25)
$$\dot{z} = xy - (8/3)z$$

The model is set out in terms of figure 10.14, which duplicates figure 4.15 with some minor changes.

Our first task is to establish any fixed points. To do this we set $\dot{x} = 0$, $\dot{y} = 0$ and $\dot{z} = 0$. From the first equation this gives the value of x and y as being equal. We can then express the second and third equation as

$$0 = rx - x - xz = x(r - 1 - z)$$
$$0 = x^2 - (8/3)z$$

From the first of these equations this implies either $x = 0$ or $z = r - 1$. If $x = 0$ then $y = 0$ and $z = 0$. If $z = r - 1$ then $x = +\sqrt{(8/3)(r - 1)}$ or $x = -\sqrt{(8/3)(r - 1)}$. We therefore have three possible fixed points

$$P_1 = (0,0,0)$$

$$P_2 = \left(-\sqrt{(8/3)(r-1)}, -\sqrt{(8/3)(r-1)}, r-1 \right)$$
$$P_3 = \left(+\sqrt{(8/3)(r-1)}, +\sqrt{(8/3)(r-1)}, r-1 \right) \qquad (10.26)$$

The first fixed point, the origin, holds for all values of r. The second and third fixed points exist in the real space only if $r \geq 1$.

Before continuing, let us use the spreadsheet outlined in figure 10.14 to investigate what is happening around the value $r = 1$. Take a value of $r = 0.5$ and the initial point $P(0) = (1,1,1)$. Then it can be observed from the various plots that the system is attracted to the first fixed point $P_1 = (0,0,0)$. Taking more values below unity shows the same behaviour of the system. Now take $r = 1$, the system is still behaving about the same. Now take a value just above 1, say 1.5, then the curves start to show loops. The system has gone through a fundamental change at the value $r = 1$, which indicates that this is a bifurcation value. In fact, for $r > 1$, the two other fixed points come into existence.

Now experiment with different values of r. Let r take on the values 5, 10, 15, 20 and 25. With a value of 5 it will be noted that the system cycles around the positive fixed point P_3. This is also true for the value 10. At the value of 15, however, something rather strange is taking place. Both fixed points P_2 and P_3 take centre stage and the system appears to move between them! It can be noted too that the system appears to be attracted more by the negative fixed point. At $r = 20$ the system is getting a little more attracted by the positive fixed point; and even more so when $r = 25$. These fixed points have been called **strange attractors**. The system gets even more chaotic when r increases above about 40.

It will be observed in this chapter all these systems that exhibit chaotic behaviour and have various types of bifurcations are nonlinear systems. Economists are only now beginning to take nonlinear economic systems more seriously. This is because of the power of computers. As we have seen in this chapter, even spreadsheets allow us to investigate some of the properties of these complex systems.

Exercises

(1)   Consider the following function

$$x(t+1) = 2x(t) - 2x^2(t) - \lambda$$

   (i)   What are the fixed points?

   (ii)   What is the bifurcation value of λ?

   (iii) What type of bifurcation does this function have?

(2)   Consider the following quadratic (Berry, 1996, p.117)

$$x(t+1) = x^2(t) - 1$$

   (i)   What are the fixed points?

   (ii)   What are the values of the attracting two-cycle?

(3)   Plot the following function for $t=0$ to 50

$$x(t+1) = 3.67x(t)(1-x(t))$$

for the initial values

(i) $x(0) = 0.2$

(ii) $x(0) = 0.2001$

Is this function sensitive to initial conditions?

(4)   In each of the following let $x(0) = 0.01$, $x(0) = 0.0105$ and t from 0 to 50.

(i)   Show that

$$x(t+1) = 2.5x(t)(1-x(t))$$

is not sensitive to initial conditions.

(ii)   Show that

$$x(t+1) = 3.62x(t)(1-x(t))$$

is sensitive to initial conditions.

(5)   Plot the Van der Pol equation from the initial point $(x(0),y(0)) = (0.5,0.5)$ for the following values of μ. Take $dt = 0.01$ and t from 0 to 1500

(i) $\mu = -1$

(ii) $\mu = 0$

(iii) $\mu = 1$

What do you conclude?

Brief answers to selected exercises

Note:

(1)   A complete set of answers to all exercises can be found on the Cambridge University Press web site.

(2)   There are an additional ten exercises per chapter and their solutions available on the Cambridge University Press web site.

Chapter 1

(1)   (i) $x = 4.167$, (ii) $x = 1$, (iii) $x = 6$

(2)   (i) $\Delta x(t+1) = 5 - 1.2x(t)$, globally stable.

      (ii) $\Delta x(t+1) = -2 + 2x(t)$, globally unstable.

      (iii) $\Delta x(t+1) = 3 - \frac{1}{2}x(t)$, globally stable.

(3)   Two-cycle cobweb with values 1 and 2.

(4)   (i) $x_1 = 0.5505$, $x_2 = 5.4495$. Both points unstable.

      (ii) $x_1 = -2$, locally unstable; $x_2 = -1$, locally stable; $x_3 = 1$, locally unstable.

(5)   (i) $x = 2.5$, globally stable.

      (ii) $x_1 = -2.7913$, locally stable; $x_2 = 1.7913$, locally unstable.

      (iii) $x_1 = -2$, locally unstable; $x_2 = -1$, locally stable; $x_3 = 1$, locally unstable.

Chapter 2

(1)   (i) $p^* = 24$, $q^* = 52$

      (ii)   Yes.

      (iii)   Equilibrium achieved sooner.

(2)   (i) $p^* = 4$, $q^* = 6$

      (ii)   No.

(3)   (i) $p^* = 24$, $q^* = 52$ Yes.

     (ii)   Yes.

     (iii)   No. Two-cycle results.

(4) $r = 0.5$, divergent oscillations.

     $r = -3$, divergent oscillations.

     $r = -0.1$, convergent oscillations.

     $r = 0.1$, convergent oscillations.

     $r = 0.5$, divergent oscillations.

(5)   (i) $p(t) = 5.6 - 0.4p^2(t - 1)$

     (ii) $p_1^* = 2.6943$, $p_2^* = -5.1949$ Only first economically meaningful.

     (iii)   Locally unstable.

(6)   (i) $p(t) = \dfrac{28}{4} - \left(\dfrac{4}{3}\right)p(t);$ $p^* = 4$, $q^* = 6$

     (ii) $p(t) = \begin{cases} 5 & p(t-1) < 3.25 \\ \dfrac{28}{4} - \left(\dfrac{4}{3}\right)p(t-1) & p(t-1) \geq 3.25 \end{cases}$

Chapter 3

(1)   (i) $Y^* = 3000$, $C^* = 2600$

     (iii)   Not attained in finite time period.

(3) $k^* = 5$

(4)   (i) $Y^* = 2355$, $C^* = 2084$, $Tx^* = 598.75$, $Yd^* = 1756.25$

     (iii)   Initial $BD = 115$, new $BD = -98.75$

(5) $NX^* = 36.667$ and falls to 3.333.

Chapter 4

(4)   (i) $x^* = 6.4$, $y^* = 20.8$ Yes, in zigzag fashion.

     (iii)   System oscillatory but convergent.

(5)   (ii) $x^* = 2.553$, $y^* = 9.787$ Yes, very slowly in a cyclical manner.

     (iii)   Convergent oscillations.

Chapter 5

(1)   (i)   New equilibrium $Y^* = 1{,}900$, $r^* = 2.5$

(ii)   New equilibrium $Y^* = 1{,}944$, $r^* = 10.6$

(3)   (i)   New equilibrium $Y^* = 54.375$, $r^* = 17.1875$

(ii)   New equilibrium $Y^* = 57.833$, $r^* = 12.917$

(iii)   New equilibrium $Y^* = 59.5$, $r^* = 13.75$

(4)   (i)   New equilibrium $Y^* = 55.75$, $r^* = 11.875$

(ii)   New equilibrium $Y^* = 54.375$, $r^* = 17.1875$

(5)   (i) and (ii) no change in equilibrium values.

Chapter 6

(1)   (i) $p^* = 30$, $y = y_n = 8$ Yes.

(2)   (i)   *Model A*: $p(t+1) = 4.8 + 0.76p(t)$

Model B: $p(t+1) = 6 + 0.7p(t)$

Both models have $p^* = 20$

(ii)   Model B converges sooner.

(3)   (i) $\Delta y(t+1) = 263.75 - 4.25y(t) - 10\pi^e(t)$

$\Delta \pi^e(t) = y(t) - 15$

(ii) $y^* = 15$, $\pi^{e*} = 20$

(iii) π^e-isocline vertical at 15; y-isocline is $\pi^e = 26.375 - 0.425y$

(iv)   Counterclockwise and divergent.

(4)   (i) $y^* = 60$, $\pi^{e*} = 10$

(ii)   New equilibrium $y^* = 60$, $\pi^{e*} = 5$

(5)   New equilibrium $y^* = 50$, $\pi^{e*} = 10$ Counterclockwise and convergent.

Chapter 7

(1)   (ii)   Cumulative sales under five years is 117.465; under ten years is 122.067. Choice: five-year sales plan.

(2)   (i) $F_1^* = 1$, $F_2^* = -0.25$

(ii)   56

(3)   (i) $q_1 = 1.5$, $q_2 = 3$

    (ii) $q_1(t) = 3 - \frac{1}{2}q_2(t-1)$

            $q_2(t) = 3.75 - \frac{1}{2}q_1(t-1)$

    (iii)   Yes.

(4)   (i) $q_1 = \dfrac{9}{4}$, $q_2 = \dfrac{9}{4}$

    (ii) $q_1(t) = 3 - \frac{1}{3}q_2(t-1)$

            $q_2(t) = 3 - \frac{1}{3}q_1(t-1)$

    (iii)   Yes.

(5)   (i) $q_1 = \dfrac{9}{2}$, $q_2 = \dfrac{9}{2}$, $q_3 = \dfrac{9}{2}$

    (ii) $q_1(t) = 9 - \frac{1}{2}q_2(t-1) - \frac{1}{2}q_3(t-1)$

            $q_2(t) = 9 - \frac{1}{2}q_1(t-1) - \frac{1}{2}q_3(t-1)$

            $q_3(t) = 9 - \frac{1}{2}q_1(t-1) - \frac{1}{2}q_2(t-1)$

Chapter 8

(1)   (i)   Origin.

    (ii) $y = -\dfrac{1}{2}x$ $(\dot{x}=0)$

            $y = -3x$ $(\dot{y}=0)$

    (iii)   Stable arm $y = -1.22475x$; unstable arm $y = 1.22475x$

(2)   (i)   Origin.

    (ii) $r = -2$, $s = 6$ Stable arm $y = -x$; unstable arm $y = \dfrac{5}{3}x$

(3)   (i)   Fixed-point origin; $r = -1$, $s = 3$ hence saddle-point.

    (ii)   Fixed-point origin; $r = -8.65685$, $s = 2.65685$ hence saddle-point.

(4)   (i) $x^* = -2$, $y^* = 1$

    (ii) $r = -1.73205$, $s = 1.73205$

    (iii)   Stable arm $y = -4.4641 - 2.73205x$;
           unstable arm $y = 2.4641 + 0.73205x$

(5) (i) $\bar{s} = 150$, $\bar{p} = 150$

(ii) Dynamic equations:

$\dot{p} = -0.004(p - \bar{p}) + 0.004(s - \bar{s})$
$\dot{s} = 5(p - \bar{p})$

Stable arm: $\dot{p} = 154.303065 - 0.0286871s$ through $\bar{p} = 150$

Unstable arm: $\dot{p} = 151.217 - 0.0286871s$ through $\bar{p} = 147$

Chapter 9

(1) (i) $b(t) = 0.064 + 1.015b(t + 1)$

(ii) $b^* = -4$ Creditor.

(iii) Rise.

(2) (i) $t = 19$.

(ii) $t = 21$

(3) (i) $g - nt = 0.05$.

(ii) $g - nt = -0.01$

(5) (i) $g - nt = -0.011$

(ii) $g - nt = -0.012$

(iii) Waiting leads to larger adjustment.

Chapter 10

(1) (i) $x^* = \dfrac{1 \pm \sqrt{1 - 8\lambda}}{4}$

(ii) $\lambda = \dfrac{1}{8}$

(iii) Saddle-node bifurcation.

(2) (i) $x^* = \dfrac{1 \pm \sqrt{5}}{2}$

(ii) $-1, 0$

(3) Yes.

(5) (i) $\mu = -1$, converges in clockwise motion.

(ii) $\mu = 0$, limit cycle, clockwise motion.

(iii) $\mu = 1$, limit cycle, clockwise motion.

Further reading

Beardshaw, J., Brewster, D., Cormack, P. and Ross, A. (1998) *Economics. A Student's Guide*, 4th edn., London: Addison-Wesley Longman.

Begg, D.K.H. (1982) *The Rational Expectations Revolution in Macroeconomics*, Oxford: Philip Allan.

Berry, J. (1996) *Introduction to Non-Linear Systems*, London: Arnold.

Burda, M. and Wyplosz, C. (1997) *Macroeconomics: A European Text*, 2nd edn., Oxford: Oxford University Press.

Chiang, A.C. (1984) *Fundamental Methods of Mathematical Economics*, 3rd edn., New York: McGraw-Hill.

Dornbusch, R. (1976) Expectations and exchange rate dynamics, *Journal of Political Economy* 84, 1161–76.

Ezekiel, M. (1938) The cobweb theorem, *Quarterly Journal of Economics* 52, 255–80.

Ferguson, B.S. and Lim, G.C. (1998) *Introduction to Dynamic Economic Models*, Manchester: Manchester University Press.

Gärtner, M. (1997) *A Primer in European Macroeconomics*, London: Prentice-Hall.

Goodwin, R.M. (1947) Dynamic coupling with especial reference to markets having production lags, *Econometrica* 15, 181–204.

Judge, G. (2000) *Computing Skills for Economists*, Chichester: John Wiley.

Mahajan, V. and Peterson, R.A. (1985) *Models for Innovation Diffusion*, Beverley Hills: Sage.

Pfitzner, C.B. (1996) *Mathematical Fundamentals for Microeconomics*, Oxford: Blackwell.

Phillips, A.W. (1958) The relationship between unemployment and the rate of change of money wage rates in the UK, 1861–1957, *Economica* NS25.

Samuelson, P.A. (1939) Interaction between the multiplier analysis and principle of acceleration, *Review of Economic Statistics* 21, 75–8.

Sandefur, J.T. (1990) *Discrete Dynamical Systems*, Oxford: Clarendon Press.

Shone, R. (1997) *Economic Dynamics*, Cambridge: Cambridge University Press.

Varian, H.R. (1999) *Intermediate Microeconomics*, 5th edn., New York: W.W. Norton.

Waugh, F.V. (1964) Cobweb models, *Journal of Farm Economics* 46(4), 732–50.

Whigham, D. (1998) *Qualitative Business Methods Using Excel*, Oxford: Oxford University Press.

Index